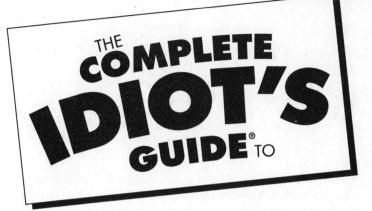

THE COMPLETE IDIOT'S GUIDE® TO

Adult ADHD

*by Eileen Bailey, and
Donald Haupt, M.D.*

ALPHA

A member of Penguin Group (USA) Inc.

To my family and my patients and teachers.—Dr. Don Haupt
To my husband, George, and my children Derek, Czar, Deara, Evelyn, and Soloman.
—Eileen Bailey

ALPHA BOOKS

Published by the Penguin Group

Penguin Group (USA) Inc., 375 Hudson Street, New York, New York 10014, USA

Penguin Group (Canada), 90 Eglinton Avenue East, Suite 700, Toronto, Ontario M4P 2Y3, Canada (a division of Pearson Penguin Canada Inc.)

Penguin Books Ltd., 80 Strand, London WC2R 0RL, England

Penguin Ireland, 25 St. Stephen's Green, Dublin 2, Ireland (a division of Penguin Books Ltd.)

Penguin Group (Australia), 250 Camberwell Road, Camberwell, Victoria 3124, Australia (a division of Pearson Australia Group Pty. Ltd.)

Penguin Books India Pvt. Ltd., 11 Community Centre, Panchsheel Park, New Delhi—110 017, India

Penguin Group (NZ), 67 Apollo Drive, Rosedale, North Shore, Auckland 1311, New Zealand (a division of Pearson New Zealand Ltd.)

Penguin Books (South Africa) (Pty.) Ltd., 24 Sturdee Avenue, Rosebank, Johannesburg 2196, South Africa

Penguin Books Ltd., Registered Offices: 80 Strand, London WC2R 0RL, England

International Standard Book Number: 978-1-61564-006-5
Library of Congress Catalog Card Number: 2009938585

12 11 10   8 7 6 5 4 3 2 1

Interpretation of the printing code: The rightmost number of the first series of numbers is the year of the book's printing; the rightmost number of the second series of numbers is the number of the book's printing. For example, a printing code of 10-1 shows that the first printing occurred in 2010.

Printed in the United States of America

Note: This publication contains the opinions and ideas of its authors. It is intended to provide helpful and informative material on the subject matter covered. It is sold with the understanding that the authors and publisher are not engaged in rendering professional services in the book. If the reader requires personal assistance or advice, a competent professional should be consulted.

The authors and publisher specifically disclaim any responsibility for any liability, loss, or risk, personal or otherwise, which is incurred as a consequence, directly or indirectly, of the use and application of any of the contents of this book.

Most Alpha books are available at special quantity discounts for bulk purchases for sales promotions, premiums, fund-raising, or educational use. Special books, or book excerpts, can also be created to fit specific needs.

For details, write: Special Markets, Alpha Books, 375 Hudson Street, New York, NY 10014.

Publisher: *Marie Butler-Knight*
Editorial Director/Acquiring Editor: *Mike Sanders*
Senior Managing Editor: *Billy Fields*
Senior Development Editor: *Phil Kitchel*
Senior Production Editor: *Megan Douglass*
Copy Editor: *Monica Stone*

Cover Designer: *Bill Thomas*
Book Designer: *Trina Wurst*
Indexer: *Tonya Heard*
Layout: *Ayanna Lacey*
Proofreader: *Laura Caddell*

Contents at a Glance

Contents

Introduction

Approximately 4.5 percent of adults worldwide have Attention Deficit Hyperactivity Disorder (ADHD) according to the World Health Organization (WHO). That means millions of adults struggle daily with losing their keys, wallets, or important papers. They consistently forget important meetings and events, or picking up their children from school. They also miss over three weeks of work productivity each year due to symptoms of ADHD, and may have problems getting along with co-workers.

Treatment has been found to be effective in reducing impulsiveness and increasing focus for most adults; however, the majority of adults either don't know they have ADHD or have not sought medical treatment for it. That means their spouses, family members, friends, co-workers, and bosses don't know, either. They don't understand why an anniversary dinner would be forgotten, why there is consistent tardiness, or why each day must start with 15 minutes of looking for car keys. This book offers those with ADHD, as well as the millions of people associated with them, an explanation of why certain behaviors continue to happen.

For those recently diagnosed with ADHD, this book can answer many of the questions you must have. For those who were previously diagnosed, maybe years ago, this book offers many tips and suggestions for coping with symptoms on a daily basis.

Friends, relatives, and co-workers may also benefit from this book. Although we understand ADHD is not an excuse for unacceptable behavior, it can be an explanation. Helping those you interact with on a daily basis understand your ADHD may help to improve your relationships.

We hope this book will provide answers to questions, new information and a resource guide to living with ADHD.

What's in This Book

We understand you may not be a medical professional and may not want to read a book filled with medical jargon. We have tried to keep this book basic and free of too much medical terminology. When we needed to use medical terms, we have provided an explanation. There is also a glossary at the end of the book to help you better understand certain terms.

The book has been divided into six different parts to make it easier to keep track of where you are and what you have read.

Part 1, "Understanding Adult ADHD," covers all the basic information. It explains exactly what ADHD is and what it isn't. We explain the three main types of ADHD, and what the terms ADD and ADHD mean. Finally, we discuss some of the other medical conditions commonly associated with ADHD.

Part 2, "Treatment of ADHD," covers the different treatment options available for helping to alleviate symptoms of ADHD. We explain all about medication for ADHD, and provide insights to help you decide if medication is the right treatment for you. We also help you by offering steps you can take when looking for the right medical professional. Alternative and complementary treatments are also discussed, letting you know which ones may help and which ones you may want to avoid. Finally, we talk about coaching, explaining what an ADHD coach is and how a coach can help you reach your goals.

Part 3, "ADHD and Relationships," discusses how ADHD impacts marriage and how you and your spouse can work together to focus on the positives within the relationship. In addition, there is information on different types of relationships, such as parents and siblings, friendships, and co-workers. Finally, we talk about communication, the cornerstone to good, working relationships, and some of the obstacles to communication commonly seen in adults with ADHD.

Part 4, "ADHD at Work," concentrates on helping adults with ADHD succeed at work. We provide plenty of suggestions and tips for dealing with hyperactivity, impulsiveness, inattention, and disorganization in the workplace. We also discuss federal laws that help protect individuals with disabilities, and how you can become your own advocate.

Part 5, "Managing ADHD in Daily Life," provides many tips and suggestions for coping with secondary symptoms of ADHD, such as procrastination, difficulty prioritizing, and hypersensitivities. Lastly, we discuss how ADHD impacts emotions and give suggestions to help manage emotions on a daily basis.

Part 6, "ADHD Through Different Stages of Life," talks about how ADHD can appear differently throughout the life span. From young adults heading off to college to senior citizens, this part gives you lots of information on dealing with ADHD symptoms during each phase.

Extras

We have packed a lot of information into this book on living with ADHD as an adult. The following sidebars include even more:

The Lowdown

These sidebars provide helpful tips and suggestions for coping with, and managing, the daily symptoms of ADHD.

def•i•ni•tion

These help to provide explanations for some of the medical terminology often used when discussing ADHD.

Think It Over

Managing ADHD may have issues and warnings you should be aware of. This sidebar calls attention to an important area of concern.

The Scoop

There's lots of surprising but pertinent information about ADHD. This sidebar points out some interesting facts to help you better understand ADHD.

Acknowledgements

Donald Haupt, M.D.: Thanks to my wife, whose love, sense of humor, and support help me immeasurably every day. Thanks to my kids, who show me new ways of seeing the world. Thanks to my mother, Claire, and late father, Abram, who gave me a strong foundation and structure to grow on. Thanks to Anthony Rostain, M.D., who gave the first lecture I heard on adult ADHD. And a special thanks to my patients, who continuously enlighten and inform me.

Eileen Bailey: I would like to thank my husband, who continuously offers his support, encouragement, and love each and every day. Thank you to all of my children. My son Derek, for whom I began this journey and who inspires me with his courage to face each new day, despite the obstacles in his life. My stepdaughters, Sharaczar and Shaldeara, who bring happiness into our home each time they visit. My younger children, Evelyn and Soloman, who rose to the occasion, helped out around the house, and gave up summer activities to allow their mother to spend the summer writing and never fail to bring a smile to my face.

Both of us would also like to thank our agent, Marilyn Allen, for believing in us and helping to make this book a reality.

Trademarks

All terms mentioned in this book that are known to be, or are suspected of being, trademarks or service marks have been appropriately capitalized. Alpha Books and Penguin Group (USA) Inc. cannot attest to the accuracy of this information. Use of a term in this book should not be regarded as affecting the validity of any trademark or service mark.

Part 1

Understanding Adult ADHD

Whether you were recently diagnosed with ADHD, have been diagnosed for several years, or have a friend or family member with ADHD, you probably have a great deal of questions. Part 1 answers many of those questions.

From learning about the three types of ADHD and how symptoms impact adults to sorting out the myths from the facts, we provide factual information to help you better understand adult ADHD.

Often, ADHD does not travel alone, and with over 60 percent of individuals with ADHD diagnosed with another disorder at some time in their lives, it is important to know about disorders such as depression, bipolar disorder, and learning disabilities. This part will help you discover why comorbid conditions can interfere with treatment and what you should expect from your doctor when you have two or more conditions.

Chapter 1

About ADHD

In This Chapter

- ◆ ADHD through the past 100 years
- ◆ Major subtypes of ADHD
- ◆ Adult vs. childhood ADHD
- ◆ A self-screening test for ADHD

ADHD used to be considered a childhood disorder. Only recently did we begin to understand that symptoms of ADHD frequently continue into adulthood, which has led to an outpouring of research and advances in the diagnosis, treatment, and understanding of adult ADHD. If you are one of the many adults who have spent years dealing with a low self-image, lost jobs, and failed relationships because of symptoms of ADHD, this is good news.

We have come a long way from using the term "minimal brain dysfunction" just a few decades ago, to ADHD becoming one of the most researched disorders of all times. Even so, for those living with adult ADHD, there is so much that is not yet understood. For example, do you pay too much attention or not enough attention? Are you still hyperactive or just restless and bored? Will you ever learn to be organized?

Diagnosing adult ADHD can be tricky; information from childhood is needed but not always available. Living with undiagnosed ADHD increases your risk of developing depression or anxiety. Your ADHD may have been misdiagnosed in the past, delaying the treatment you need. In this chapter, we'll explore what you need to know about ADHD and what it looks like in adults.

The History of ADHD

It would seem that ADHD is a new disorder, recently discovered, with symptoms only noticed in the past few decades. In reality, symptoms of ADHD have appeared in literature as early as 1844. A poem written by Dr. Heinrich Hoffman, a German psychiatrist, appearing in the book, *Der Struwwelpeter* (Shock-haired Peter), describes a young boy who won't sit still.

> *... But fidgety Phil,*
> *He won't sit still;*
> *He wriggles*
> *And giggles,*
> *And then, I declare*
> *Swings backwards and forwards*
> *And tilts up his chair ...*

Almost 50 years later, in 1902, Dr. George F. Still, a member of the Royal College of Physicians in London, England, provided the first published work with his observations of "an abnormal defect of moral control." His observations of schoolboys, not necessarily "bad" boys but boys who had trouble paying attention and impulsively stumbled into trouble, are similar to what we know today as attention deficit hyperactivity disorder. Even though Dr. Still used the name "Defect of Moral Control," he saw this as a medical diagnosis.

> **The Scoop**
>
> Many famous people throughout history, such as Benjamin Franklin, have shown characteristics of ADHD. Benjamin Franklin had 16 different careers and showed signs of impulsivity—regardless of what he knew about writing and international diplomacy, he went kite-flying in an electrical storm.

Later, in 1933, two researchers, Kahn and Cohen, described "Organic Drivenness, a brain stem syndrome and an experience." The symptoms included difficulty or inability to engage in quiet activities, clumsiness, and impulsiveness. These same symptoms have appeared in other medical research papers under different names.

The use of stimulants to treat children with behavioral problems first emerged in 1937. Dr. Charles Bradley began treating children with headaches with Benzedrine (a *stimulant medication*). This medication did not improve the headaches but teachers began noticing immense improvements in both behavior and schoolwork for these children. Students and teachers began to refer to the medication as "arithmetic pills."

def•i•ni•tion

Stimulant medications, commonly used to treat ADHD, increase dopamine and norepinephrine, neurotransmitters in the brain. It is generally accepted in the medical community that a low level of dopamine in the prefrontal cortex contributes to symptoms of ADHD.

It was still more than 25 years later before stimulant medication was used to treat symptoms of ADHD. In 1956, methylphenidate (Ritalin) was introduced as a treatment for children with hyperactivity; use of this medication became more accepted in the early 1960s. At that time, ADHD was called "minimal brain dysfunction," however, hyperactivity was the only symptom treated. By the late 1960s the name changed once again to "hyperkinetic disorder of childhood," although hyperactivity was still considered the main symptom.

During the 1970s additional symptoms such as lack of focus, daydreaming, and impulsiveness were associated with hyperkinetic disorder of childhood. In 1980, the names attention deficit disorder with hyperactivity; attention deficit disorder without hyperactivity (a.k.a. ADD); and attention deficit disorder, residual type (a.k.a. Adult ADHD) were added to *The Diagnostic and Statistical Manual (DSM) of Psychiatric Disorders*. At this time, ADHD and ADD were thought to be separate disorders.

In the 1970s, Dr. Paul Wender, noticed the same symptoms in the parents of the children he was treating for hyperactivity and inattention, leading him to further study this syndrome in adults. Prior to this, it was felt the syndrome rarely existed past the teenage years. Although he published a paper on adults, which was replicated in the 1980s, it was not until the 1995 book *Driven to Distraction*, by Dr. Edward Hallowell and Dr. John J. Ratey, that adult ADHD began to receive serious attention.

The name used today, attention deficit hyperactivity disorder, came about in 1987. This name replaced the three names coined in 1980 and combined all three to create one disorder. It was not considered a behavioral disorder but rather a medical diagnosis that could cause behavioral problems. These behavioral problems were seen as different than those caused by divorce or other emotional turmoil.

Since 1987, many different medications have been introduced, and people diagnosed today have a deeper understanding of ADHD as well as more options for treatment. ADHD has been the subject of so many different research studies that in 1998 the American Medical Association stated it was one of the best researched disorders of all time.

ADHD Today

ADHD is now recognized as a medical diagnosis. ADHD is a *spectrum disorder*, meaning that one person may have mild symptoms and another may have more serious symptoms. There is no specific look or feel of ADHD. It may be, and often is, different in each person.

The three main symptoms—hyperactivity, impulsiveness, and inattention/distractibility—appear in varying degrees. One person may have extreme impulsiveness; another may not have problems with impulsiveness but can be very hyperactive. Michael, an adult with ADHD, often interrupts others when they are talking, has financial problems because of impulsive spending, and finds himself overloaded at work because of impulsively taking on new projects. Sarah, on the other hand, loses a great deal of time each day searching for keys and other items she has "misplaced," has many projects started but never finishes any of them, and has a hard

def•i•ni•tion

Spectrum disorder is a term used in psychiatry to describe conditions associated with a particular disorder and varying degrees and subtypes of the disorder.

time following conversations because she's distracted by what is going on around her. Both of these adults have ADHD, but their symptoms don't look anything alike.

Who Has ADHD?

Between 3 and 7 percent of all children in the United States have been diagnosed with ADHD. That means approximately 4.5 million children; or assuming an average class size of 23, at least one child in every classroom nationwide has been diagnosed with ADHD.

Currently, more boys are diagnosed than girls (9.5 percent of boys and 5.9 percent of girls), but that doesn't necessarily mean more boys have ADHD. ADHD, predominately inattentive type, more frequently seen in girls, may be missed in childhood, mistaken for shyness, and not diagnosed until later in life.

It was once thought that a person would grow out of ADHD, but it is now understood that many adults continue to have symptoms. Somewhere between 2 and 5 percent of all adults (around 50 percent of those with childhood ADHD) struggle with symptoms well into adulthood.

The Biology of ADHD

No one knows for sure what causes ADHD. It is considered hereditary, but which genes cause ADHD is still not known. Scientists believe the genes that regulate dopamine in the brain are involved with the risk of developing ADHD.

A study completed in 2002 examined brain activity in children with ADHD. This research showed the front portion of the brain, the prefrontal cortex, was less active. Some areas of the brain were smaller in children with ADHD, but caught up in size as the children grew. It's not clear whether these differences in the brain are the cause of ADHD, or part of the syndrome.

If you are a child with one parent with ADHD, you have a 50 percent chance of developing ADHD. Some researchers indicate that approximately 75 percent of all people diagnosed with ADHD have a family history of ADHD.

This means that approximately one fourth of all cases of ADHD may be caused by something else (or a family history of ADHD is not known because of lack of diagnosis). Cigarette smoking or drinking during pregnancy may lead to ADHD according to a number of studies. This risk is small; most women who smoke or drink do not go on to have children with ADHD, but the association is still there, and is a further reason not to smoke or drink alcohol during pregnancy. Exposure to lead in the preschool years, such as in old paint or plumbing fixtures, may also increase the risk of a child developing ADHD. Some brain injuries have symptoms similar to those behaviors found in children with ADHD, as well.

> **Think It Over**
>
> Some researchers believe that environmental factors only increase the risk of developing ADHD if the child is genetically susceptible to ADHD to begin with.

Additional causal theories include malnutrition during infancy, exposure to certain toxins during pregnancy, a resistance to thyroid hormones, and dietary deficiencies. However, there is not enough evidence currently to support these theories.

The Three Main Types of ADHD

DSM stands for *The Diagnostic and Statistical Manual*. It is published by the American Psychiatric Association and outlines diagnostic criteria for mental illnesses. It was first published in 1952 and has been revised five times since then. (We are now using DSM-IV-TR.) Each revision contains more precise descriptions of specific mental illnesses and criteria for each based on extensive research. The newest revision is due to be published in 2012 and will no doubt include updated definitions, possibly including adult ADD. For now, descriptions and symptoms of ADHD are geared toward children and must be translated into how symptoms manifest in adulthood. According to the DSM-IV-TR, symptoms must be present within the last six months, have appeared before age seven, and be present in at least two environments (for example, home and work).

There are three main types of ADHD: hyperactive/impulsive type, inattentive type, and combined type.

Hyperactive/Impulsive Type

The hyperactive/impulsive type of ADHD is exactly as the name implies. It is characterized by excessive energy and acting without thinking first. Some example characteristics include ...

- Fidgeting.

- Trouble sitting still, even when required.

- Difficulty enjoying quiet activities.

- Excessive talking.

- Constant movement.

- Blurting out answers, even before someone has finished asking a question.

- Interrupting when others are talking.

- Difficulty waiting for your turn, even in conversations.

Hyperactivity in adults can also show up as restlessness, being easily bored, constant doodling or tapping feet, and participating in high-risk activities.

Inattentive Type

Inattention and distractibility can show up in many different ways and is not limited to paying attention while someone else is speaking (although that is part of it). Some examples of inattention/distractibility are ...

- Not paying attention to details.

- Making careless mistakes.

- Difficulty sustaining attention.

- Seeming as if you are not paying attention.

- Not completing tasks or projects.

- Disorganization.

- Avoiding situations and tasks that require a sustained mental effort.

- Being easily distracted.

- Forgetfulness.

If you are diagnosed with inattention/distractibility, you may not have been diagnosed until your teen or adult years. This type of ADHD is frequently overlooked, especially in young children.

The Combined Type

If you have at least six symptoms of both the hyperactivity/impulsiveness type and the inattention type, you would be diagnosed with ADHD, combined type. People with combined type may have more problems with distractibility and impulsiveness than those diagnosed with inattentive type.

Additionally, people diagnosed with combined type ADHD have more psychological distress, use more psychiatric services, and are at a higher risk for alcohol/drug use, and suicide. Learning disabilities are also more prevalent in individuals diagnosed with combined type ADHD.

How Symptoms Manifest in Adults

Not long ago, ADHD was considered a childhood disorder. Because hyperactivity lessens as a child grows up, it was assumed that you "grew out of ADHD." The DSM-IV-TR (diagnostic criteria) reflects this assumption. Phrases such as, "Often loses things needed for tasks and activities (such as toys, school assignments, pencils, books, or tools)" indicate symptoms for children, but this does not always equate to how symptoms show up in adults. The following should not be used as a diagnostic tool but instead provides some examples of how the major symptoms of ADHD may show up in adults.

Hyperactivity Equals Restlessness

Hyperactivity is easy to spot in children. They can't sit still, fidget constantly, and sometimes act as if driven by a motor, going nonstop from morning until night. Generally, hyperactivity changes as you mature. Your excess energy may seem more like restlessness. You become bored easily and may move from job to job. Each job loses its interest once you learn the skills needed and you begin to feel an intense need to move on. Hyperactivity may also show up as fidgeting, playing with a pencil, doodling, continuously tapping your feet, or feeling the need to get up and move around. High-stimulus activities hold your interest longer.

Impulsiveness in Adults

Impulsiveness is acting before thinking. You may interrupt other people while talking or answer their question before they even finish it. You may blurt out remarks that are inappropriate or hurtful, or engage in high-risk behaviors. Some adults with ADHD impulsively spend money, causing financial problems at home. Usually people who are impulsive have a low frustration threshold. Impulsiveness may be seen as confidence to people around you. You may require instant and continuous gratification to keep your interest level up.

Inattention or Paying Too Much Attention?

People debate the term inattention when describing ADHD. Some say it would be more correct to say that the problem lies instead on filtering stimuli. For example, you may not be able to ignore the ringing phone, the conversation taking place in the other room, the children crying, or the television blaring. Instead, you pay attention to everything, becoming overwhelmed by the amount of stimuli around you.

Inattention can also show up as forgetfulness, even when something is important. Many parents with ADHD have forgotten to pick up their child from school or have had utilities shut off because they simply forgot to pay the bills.

Distraction is certainly a major issue. Imagine yourself gardening when you hear the phone ring. You go inside to answer the phone, stop to get a drink, watch a few minutes

The Scoop

Inattention in adults with ADHD can show up as misjudging the amount of time that has passed or not being able to judge how much time a task will take.

of television, talk to your spouse, get the mail, and then start another project—completely forgetting about the gardening.

Disorganization as a Way of Life

How many times have you lost your keys, your wallet, or some piece of paper with important information on it? Disorganization in adults with ADHD is probably one of the most frustrating symptoms. Children in school hear it all the time, "If you would just be more organized, you would be able to find your homework …." Organization for the adult with ADHD is as elusive as a needle in a haystack.

The Impact of ADHD on Executive Functioning

Executive functioning refers to the ability to reason, plan, and organize information in order to complete tasks, and shift attention from one task to another. It helps in self-regulation of behaviors. Some of the ways executive functioning helps are …

- Planning
- Organizing
- Multitasking
- Using information from past experiences in current situations
- Completing tasks on a schedule
- Checking progress made and adjusting or changing course when necessary to complete a task
- Managing, keeping track of time, and planning for the future
- Understanding relationships and group dynamics including conversation skills, such as taking turns talking
- Controlling emotions
- Asking for help when needed
- Seeking additional resources when needed

Recent research has shown deficits in executive functioning in many children, adolescents, and adults with ADHD. When *comorbid* conditions or learning disabilities are present, these deficits interfere with daily life even more. Many experts consider executive functioning deficits to be the core problem of ADHD.

def•i•ni•tion

Comorbid (sometimes called coexisting) refers to a disease or condition that exists with another condition. For example, a person can have both ADHD and depression and have symptoms of both disorders.

Deficits in executive functioning may cause problems with working memory (those items held in the memory only for short periods while they are being used, like the RAM in your computer), slow processing speed, written expression, prioritizing, organizing, and math calculations.

The Lowdown

Executive functioning deficits cause problems with planning. You might want to take the time to break large projects down into small tasks or steps and create goals for each step. This can make reaching your goal much easier.

Diagnosing Adult ADHD

The diagnostic process usually begins with a visit to your family doctor or mental-health professional. A complete family history should be taken. Since ADHD begins in childhood, you'll answer numerous questions about your childhood. You may need to enlist family members to report on your behavior during your childhood. Your doctor will also ask about your current health. You may be asked to complete a questionnaire about behaviors, academics, relationships, and job performance. Your doctor may also require a complete physical to rule out whether symptoms are a result of an underlying physical illness. Illnesses such as hypo- or hyperthyroidism can cause symptoms similar to ADHD.

Checklists and Rating Scales

A number of different *rating scales* and checklists are available to help in the diagnosis of children for ADHD. Since adult ADHD has only recently been recognized, there are still only a few rating scales available for adults.

> **def•i•ni•tion**
>
> A **rating scale** is a collection of questions to determine the number of characteristics and behaviors, consistent with ADHD symptoms, a person may have. Rating scales have been developed by medical professionals based on symptoms shared by a large number of people.

Connors Adult ADHD Rating Scale (CAARS) is one such tool. This rating scale has questions on nine separate areas: inattention, hyperactivity, impulsiveness, executive function, memory, self-image, relationships, learning problems, and mood disturbances. This scale is accurate in approximately 85 percent of adults.

The Adult ADHD Self-Report Scale (ASRS) is a checklist created by the World Health Organization and can be used as part of the overall screening process.

As more and more is understood about adult ADHD, additional checklists and rating scales will undoubtedly emerge.

Difficulty in Diagnosing Adult ADHD

As an adult, remembering specific details of your childhood can be hard. You may remember generalities, such as not liking school or having a hard time in math, but specifics may elude you. Since a diagnosis of ADHD requires that ADHD begin in childhood, this may require information not readily available. Ideally, you could use copies of report cards with notations from teachers, but, chances are, you no longer have these documents. You may need to enlist the help of parents or other family members to help in remembering what symptoms of ADHD you exhibited during your childhood. In many cases, your description of your childhood, especially experiences in school, will suffice.

Misdiagnosis also can stand in the way of an accurate diagnosis. Some adults with ADHD may have been previously diagnosed with depression, anxiety, or learning disabilities. It is possible for these other conditions to exist alongside ADHD; however for some, the previous diagnosis may stand in the way of discovering adult ADHD. A complete medical history is important. This can help to differentiate diagnoses. Finding an accurate (and complete) diagnosis may require that you, and your doctor, dismiss a previous diagnosis and begin again.

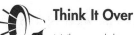

Think It Over

When adults are faced with long-term stressful situations (such as a divorce that goes on for several years) signs of restlessness or inattention can appear to be chronic, even though they are situational and not part of adult ADHD.

Environmental factors, including stress, can also cause inattention, distractibility, and restlessness. You should share with your doctor any current situations that may be causing undue or extreme stress in your life. Making the doctor aware of current life events can help not only in having an accurate diagnosis, but can help you to cope with stressful situations.

Symptoms of adult ADHD can create problems in relationships, job performance, and daily life. Many adults have found that treatment improves their lives in many different ways, but an accurate diagnosis is essential to creating an effective treatment plan. You should be honest and open with your doctor, explain why you believe you have adult ADHD, what symptoms are causing you the most problems, and share as much as you can about your past experiences. This will allow you and your doctor to determine the best course of action.

The Difference Between ADD and ADHD

Do you have ADD? Or ADHD? There is a great deal of confusion over the terms ADD and ADHD. Sometimes ADD is used to describe ADHD without the hyperactivity. Sometimes people say ADD simply because it has one less letter and is easier to say. The correct medical term is ADHD, and if you don't have hyperactivity, the correct phrase is "ADHD, predominately inattentive type." But since that's quite a mouthful, the term ADD will probably continue to indicate "without hyperactivity," and, to keep things simple, we'll use the terms ADD and ADHD, too.

It is also a common perception that girls have ADD and boys have ADHD. It is true that the majority of females are diagnosed with ADD, but many girls are diagnosed with ADHD, hyperactive/impulsive type, and plenty of boys have been diagnosed with inattention rather than hyperactivity. Gender, therefore, isn't a good predictor of how someone will be diagnosed.

There are, however, some distinct characteristics of each. An ADD diagnosis can be more difficult or may be delayed until children are older. Often, children with ADHD are diagnosed by elementary school, because the hyperactivity is easy to see. Children with ADD may be seen as shy or underachievers and may not be diagnosed until the teen years or older.

Hyperactivity is more consistent than inattention. It is easier to recognize and it is often discovered earlier. Inattention is more inconsistent. You may be able to pay attention, even *hyperfocus*, on those things that hold your attention, especially high-stimulus activities. You may not be able to focus on activities and tasks that are boring or repetitive. During these activities, you can be easily distracted. Shifting attention, or moving from task to task, can be extremely difficult. This inconsistency is confusing and can make it more difficult to diagnose ADD.

def•i•ni•tion

Hyperfocus is the ability to focus so intently on one specific task that you may become oblivious to the world around you.

If you are hyperactive, you are more apt to be outgoing and may find it easier to meet people, but find it more difficult to bond and create deeper friendships. If you are inattentive, it may be harder for you to meet people, but you may have deeper and more lasting friendships. Both ADD and ADHD, however, may cause problems in social situations, especially in following conversations and the tendency to blurt out inappropriate remarks.

As far as treatment, there isn't much of a difference between ADD and ADHD. The same medications are used to treat both. The only difference would be in the types of behavior strategies used. For example, if you are hyperactive and impulsive, behavioral strategies would be geared toward curbing impulses and managing hyperactivity by using strategies such as getting up and moving around. With inattention, strategies might be using technology to help with time management.

A Five-Question Screening Test

This test is for screening purposes only. It can help determine if you should seek further professional help. It does NOT replace a professional evaluation.

1. **Were you diagnosed with ADHD (or an equivalent condition) as a child?**

    a. Yes

    b. No formal diagnosis but teacher comments, my parents' memories, and my own recollections fit the symptoms of childhood ADHD

    c. No

2. **Do people complain that you forget tasks, appointments, or promises?**

    a. Yes, both at work and in my personal life

    b. Sometimes, but mostly outside of a structured setting (work, school)

    c. Infrequently

3. **Do you have trouble focusing on tasks and details or shifting attention from one task to another?**

    a. Yes, especially if the task is boring or repetitive

    b. Sometimes

    c. Rarely—I love column addition!

4. **Do you have trouble sitting still?**

    a. Yes, I can't!

    b. For more than 15 minutes, unless I'm engrossed in a movie or show, and even then I'm a restless fidgeter

    c. No

5. **When you have to prioritize tasks or steps in a project or get organized, can you?**

   a. No, I'm all over the place, like a bee in a flower patch

   b. Only with great effort, or if overseen by a teacher or supervisor

   c. Organization is my middle name! Literally

Scoring: Give yourself five points for each "a" answer, three points for each "b" answer, and one point for each "c" answer.

If your score totals higher than 15 points, you should be evaluated for ADHD.

If you scored between 10 and 15 points, you would probably benefit from an evaluation.

If your score is between 5 and 10 points, you are within normal limits.

The Least You Need to Know

◆ Stimulant medications were first used as a treatment for behavioral disorders in 1937.

◆ Most ADHD is considered hereditary. Bad parenting or diet does not cause ADHD.

◆ ADHD in adults still has major symptoms of hyperactivity, impulsiveness, and inattention/distractibility, but these can look different in children and adults.

◆ Symptoms of adult ADHD can create problems in relationships, job performance, and daily life.

◆ One of the difficulties in diagnosing adult ADHD is that symptoms must be present in childhood, but personal and family recollections are often enough to make a diagnosis.

2

Debunking Myths About ADHD

In This Chapter

- ◆ ADHD is a real disorder
- ◆ Diet and ADHD
- ◆ ADHD's role in learning situations
- ◆ Girls get ADHD, too

Over the years, a great deal of research has been done on the causes, the symptoms, and the treatment of ADHD. Despite this many myths, misconceptions, and misunderstandings still exist. Critics assert parents would rather drug a child than deal with playfulness, and adults who claim ADHD really just want an excuse for their behavior.

Misleading information can stop someone from seeking treatment. For example, imagine a woman who has spent years fighting disorganization and distractibility. When her neighbor insists ADHD is just an excuse, instead of speaking up, she feels ashamed. She feels guilty for looking for answers instead of trying harder.

Those of you with ADHD, take heart! In this chapter, we're going to give you scientifically validated facts and information so you may refute the misinformed folks, or at least so you can tune them out.

Myth: ADHD Is Not a "Real" Disorder

"Everyone gets distracted sometimes, it's no big deal, you just have to focus more." How many times have you heard similar words from neighbors, friends, or co-workers? This type of sentiment is still around, despite the immense amount of accurate information available. Critics of ADHD still claim ADHD is not a "real" disorder. With judgments based on emotion and no scientific data, critics will accuse people with ADHD of simply wanting to sweep poor behavior under the carpet instead of taking responsibility. Or some may rant about how the psychiatrists and pharmaceutical companies got together and made up a diagnosis in order to increase profits.

> **Think It Over**
>
> There is a great deal of information on ADHD today. There are hundreds of websites and books touting all kinds of information and written by all kinds of people. Make sure the information you read comes from a reliable source.

There are a few points critics frequently bring up to back up their claims of ADHD being a fake diagnosis. The following discusses the statements from critics and offers evidence to dispute each point:

There is no definitive medical test for ADHD.

> **The Scoop**
>
> There are physical illnesses that can also be diagnosed without a laboratory or medical test. Migraine headaches are normally diagnosed based on medical history and a discussion of symptoms, much the same way as ADHD is diagnosed.

Diagnosis of ADHD is subjective. This is true. There is no laboratory or medical test that will tell you if you have ADHD. It is diagnosed through a family history and a discussion of symptoms. This, however, does not take away from the fact it is a real diagnosis. Some medical conditions are also diagnosed this same way.

Symptoms of ADHD are personality traits rather than symptoms and are not consistent.

Honest, trustworthy, compassionate, loyal—these are personality traits. Hyperactivity and inattentiveness/distractibility are not personality traits. Symptoms do vary in degrees based on the individual person. We already know that hyperactivity is not present in all cases of ADHD, and some people are more easily distracted than others. This is obvious based on the different subtypes of ADHD. Even so, core symptoms must be present before a diagnosis can be made. Diagnostic criteria say these symptoms must appear before age seven and be present in two separate environments. Doctors experienced in diagnosing ADHD are able to differentiate character traits from symptoms of ADHD.

Symptoms of ADHD are too general and can be explained by life situations.

Critics say, for example, hyperactive children are simply active, playful children, or they may be overly active due to emotional overload or lack of discipline. Again, this point is true, to a degree. Tired or over-whelmed children may become agitated and hyperactive. Children from an undisciplined home may act up. Adults who are stressed may be pre-occupied and forgetful. The difference is in the consistency of symp-toms. When distractibility occurs because you are preoccupied with a problem at work, your attention returns once the problem is solved. When you have ADHD, inattention/distractibility is a consistent pres-ence in your life, not situational.

ADHD is a real diagnosis. It has been recognized as a neurobiological disorder by all major medical, psychiatric, psychological, and educa-tional associations and organizations. It is listed as a disorder or dis-ability by all branches of the U.S. government. This recognition is not like getting some honorary award. Recognition comes after reviewing hundreds of studies. The medical diagnosis of all physical and mental conditions is accepted through this same process.

Myth: Bad Parenting Causes ADHD

According to some critics, ADHD is simply an extension of poor par-enting and chaotic households or is caused by a lack of discipline in the home. Most parents of children with ADHD have heard, at one time or

The Lowdown

When parents have ADHD themselves, trying to discipline children can be overwhelming. Using charts and other behavioral strategies can help make discipline more consistent.

another, "All he really needs is some good old-fashioned discipline." This myth has caused many parents to feel guilty and to harbor feelings of shame about their child's ADHD.

Bad parenting simply does not cause ADHD. ADHD is a neurobiological disorder. Discipline can no more "cure" ADHD than it can make a blind person see. In fact, Dr. Russell Barkley has shown that using strong discipline on children with ADHD may actually worsen symptoms rather than improving them.

It can also be true that symptoms worsen when households are chaotic and do not include consistent discipline. Children with ADHD thrive in structured, consistent environments. Parents who provide clear rules with consistent and positive discipline, and consequences for misbehaviors, find symptoms of ADHD to be more manageable.

Myth: Diet or Too Much Sugar Causes ADHD

In the late 1960s, Dr. Ben Feingold created an elimination diet. This diet eliminated artificial coloring, flavoring, sweeteners, and preservatives. It assumed the increase in hyperactivity and behavioral problems were a result of the artificial ingredients in processed foods. Originally used as a diet for allergies, Dr. Feingold noticed a change in children's behaviors when using this diet. According to Dr. Feingold, this diet helped children with hyperactivity about one half the time.

Think It Over

Food plays an important role in how we feel and may affect our moods. Eating a well-balanced diet is always important to our health. Be careful of diets that claim to cure ADHD. There is no "cure" for ADHD.

The problem is science and research have not backed up the claims that diet or sugar cause hyperactivity, or any other symptoms of ADHD. In 1994, Dr. Richard Milich and Dr. Daniel Hoover completed one of the more interesting studies on diet (published in *The Journal of Abnormal Child Psychology*). A total of 31 boys between the ages of five and seven were given drinks with a sugar substitute. Previous to the study, their mothers had indicated sensitivity to sugar. Half of the mothers were told their son received sugar and half were told their son received a sugar substitute. The mothers who believed their children received sugar reported more hyperactive behaviors; they were more critical of their child's behavior and hovered over their child more. The mothers who believed their child received a sugar substitute were more relaxed with their child and got along better with their child.

This study questions whether improved behavior is a direct result of eliminating sugar from the diet or whether it has more to do with the reaction of the mother. In other words, is it the diet itself that creates a change in behavior, or did the added structure and monitoring of the child's behavior cause improvement?

A proper and well-balanced diet is integral to maintaining health. Eating properly can lower a person's risk of developing a number of health conditions, such as heart disease. However, the National Resource Center for ADHD indicates that scientific studies have not supported diet alone as an effective treatment for ADHD.

Myth: ADHD Is a Kid's Disorder

The Diagnostic and Statistical Manual states symptoms of ADHD must be present before the age of seven to make a diagnosis. One of the main symptoms of ADHD, hyperactivity, seems to lessen, or at least changes, as a person grows and matures. This leads some people to believe ADHD is a childhood disorder. At least half of all children with ADHD, however, will continue to have symptoms of ADHD into adulthood.

Dr. Paul Wender researched and introduced the concept of adult ADHD back in the 1970s. Dr. Wender treated children with ADHD and observed parents of those children also experiencing symptoms of ADHD. Although he published articles on the subject, not until 1995, when the book *Driven to Distraction* (Hallowell and Ratey) was released, was adult ADHD accepted by the general public and much of the medical community as a valid diagnosis.

Today, many adults are finding out about their own ADHD after bringing their child to the doctor for ADHD. Completing checklists or reading information and learning about ADHD brings back memories of their own childhood. Then they may discuss their own symptoms with the doctor, discovering there is a medical reason for many of the behaviors with which they have struggled throughout their lives.

The Scoop
I (DH) have treated several families in which two to four people have ADHD. It usually begins when I see a college student who is diagnosed, and soon one of the parents calls and says they have read up on ADHD and think they may have the problem, then a sibling in college, and so on. Sometimes even aunts, uncles, and cousins come in for evaluation!

Without treatment, symptoms of ADHD can continue to cause impairment and problems. Some adults experience problems at work and in relationships. Some develop depression or anxiety, or turn to substance abuse as a way of self-medication.

With advances in research and greater understanding of ADHD, more and more adults are seeking out diagnosis and treatment, learning they do not need to live with the debilitating impact of ADHD.

Myth: ADHD Medications Cause Addiction

One myth surrounding the treatment of ADHD is that children who are given medication to treat the symptoms will grow up to use, abuse, and become addicted to other substances, such as cocaine.

Teens and adults with ADHD are more likely to abuse drugs. For those with comorbid conditions (bipolar disorder, depression, and so on) the risk is even higher. But, the risk is actually less for those who have been treated with stimulant medications. A review of six studies (Wilens, et al, 2003, *Pediatrics*, Vol 111) showed youth who had not been treated with stimulant medications were twice as likely to abuse substances during their teen years.

A number of critics also believe ADHD medications are, themselves, addictive. One study showed a correlation between how quickly a drug was effective with the risk of addiction. Cocaine, when snorted, causes a reaction within seconds. Stimulant medications, on the other hand, can take up to an hour to be effective. Many studies have shown that stimulant medications, when taken as prescribed, are not addictive.

Myth: ADHD Is a Learning Disability

A common misconception about ADHD is that it is a learning disability (LD). A learning disability makes learning hard because of problems with processing information or retrieving information previously learned. ADHD, on the other hand, can cause problems in learning because you become distracted, or constant activity causes you to miss details.

There are other differences between ADHD and an LD. ADHD is a medical diagnosis. It is not (and cannot be) diagnosed by educational professionals. LDs are not medically diagnosed and are most often identified within the school. (Some people have an independent evaluation by a private psychologist.)

ADHD also impacts a person globally. LDs are specific to one area. For example, a math LD interferes with a person's ability to complete math. It does not cause problems in reading. Symptoms of ADHD, such as inattention, remain more constant whether learning history or math. ADHD does not interfere with just one area of your life but in many areas.

Despite the differences, neither ADHD nor learning disabilities have any impact on intelligence. Some of the same strategies help whether you have an LD or ADHD, such as minimizing distractions, breaking large projects into smaller tasks, and using technology for reminders. During the school years, lumping these strategies together can add to the confusion and give the impression that ADHD is a type of LD.

Myth: Only Hyperactive People Have ADHD

There is no doubt about it, hyperactivity is easier to spot than inattentiveness. In terms of ADHD, it is, or at least it has been in the past, the squeaky wheel that gets the grease. Quiet, shy, or withdrawn children frequently get passed by, seen as underachievers or lazy. Hyperactive children get lots of attention—because they're driving their parents, teachers, siblings, and peers crazy!

The Lowdown

Adults with inattention can find it difficult to complete unpleasant tasks, such as paying the bills. Try enlisting the help of a friend (or spouse) to sit with you while you are completing the task. The other person doesn't need to do anything but, by being there, can add motivation to complete the unpleasant task.

Past descriptions of ADHD (hyperkinetic disorder of childhood or minimal brain dysfunction) listed hyperactivity as the main symptom. By the 1970s, additional symptoms of inattention and impulsiveness were added to the diagnostic criteria, but hyperactivity still received the most attention. Today, inattention and distractibility are seen as major symptoms. Hyperactivity is not necessary for a diagnosis of ADHD.

Myth: ADHD Is a Male Disorder

The majority of people diagnosed with ADHD are male. For every girl diagnosed, there are three boys diagnosed (the National Alliance on Mental Illness). A report issued by the surgeon general in 2001 stated, "girls are less likely to receive a diagnosis and treatment for ADHD than boys, despite the need."

Girls are often diagnosed with ADHD, inattentive type. Girls with inattention may be seen as ditzy, spacey, or not academically inclined. Girls also have a higher rate of depression and other mood disorders, self-esteem issues, anxiety, and problems with family relationships, than boys with ADHD. This may be linked back to girls not being diagnosed as early. Kathleen G. Nadeau, in her book, *Understanding Girls with AD/HD*, explains that girls are diagnosed less often because girls tend to be less rebellious and less defiant than boys.

The problems girls experience might be explained by the fact that symptoms are often brushed aside. Girls are left to deal with the inability to pay attention or focus on their own. Many probably believe they are stupid or slow, because no matter how hard they try, they still daydream rather than pay attention.

Fortunately, recent understanding that ADHD, inattentive type, is just as debilitating and just as harmful has led to greater understanding and an increase in the number of diagnoses of girls, as well as girls being diagnosed earlier.

Myth: People with ADHD Are Not Smart

Children with ADHD frequently do not do as well in school as their non-ADHD classmates. Because of this, they are considered to be "not as smart." In fact, ADHD does not impact intelligence. In some cases, *IQ* tests can show lower scores for people with ADHD, frequently showing up as a wide gap between high "verbal" and low "performance" scores. Taking an IQ test requires sustained attention and focus, the exact areas those with ADHD have problems with. This does not mean people with ADHD are not as intelligent. It means they have a problem with attention while taking an IQ test.

According to a study published in *Clinical Pediatrics* (2005), 31 children with ADHD took an IQ test prior to receiving treatment for ADHD. One year later, the same test was given to the same children. Those children on medication (24 of the 31 children) received significantly higher IQ scores on the second test.

ADHD does not impact intelligence; however it may impact the ability to use, or focus, intelligence, especially without treatment.

def•i•ni•tion

IQ, or intelligence quotient, is the ratio of tested mental age to chronological age times 100.

Myth: ADHD Is Overdiagnosed

One of the largest criticisms of ADHD is the increase in the number of diagnoses over the last several decades. Critics believe this increase emphasizes that this is a fake or made-up disorder, and that more and more people are relying on a "disorder" rather than discipline.

The Scoop

Some experts believe 4 of every 100 adults in the United States have ADHD, and that, rather than being overdiagnosed, adult ADHD is under-diagnosed.

According to the Centers for Disease Control, the diagnosis of ADHD has increased by an average of 3 percent a year between 1997 and 2006. This does not mean ADHD is overdiagnosed, but may instead point to ADHD being underdiagnosed in previous years.

There are a number of reasons why the number of people diagnosed with ADHD may have increased:

◆ There has been an increased awareness of ADHD. More and more people understand what symptoms are involved, what these symptoms look like and, because of that, more and more people are seeking a diagnosis and treatment for things they may have seen as character flaws in the past.

◆ Girls are more likely to be diagnosed today than even 10 years ago. Understanding not only hyperactivity but also the different subtypes of ADHD has led to a greater number of people diagnosed with ADHD.

◆ Adults are now being diagnosed with ADHD. This is no longer seen as only a childhood disorder and we now know at least 50 percent of children with ADHD continue to experience symptoms into adulthood.

◆ Characteristics once thought of as character or personality flaws, such as chronic tardiness, forgetfulness, disorganization, or consistent underachievement might actually be symptoms of adult ADHD. The more we understand adult ADHD, the more adults will seek treatment.

◆ Children born prematurely or with a low birth weight are at a higher risk of developing ADHD. These children are more apt to survive today than in the past due to medical advances.

- We live in a more fast-paced, technological age. Many more jobs today require people to sit still for longer periods of time. This can make symptoms of ADHD more noticeable than in the past.

- Two-income families and today's style of home life make ADHD more noticeable. In the past, when moms stayed at home, life was simpler. Today, with both parents often working outside the home, households need to be more organized and children need to take on more responsibilities. Disorganization in adults and emotional immaturity in children may be more noticeable today than a few decades ago.

The Least You Need to Know

- ADHD is not just a childhood disorder. As far back as 30 years ago, Dr. Paul Wender introduced the subject of adult ADHD.

- The increase in the number of diagnoses of ADHD in the past few decades can be explained by increased awareness, different lifestyles, and a greater understanding that ADHD impacts girls and adults, as well as boys.

- Hyperactivity is one of the major symptoms of ADHD however, it does not need to be present to have a diagnosis. ADHD, inattentive type, is a subtype where the main symptom is inattention/distractibility and may not include hyperactivity.

- Medications used to treat ADHD do not cause later addictions in the doses prescribed. As a matter of fact, some studies have shown that children treated with stimulant medications may be at less risk of substance abuse during adolescent years than those with untreated ADHD.

- Girls with ADHD are at a higher risk of developing depression or anxiety, especially if the ADHD has gone undiagnosed or untreated.

Chapter 3

Related Conditions

In This Chapter

- ◆ Conditions commonly associated with ADHD
- ◆ How comorbid conditions complicate treatment
- ◆ Exploring which condition should be treated first

ADHD by itself can cause impairment, but add other conditions, such as depression, anxiety, or bipolar disorder and you have an array of symptoms that can wreak havoc in your life. Sometimes these conditions are secondary, meaning they have developed as a result of dealing with symptoms of ADHD. In these cases, once ADHD is managed, the symptoms of the secondary disorder may resolve themselves. In other cases, these conditions are a second, separate condition and both must be treated.

In this chapter, we'll discuss some of the most commonly associated disorders and tell you what symptoms to be aware of. We'll also discuss how each is treated and how to determine which condition should be treated first.

What Is a Comorbid Condition?

Comorbid, sometimes called coexisting, means having two or more diagnosable conditions at the same time. For example, a person can be diagnosed with both ADHD and depression.

During the diagnostic process comorbid conditions can cause problems. Many conditions can share or overlap some symptoms of ADHD. For example, a symptom of both ADHD and anxiety disorder is "difficulty concentrating." It is important for patients to answer honestly questions asked by their doctors or on questionnaires. It is equally important for doctors to take a family history and be aware of other disorders that may be causing symptoms. Family doctors do not always have the experience or knowledge to diagnose ADHD, especially when other mental conditions may be present. Since accurate diagnosis is extremely important in creating an effective treatment plan, you may want to work with a mental-health professional who specializes in adult ADHD.

> **The Scoop**
>
> As many as two thirds of all children and adults diagnosed with ADHD will also be diagnosed and treated for a second mental-health condition sometime in their life.

Depression

Almost one half of adults with ADHD may also have signs of depression or *dysthymia*. Depression can be caused by genetics, but environmental factors (for example, the loss of someone close) may also play a role. Many times ADHD is diagnosed in childhood and depression later, in the teen or adult years. When ADHD has not been diagnosed in childhood, depression may be diagnosed first, especially in women.

def•i•ni•tion

> **Dysthymia** is a chronic form of depression. Symptoms are generally not as severe but occur almost every day. Symptoms must be present for at least two years in adults, and one year in children, before a diagnosis can be made.

Signs of depression can include:

◆ Feeling sad, feeling hopeless, or crying spells (without cause)

◆ Loss of interest in daily activities or in activities that you once enjoyed

◆ Insomnia

◆ Trouble focusing or paying attention

◆ Indecisiveness

◆ Irritability, easily annoyed

◆ Feeling tired or easily fatigued

◆ Weight gain or loss without trying

◆ Unexplained physical complaints (headaches, stomachaches)

◆ Feelings of guilt

◆ Suicidal thoughts or behaviors

Depression symptoms can vary in severity. You may have an overall feeling of sadness without knowing or understanding why, or feel worthless, hopeless, or suicidal. People with depression sometimes describe feeling as if there is a black curtain around them. You do not simply "get over" depression.

A number of different types of antidepressants are available today. For some people, antidepressants alone may help symptoms of both ADHD and depression, but other people may need both an antidepressant and medication for ADHD.

Bipolar Disorder

Bipolar disorder was previously known as manic depression. People with bipolar disorder experience extreme highs (mania) and extreme lows (depression). Mania can include feelings of grandiosity, excitability, or giddiness. Other symptoms of bipolar disorder include:

◆ Irritability

◆ Mood swings

- Hyperactivity

- Racing thoughts

- Impulsiveness

- Depression, lethargy

- Trouble waking up in the morning

Periods of mania can last anywhere from one day to several months, normally followed by severe depression; or moods can cycle very rapidly, sometimes changing from mania to depression in a matter of minutes or hours.

Think It Over

Up to 80 percent of individuals with bipolar disorder can meet the diagnostic criteria for ADHD. Some experts believe ADHD should be diagnosed only after bipolar disorder has been ruled out.

Treatment for bipolar disorder, usually a mood stabilizer such as lithium or valproate, takes precedence over treatment for ADHD, since without stabilizing moods, treatment for ADHD will not be as effective. For some people stimulant medications can trigger periods of mania, so it's important to carefully monitor the use of ADHD medications in people with bipolar disorder.

Anxiety Disorders

Anxiety disorders occur in anywhere from 25 to 40 percent of adults with ADHD. Frequently, anxiety symptoms are not readily apparent or are confused with symptoms of ADHD. Symptoms of anxiety include:

- Consistent or constant worrying for no apparent reason

- Difficulty concentrating

- Insomnia

- Restlessness or irritability

- Feelings of dread or always anticipating the worst

- Feeling tense or jumpy

Anxiety or panic attacks may also occur. These are periods of extreme anxiety and are accompanied by pounding heart, sweating, shaking, and breathing problems. Anxiety attacks occur without reason, sometimes in your sleep.

People with both anxiety and ADHD often have more social and relationship problems than those with only ADHD.

The most effective treatment for anxiety is a combination of cognitive behavior therapy and medication. Stimulant medications can sometimes cause an increase in anxiety symptoms, but some people with anxiety disorder and ADHD find stimulant medications help calm symptoms.

Obsessive Compulsive Disorder

Obsessive compulsive disorder (OCD) has two major symptoms, obsessions and/or compulsions. Obsessions are persistent thoughts or images that will not go away. These thoughts or images usually cause anxiety and intrude into daily activities and everyday life. Examples of obsessions are fears about being contaminated by germs or committing a violent act. Obsessions may also include an extreme need for order. For example, someone may need all of their shoes lined up in a particular order and will not be able to concentrate or go on with other activities of life unless he or she fixes the shoes.

The Lowdown

Stress often triggers symptoms of OCD and worsens symptoms of ADHD. Learning relaxation techniques such as deep breathing exercises can help you cope with symptoms of both.

Compulsions are rituals or repetitive behaviors that must be completed in an effort to alleviate fear and anxiety. For example, washing hands over and over to eliminate the fear of being contaminated by germs. Other common compulsions include:

◆ Checking excessively to be sure the stove is turned off or doors are locked

◆ Eating foods in a particular order

◆ Repeating a word or phrase over and over

People with OCD understand their thoughts or actions are irrational but feel powerless to stop. Obsessive compulsive disorder is a type of anxiety disorder, and treatment would be the same as general anxiety: a combination of cognitive behavior therapy and medication. Some research indicates up to 70 percent of people with ADHD will develop at least some OCD symptoms.

Learning Disabilities

Up to one half of all people with ADHD may have a learning disability as well. Learning disabilities create problems in reading, calculations, writing, and visual or auditory perception. Learning disabilities do not impact symptoms of ADHD; for example, people with ADHD and dyslexia are not more hyperactive or inattentive than those with ADHD alone. Learning disabilities, however, can impact school and work performance and, in turn, can impact self-esteem and relationships.

Medication for ADHD does not improve a learning disability, but can indirectly help people with learning disabilities. Improving ADHD symptoms can help focus and concentration, thereby allowing those with ADHD to develop better strategies for coping with their learning disability.

Substance Abuse and Other Addictive Behaviors

Numerous studies have shown adults with ADHD are at a higher risk of substance abuse than their non-ADHD peers. In addition, substance abuse is more likely to begin at an earlier age in people with ADHD. (Contrary to popular belief, the use of stimulant medications for ADHD has not been shown to increase the risk of substance abuse.)

> **The Scoop**
>
> Individuals with untreated ADHD are twice as likely to develop substance abuse as those who are prescribed stimulant medications to treat their symptoms of ADHD.

Impulsiveness and behavioral problems may contribute to the high rate of substance abuse. Some scientists believe genes contribute to the link between ADHD and substance abuse. If you have ADHD and someone in your family has been diagnosed with substance abuse, your risk of substance abuse is even higher.

Also, when ADHD is not treated, people often seek out potentially addictive stimulants, like high-dose methamphetamine or cocaine, to "treat" their ADHD. This may work initially in lower doses but, for most people, the doses rapidly get higher and they become addicted.

When treating ADHD in someone with a history of substance abuse, your doctor will need to weigh the benefits of stimulant medications with the risks, especially if you have been sober less than a year. Long-acting stimulant medications offer less of a chance of abuse. Substance abuse and ADHD should be treated simultaneously once initial sobriety has been achieved. Treating ADHD may increase the chances of substance abuse treatment being more successful.

Other Common Comorbid Conditions

Although the previous conditions are some of the more common comorbid conditions, they certainly are not the only ones. ADHD can occur with any condition.

Sleep disorders are also common in people with ADHD. Many adults with ADHD complain of not being able to turn off racing thoughts long enough to fall asleep. Some adults with ADHD may wake up several times throughout the night, resulting in poor sleep. Symptoms of sleep disorders include inattention and inability, or difficulty, concentrating.

Between 40 and 50 percent of adults with ADHD also have signs of conduct disorder or oppositional defiant disorder. Symptoms include being argumentative, short tempered, or not following rules. Aggression and social problems are sometimes helped by stimulant medication treatment. For some, the addition of an antidepressant or mood stabilizer helps as well.

The Lowdown

Recent research has shown that stimulant medication taken in the evening may actually help adults with ADHD improve their mood during the evening hours, fall asleep quicker, and wake up less often during the night.

How Does a Comorbid Condition Complicate Treatment?

Individuals with ADHD plus another psychiatric disorder find life more difficult and treatment for ADHD more complicated. It is a challenge for doctors to develop effective treatment plans that incorporate all symptoms.

def•i•ni•tion

Cognitive behavioral therapy is based on the premise that our thoughts, not external things, define our behaviors. It works to change thought processes to improve how we feel about a situation.

Although a combination of medication and behavioral therapy is important when treating ADHD alone, it is even more important when you have one or more additional psychiatric disorders. Adding therapy (talk, *cognitive behavioral therapy*, or both) can increase the chances of treatment being successful.

Just as the symptoms of other conditions can interfere with a diagnosis by masking symptoms of ADHD, they can also interfere with treatment as well. If you are crippled with feelings of anxiety or too depressed to act on learning new skills, it is hard to create a structure in your life to help improve inattentiveness or impulsiveness. It may also be difficult to determine which symptoms of ADHD need to be addressed if they are hidden behind depression, mania, or anxiety symptoms. Mental-health professionals will need to work with the patient to, at the very least, lessen symptoms of other disorders in order to effectively treat ADHD.

Medications can also complicate treatment in the following ways:

- ◆ Stimulant medications can increase anxiety.
- ◆ Stimulant medications can trigger a manic episode.
- ◆ Antidepressant medications can worsen ADHD symptoms.

This is not to say these medications should be avoided or someone should forego treatment for one condition. A mental-health professional can closely monitor medication to determine the correct dosage and combination to improve symptoms. For example, symptoms of ADHD may aggravate anxiety, so by using stimulant medications to reduce symptoms of ADHD, the anxiety may be more controlled and easier to treat.

What Condition Is Treated First?

The first rule is: Treat the most distracting or destructive condition first. That means, which symptoms are most interfering with your daily activities? Is it the inattentiveness of ADHD or is it the mood swings from bipolar disorder? Frequently, mood disorders will be treated first because either the lows of depression or the mood swings of bipolar disorder are more difficult for a person to cope with. ADHD will be easier to manage after moods have been stabilized.

Antidepressants, often used to treat depression, bipolar disorder, and anxiety can take approximately three weeks to work. Short-acting ADHD medications are effective within an hour. Because of this, when a dual diagnosis is made, antidepressant medications may be started first. ADHD medications can then be added as needed.

The second rule is: Don't forget the ADHD! As the depression, mood swings, or anxiety start to improve, keep an eye out for the ADHD symptoms that may have been hiding behind the other disorder all along. In some cases, the ADHD may have been part of the cause and treating it helps greatly in relieving the other symptoms.

> **Think It Over**
>
> Certain antidepressants (SSRIs and SSNRIs) can cause dangerous drug interactions when taken with some stimulant medications. Make sure your doctor knows all of the medications you are taking and be aware of the possible side effects from combining medications.

Substance abuse is somewhat different in that it should always be treated first. Since there is the potential for abuse with stimulant medications, it is recommended to have at least six months of sobriety (and a commitment to continued sobriety) before beginning medication for ADHD.

Additional treatments, such as therapy and behavioral strategies, can be simultaneous with treatments for other conditions.

The Least You Need to Know

◆ Many mental-health conditions can coexist with, or be caused or complicated by, ADHD.

◆ These comorbid conditions often must be treated in order to clearly see the ADHD.

◆ Treating the ADHD is often helpful in improving the comorbid condition.

◆ The most serious symptoms of the comorbid condition should be treated first, especially for substance abuse.

Part 2

Treatment of ADHD

Many different options are available for the treatment of ADHD and it can be hard to know what is best—or how to tell the difference. You may wonder if medication is the only treatment or if the alternative treatments work.

This part will explore the various types of treatment, explain the role of medication in treatment, and discuss whether or not adults with ADHD can benefit from therapy. We'll also talk about the best way to go about setting up a treatment plan.

There are many alternative and complementary treatments for ADHD and it is hard to know which ones are worthwhile and which ones should be ignored.

Finally, we address ADHD coaching, a viable solution for many adults with ADHD. Coaching may help you stay on track and reach your goals.

Chapter 4

Medical Treatment of ADHD

In This Chapter

- ◆ Deciding if medication can help you
- ◆ Managing symptoms with therapy
- ◆ Finding a doctor

You wouldn't think that treating adult ADHD would be much different than treating childhood ADHD; after all, it's still ADHD, right? Possibly, but there are various complications in the medical treatment of adults. First, adults who haven't been diagnosed in childhood have been dealing with symptoms all their life. Symptoms such as forgetfulness, chronic tardiness, or poor social skills may have taken their toll, causing failures in relationships and jobs. Feelings of being inadequate or being a failure can lead to substance abuse, depression, or anxiety, complicating both the diagnosis and the treatment of adult ADHD.

Health problems may interfere as well. Besides mental-health issues, adults with ADHD may not take care of their health, forgetting doctors appointments or medication, even for a chronic health condition. Impulsiveness can lead to overeating, compulsive eating, or grabbing junk food. Medications for other health conditions may interfere with treatment for ADHD, limiting options.

In this chapter, we will review the medical options available for adults with ADHD, learn the difference between stimulant and nonstimulant medications, and explain why therapy helps in managing symptoms of ADHD.

When to Seek Medical Attention

What makes you think you have ADHD? Are you easily distracted? Maybe you can't sit still, or you have gone through job after job, getting bored and restless soon after starting? Maybe you have recently been diagnosed, or maybe you are wondering if you have ADHD. If you are an adult and have not yet been diagnosed, you might be wondering whether it is time for you to see a doctor.

Chapter 1 contains a self-test that may give you an idea of whether or not you should see a doctor. But your answers to the following questions might also provide a clue:

◆ Are you in constant motion or do you consistently fidget?

◆ Have you changed jobs frequently throughout your adult years?

◆ Do you have projects lying around that you are anxious to start but then you lose interest and never finish?

◆ Do you have a poor concept of time?

◆ Are you chronically late?

◆ Do you lack personal skills and have a history of failed relationships?

◆ Do you have financial problems due to impulsive spending or an inability to follow a budget?

◆ Do you have symptoms of depression?

Think It Over

Drivers with ADHD are four times more likely to be in a car accident, get a ticket, or run a stop sign than drivers without ADHD. Using stimulant medications decreases the risk.

Some adults with ADHD struggle with these issues on a daily basis and have for many years. They may have assumed these are not symptoms of a disorder but rather personality flaws. Obviously, this is not true. Sometimes, it just takes finding the right treatment plan.

The Role of Medication

Stimulant medications have been used effectively to treat ADHD for many years. Surprisingly, even though they are stimulants, they work to decrease hyperactivity and impulsiveness and help to increase attention and executive functioning.

Is Medication Right for You?

Medication for ADHD is highly debated, and it's not right for everyone. It may not be effective (studies show stimulant medication to be effective in 70 to 75 percent of adults with ADHD), it may interfere with other medications you are taking, or you may choose to use behavioral strategies and other therapeutic measures rather than medication.

Despite the controversy, medication does not change you or make you act differently. It will allow you to better manage symptoms of ADHD. For most of you with ADHD, medication will be an important part of your treatment.

Stimulant Medications

Stimulant medications are commonly prescribed and have been found to be most effective for adults with ADHD. There are two main types of stimulant medications (amphetamines and methylphenidate), and there are short- and long-acting versions of each.

The following table lists each medication and how long you can expect a dose to last.

Generic Name	Brand Name	Usual Length of Action (in hours)
Methylphenidate (short acting)	Ritalin, Focalin	Between 2.5 and 4 hours
d-,1-Amphetamine	Adderall, Dexedrine	Between 4 and 5 hours
Methamphetamine	Desoxyn	Between 4 and 5 hours
Methylphenidate, medium or long acting	Ritalin SR, Ritalin LA, Metadate CD, Concerta	Ritalin SR and Ritalin LA: 8 hours Metadate CD: between 6 and 8 hours Concerta: 12 hours
Amphetamine	Adderall XR, Vyvanse	Adderall XR: 10 hours Vyvanse: between 12 and 13 hours

Stimulant medications work by increasing certain chemicals in the brain. Each medication does this in a different way. For this reason, medications may have a different effect on symptoms of ADHD, depending on the individual and on how fast the medication is metabolized. If you don't respond to one medication, you may find benefits from a different type of medication.

The Lowdown

Stimulant medications can cause a mild increase in blood pressure or heart rate. Having these checked before you begin taking stimulant medications, and every three to six months while on the medication, makes good sense.

Many people tolerate stimulant medications without side effects interfering with their daily life. However, some common side effects can include loss of appetite, insomnia, and a mild increase in heart rate or blood pressure. Some of these side effects will disappear after taking the medication for a few weeks. Once you stop the medication the side effects stop, too.

With all stimulant medications, there is a slight risk of addiction, especially if you use them in higher doses or in ways other than recommended. This risk is higher if you have a past history of substance abuse, especially if you are not in a recovery program or have been sober for less than one year. The risk also seems to be a bit higher with methamphetamine.

The Scoop

Mary (not her real name) went for treatment for ADHD and depression. She had been addicted to cocaine but had been sober for over a year. Wellbutrin helped her depression and also provided some help with her ADHD symptoms. Once her depression stabilized, Mary started on Adderall as well. Two years later, Mary is still doing well. There are no signs of substance abuse and both her depression and ADHD symptoms are greatly improved.

Nonstimulant Medications

In recent years, a few nonstimulant medications have been introduced for treating ADHD. Atomoxetine (Strattera) was the first one approved by the FDA for adult ADHD. This medication is frequently used as a second- or third-line treatment option for adults with ADHD, as it seems to be less effective.

Because Strattera is not a controlled substance, there is little or no chance of it being abused or causing dependence after prolonged use and it can be prescribed for more than 30 days. This medication needs to be taken daily and you will need to take it for two to three weeks before it is effective.

Nonstimulant medications also have side effects, such as nausea, loss of appetite, mood swings, or drowsiness. Most of these side effects disappear after a few weeks of taking the medication. There have been a small number of cases of liver problems with Strattera, so it is wise to have your liver function evaluated beforehand and every six months while on Strattera.

Off-Label Medications for ADHD

Sometimes doctors will prescribe medications *off-label*. This can be seen as "improvising." Sometimes, medications have been found to be effective in treating symptoms of a disorder or illness by accident. This can happen when a doctor prescribes medication for one illness and the patient finds it improves symptoms of another illness or disorder as well. For example, certain blood-pressure medications and antidepressants have been found to be helpful in treating symptoms of ADHD.

def•i•ni•tion

> A drug is considered **off-label** when it is prescribed to treat a medical condition other than the one for which the Food and Drug Administration (FDA) has approved it. The prescribed medications have been approved by the FDA, but for a different medical condition. One study showed that at least one fifth of all prescriptions written are off-label.

Some commonly prescribed off-label medications for adult ADHD include:

◆ Bupropion (Wellbutrin) is an antidepressant medication and may be prescribed if you have not been helped by stimulant medications or can't tolerate the side effects.

◆ Modafanil (Provigil) is used to treat narcolepsy. It is not considered very effective in treating ADHD but may work if other medications are ineffective.

◆ Catapres (Clonidine) and guanfacine (Tenex) have been primarily used for children. These medications are not a good first choice but are sometimes used in conjunction with stimulant medications. They may be prescribed alone if stimulant medications can't be tolerated.

Special Considerations

When medications are prescribed to treat adults with ADHD, there are a number of considerations and special circumstances:

◆ Liver and kidney function in adults may be weaker than in children. Since ADHD medications can have a negative effect on both the liver and kidneys, adults may need less medication and the medication may stay in the system longer.

◆ Adults are more likely than children to be taking medications for other medical conditions, such as diabetes or high blood pressure. Doctors need to be aware of possible drug interactions.

◆ Side effects from other medications can mimic or worsen symptoms of ADHD, causing confusion over whether the ADHD medication is working correctly or whether it is even needed.

♦ Adults with ADHD may have other medical conditions, such as heart disease, which should be closely monitored while taking stimulant medications.

Despite potential problems, most adults tolerate stimulant medications well. As with children, they are still the most commonly prescribed and effective treatment for ADHD.

Clinical Pearls

A "clinical pearl" is a term doctors use to describe nuggets of information gleaned from reading, experience, and discussion with colleagues. Here are a few that I (DH) have found about using stimulants for adult ADHD:

For adults, begin with a shorter-acting medication. Every person differs a little in his or her response and the dose needed to help them. Shorter-acting medications give more flexibility to figure out the dose needed.

I usually begin with Adderall. In the average adult its effect lasts about 4 hours, while methylphenidate only lasts about 2.5 hours. That's a lot of doses to remember over the course of a 16-hour day!

> **The Lowdown**
>
> Many people use caffeine to help their ADHD (though it is not a very good "treatment"). When taking a stimulant medication, caffeine can make you feel "jumpy." Reducing your caffeine intake can help you when deciding if a medication is right for you.

When the shorter-acting medication is established, many people prefer a once or twice-a-day medicine (less chance of forgetting). Vyvanse works for 12 to 13 hours in most people (it's only effective after it has been digested). Adderall XR works for about 8 hours. The choice depends on your specific needs and the length of time you need the medication to work.

When insomnia shows up as a side effect, I look carefully at exactly what the dose schedule is and what is meant by, "I can't sleep." Most often, the last dose of the day is being taken before 6 P.M. and the medication is out of your system by the time an 11 P.M. bedtime rolls around. Usually, it's not that you get in bed at 11 and can't sleep; rather, it's that your ADHD by that time is in high gear and you are hyper-focused on some other activity and forget to go to bed! In these cases, I recommend that my patients try a dose, or a half dose, of stimulant about two hours before bedtime. Many people with ADHD become relaxed with stimulants, just like the hyperactive child calms down with them. With your executive functioning working, it is a lot easier to get up from what you're doing and go to bed.

The Lowdown

Stimulant medications can sometimes help you get to sleep. One woman put it this way, "It helps me to focus on going to sleep instead of on all those thoughts banging around in my head." (Please remember, it is important to talk with your doctor before changing how you take your medication.)

If loss of appetite is a problem, take the medication after meals.

FDA-approved doses of stimulants have been best researched in children. Your doctor may suggest a higher dose for you.

As always, if you have any doubts or questions about your treatment, ask! A good doctor welcomes, and does his or her best to answer, all questions about your condition and treatment. There is no such thing as a "stupid" question!

Therapy

The goal of therapy is to affect a positive change in the patient's actions and behaviors. Therapists are trained to understand your problems through listening to your words (and what you leave unspoken), your body language, and your tone of voice. Preferably, the therapist you choose will have been trained, and have experience treating, ADHD and will be familiar with problems and questions commonly associated with adult ADHD.

If ADHD Is Biological, Why Is Therapy Important?

Therapy is frequently a part of an overall treatment plan for adult ADHD. Medication, although an integral part of treatment, works for between 60 and 80 percent of adults with ADHD, leaving a number of adults searching for additional means to manage symptoms. In addition, medication does not cure ADHD nor take away all symptoms. Therapy can help fill in the blanks.

Another reason for therapy is that secondary problems, such as low self-esteem, social-skills deficits, stress, or feelings of inadequacy, incompetence, and helplessness can develop after years of living with ADHD. Psychotherapy can help in coping with these issues.

> **Think It Over**
>
> Therapy helps many people, but there are no guarantees. If your therapist or counselor guarantees or makes promises about the outcome of therapy, it is time to look for a new therapist or counselor.

Psychologist, Psychiatrist, Counselor, Social Worker?

Many different health professionals may be involved in your treatment. It is important to understand what each medical professional can do and the role each may play in your treatment.

- **Psychiatrist:** A psychiatrist is a medical doctor (M.D.). In addition to completing medical school, psychiatrists have undergone specialized training and education on the treatment and prevention of mental and emotional disorders. A psychiatrist can diagnose and treat illness as well as prescribe medication. Some neurologists also have experience in treating ADHD.

- **Psychologist:** A psychologist has received either a Master's degree or doctorate degree in psychology. A psychologist can diagnose and treat mental or emotional illness. They cannot prescribe medication in most states.

- **Therapists and counselors:** Therapists and counselors generally have at least a Master's degree and most have additional clinical training. There are a number of different certifications and licenses available to therapists and counselors, including, marriage and family therapists or clinical counselors. Therapists and counselors cannot prescribe medication.

◆ **Psychopharmacologists:** These are medical doctors (M.D.) that specialize in treating mental and emotional disorders with medications. Many times psychopharmacologists will work with family doctors or pediatricians to develop a treatment plan.

◆ **General practitioner/family doctor:** This is your primary-care doctor and provides your medical care for your overall health. Family doctors can help to coordinate care with various specialists but often do not have specialized training to treat adult ADHD.

◆ **Nurse practitioners:** Nurse practitioners have received more training and education in diagnosing illness than registered nurses (R.N.). Some nurse practitioners specialize in mental health and can prescribe medications.

◆ **Social workers:** Social workers are licensed and can treat and diagnose ADHD and other mental illnesses. They sometimes provide counseling or therapy and work as advocates helping patients locate services and resources within their communities. They cannot prescribe medications.

Behavior Modification and Lifestyle Changes

Behavioral strategies and lifestyle changes are important to help manage symptoms of ADHD. Medications, as previously discussed, are an important part of treatment but do not take away symptoms fully. Although behavior and lifestyle changes are discussed in depth in later sections of this book, it is important to note that such strategies are an important part of overall treatment.

Choosing Medical Professionals

How effective your treatment is, will partly depend on how effective the medical professional you choose is. The right medical professional for you will make you feel at ease, will take your insurance, is convenient for you to get to, and has experience in treating adults with ADHD.

Finding ADHD Specialists

Where do you find a specialist? Some ideas include:

♦ Internet resources: CHADD and ADDA (see Appendix B for specific information on these organizations).

♦ Referral from your family doctor.

♦ Local support groups.

♦ Referrals from other adults with ADHD.

Make a list of several different professionals who you feel fit your criteria. Contact each one and set up a time to talk either by phone or in person. Ask questions about philosophies, treatment options and choices, past experience in treating ADHD, and appointment times. Based on the answers, choose one professional to begin treatment with.

You can switch professionals later if you find you do not feel comfortable or do not feel satisfied with the care you are receiving.

The Lowdown

Be considerate and keep your conversation short when interviewing a mental-health professional. This is not a time to discuss specifics about your situation but to find out whether this particular medical professional will fit your needs.

Creating a Team of Professionals

Many family doctors are not familiar with treating adult ADHD. Because of this, you may see several doctors rather than just one. If you are taking medication, your family doctor will still need to monitor your physical health. Blood pressure, heart rate, and kidney and liver function should be checked on a regular basis. Expect to see your family doctor every three to six months.

Other specialists who may be included in your team of professionals include a psychiatrist (to prescribe and monitor medication, and to diagnose and treat mental illnesses) and a therapist or counselor (to work on behavior-modification strategies, self-esteem, and other unresolved issues).

Establishing Communication Between Medical Professionals

Having different team members communicate with one another can help make sure the services you receive from various specialists are as effective as they can be. When you begin treatment with a specialist, you may want to ask about procedures for sharing information. You may need to complete forms to allow doctors to communicate with one another.

Depending on your insurance company (especially if you have an HMO or managed-care plan), your family doctor might be the point of contact or health-care coordinator. Each specialist may need to send reports to your family doctor on a regular basis. Even if your insurance company does not require it, it is a good idea to have your family doctor receive reports on medications you may be taking. This way, should you need additional medication for other health conditions, you can make correct decisions based on possible drug interactions.

Sometimes, in an emergency, your doctors may need to quickly share information with one another. Being prepared and understanding the procedures ahead of time can eliminate confusion. Talk with all of your doctors about their policies.

Creating a Treatment Plan

Although ADHD has some core symptoms it can appear differently, or cause problems in different areas of daily life, depending on the person. Based on this, treatment plans should be individualized to target the specific areas causing you the most problems.

Treatment plans may have a combination of medical/pharmacologic treatment, therapy/counseling, and behavioral/lifestyle changes. When developing a treatment plan, it is important to take comorbid conditions, if present, into consideration.

Setting Up an Effective Treatment Plan

When developing a treatment plan, a good place to start is to create a list of symptoms that are causing you the most trouble, and what you would like to change. For example:

- Being able to focus for longer periods of time.

- Working on social skills to get along better with co-workers.

- Improving low tolerance to frustration.

- Working on tardiness.

Once you have completed the list, you and your doctor may want to choose one or two items to begin working on. Once you have seen improvement in those areas, you can add additional items.

Determining if Treatment Is Effective

As you begin treatment, create a list of symptoms of ADHD and how they may impact your life. For each item, give a rating on a scale of 1-10, 10 being best. Place an "X" next to the one or two items you plan to concentrate on first. Each week or on a daily basis, rate the symptoms. This will help you to keep track of how your treatment is working. If you are beginning medication, you may see improvement in areas that you did not specifically choose to work on. (A good thing!)

A treatment chart is also a great tool to bring with you when you go to the doctor for follow-up visits. Rather than relying on your memory (or becoming frustrated because of your lack of one), the chart will give you and your doctor specific information on what has been working and where you still need help.

The Lowdown

Treatment plans for ADHD should follow the guidelines used for other chronic conditions, such as diabetes, since ADHD also continues throughout life. Long-term planning can help to manage symptoms on an ongoing basis.

The following is an example of a treatment follow-up sheet:

Areas to Work On	Importance	Rating 1-10 (10 Being Best)
Chronically late	Very important; may lose job	2
Losing items	Important but manageable	5
Interrupts others	Important	4

Health Insurance and ADHD Treatment

Health insurance plans vary and it is important to understand exactly what your plan will cover, how much your deductible will be, and what your co-payment is for both your family doctor and specialists.

Some insurance companies make it a practice to deny claims for ADHD and other mental-health issues. As a consumer, you have the right to file an appeal. The majority of states have an appeal process that insurance companies are required to follow. A study by the Kaiser Family Foundation found the majority of patients who filed an appeal won.

Before you begin treatment you should:

♦ Read your health insurance policy. Are mental-health benefits included? What are the policy limits for inpatient and outpatient benefits? What other services are included?

♦ Contact your insurance company and ask about the number of visits per year for ADHD, what type of doctor you can see, what services, if any, you must have preauthorized for payment to be approved, which medications for ADHD are approved, and what the co-payments will be for seeing your primary-care doctor, a psychiatrist, or a therapist, and for medication.

♦ Contact your state insurance office or your local Mental Health Department to find out if insurance companies are required to cover mental-health issues in your state. Ask about appeal procedures if your claim is denied so you can be prepared.

- Keep accurate records. Keep track of doctor's names, phone numbers, and addresses, as well as when you saw them, and for how long.

- Keep records on who you speak with at the insurance company, what he or she has said, and the date of the conversation. Remember, most of the time you will be speaking with a customer service representative who does not make decisions regarding benefits, so be patient, calm, and respectful.

Think It Over

Insurance companies may routinely deny claims in an effort to save money. According to the Kaiser Family Foundation, 52 percent of people appealing a claim won during the first appeal, 44 percent won on the second appeal, and an additional 45 percent won on a third appeal.

It is important to be persistent in making sure your health care is covered and paid for according to your policy and your state laws. Health costs are expensive and can add up quickly, causing financial problems when you are left to pay.

The Least You Need to Know

- Stimulant medications have been found to be the most effective in treating adult ADHD.

- When taking medication, you should be monitored for blood pressure, heart rate, and kidney and liver functions.

- Medications can last anywhere from 2.5 to 13 hours. You can work with your doctor to choose the medication best for your lifestyle.

- A treatment plan can help you focus on specific areas causing problems in your life.

- Health insurance varies based on your state laws and individual coverage. Contact your insurance company to find out your coverage.

Chapter 5

Alternative and Complementary Treatments

In This Chapter

- ◆ What are the differences between alternative and complementary treatments?
- ◆ Risks and benefits of using alternative treatments
- ◆ What methods can be added to traditional treatments?
- ◆ Types of alternative treatments

A number of alternative treatments are advertised as helping to reduce symptoms of ADHD. Some of these are unproven, some show promise, and some can be incorporated into your daily life to enhance your current treatment program.

It is hard, though, to know the difference between proven science and good advertising techniques. The U.S. Food and Drug Administration tries to police companies touting false claims about the effectiveness of a treatment, but new companies crop up all the time, offering "safer" or "better" treatments.

In this chapter, we will explore the different options available and explain what you need to know before considering one of these other treatments. We will go over which methods you can add to your daily life without any side effects, and which products and services you should steer clear of.

The Difference Between Alternative and Complementary Treatments

The term alternative treatment generally refers to any medical treatment that is not taught in (U.S.) medical schools and is not used by medical doctors on a regular basis.

This definition, however, is somewhat outdated as some medical schools now have classes on alternative treatments. And doctors are beginning to recommend some *complementary* natural treatments in addition to traditional methods. In reference to ADHD, the term "alternative treatment" often refers to any treatment other than the conventional method of treatment: medication, behavioral strategies, and sometimes therapy/counseling. Complementary treatments are those that are added to existing treatments, such as omega-3 or an exercise regimen.

def•i•ni•tion

Complementary treatments are used along with another treatment. These can be traditional treatments, such as two medications being used, or natural treatments, such as adding omega-3 to your diet as well as taking medication.

The Pros and Cons of Alternative Treatments

Traditional, or conventional, methods of treating ADHD have been widely studied and the benefits of these treatments have been well documented. Even so, some adults with ADHD seek out alternative forms of treatment. They may believe that ADHD medications are "bad," that medications for ADHD will make someone different, take away personalities, or create "zombies." Or they may just believe that natural is better. Companies selling alternative treatments, some people in the media, and outspoken critics of mental illness and medication, have scared people into believing ADHD medications are unsafe and unproven.

Not everyone looking for alternative treatments fits into one of these categories. Some people simply can't afford medical treatment and some cannot tolerate taking stimulant medications, either because it will interfere with other medical conditions or they cannot tolerate the side effects. The problem is that most alternative treatments do not provide the same benefits as stimulant medications.

In study after study, the effectiveness and safety of stimulant medications has been proven. In order for a medication to be approved by the Food and Drug Administration (FDA), scientific studies must be conducted. These studies are controlled studies and are repeated several times to be sure the results are consistent. Studies include comparing the medication to a placebo. In these cases, participants are not told whether they received the medication or the placebo until after the study has been completed. All participants in the study have the same diagnosis. The results of scientific studies are often published in scientific journals and are peer reviewed.

Natural and alternative treatments for ADHD do not need to be approved by the FDA. There are few, if any, scientific studies to back up claims of effectiveness for herbal supplements and other alternative treatments. Many companies selling these types of treatments rely instead on testimonials from people who have used the treatment. If testing was completed, it may have been on a small sample group. Unfortunately, when evaluations for effectiveness are completed in this way, the consumer is not aware of the lack of scientific data to back up claims.

In addition, dosing information, purity, and strength of supplements are not regulated by the FDA. The strength of the supplements can vary from manufacturer to manufacturer. Dosing information listed on supplements is usually based on the average adult and does not take an individual's weight into consideration.

All of this is not meant to say that alternative or complementary treatments have no place in helping you cope with and manage symptoms of ADHD. Some treatments show promise, but more research is needed to find out exactly how and whom the treatment may help. For example, EEG neurofeedback training has shown some promise, but there is not yet enough documentation to show this as an across-the-board treatment for ADHD.

Types of Complementary Treatments

Some natural methods for managing symptoms of ADHD are actually complementary, rather than alternatives. For example, exercise has been shown to improve concentration and focus. Incorporating exercise into your daily routine is certainly good for you, can help you concentrate better, and improves your overall health. So even though there are benefits to exercise, it is not considered a viable treatment for ADHD by itself.

Omega-3

Omega-3 fatty acids are essential to our health, but we do not produce these in our body. We must consume omega-3 fatty acids in the foods we eat. Fish (for example: tuna and salmon), nuts, and certain plants contain omega-3 fatty acids. Omega-3 fatty acids are thought to play a large role in brain function.

Several small studies involving omega-3 fatty acids have shown this to be a promising treatment for reducing symptoms of ADHD. One study completed at the Massachusetts General Hospital and Harvard Medical School found omega-3 fatty acids to be so effective that researchers believed it showed potential to become a first-line treatment for ADHD. Participants of the study showed an increase in cognitive skills and a decrease in ADHD symptoms. The Hallowell Center also conducted a small study on omega-3 fatty acids

Think It Over

High doses of omega-3 can lengthen the amount of time it takes your blood to clot, cause nausea, diarrhea, or other stomach problems. Before taking omega-3 supplements, talk with your doctor about the right dose for you.

and found the same results. The University of Maryland completed a study showing that children with low levels of omega-3 fatty acids had more behavioral problems than those with higher levels.

So far, studies have shown promising results for the use of omega-3 fatty acids in treating ADHD (and other mental illnesses); however, the studies have been small. Additional research is needed for us to better understand the relationship between omega-3 and ADHD, and its possible treatment uses.

You may not feel the effects of omega-3 for six weeks. If you choose to try this, give yourself enough time to see if it makes a difference.

ADHD and Exercise

Exercise, according to Dr. John Ratey, can replace stimulant medications for some people with ADHD and be a complementary treatment for others. In Dr. Ratey's book, *Spark: The Revolutionary New Science of Exercise and the Brain*, he indicates that daily exercise increases attention and improves executive functions.

Dr. Ratey began his book after hearing about a school in Naperville, Illinois, that was incorporating exercise in its students' daily routine. As expected, the children in the school had less weight problems. But more surprising was the improvement in academics and learning.

The impact of exercise on our health has long been known, and recent research has shown an improvement in memory and cognitive skills in senior citizens who exercise. It seems that exercise, however, improves the ability to learn throughout our lives.

Other positive results of exercise include reducing stress and anxiety, lowering cravings from addictions, and reducing symptoms of PMS in women. Ideally (according to Dr. Ratey), you should exercise between 45 minutes and 1 hour a day, six days a week. However, even exercising for 20 minutes per day will help to increase attention and cognitive skills.

> ### The Scoop
>
> Exercises that combine complex movements and coordination, such as martial arts, dance, and gymnastics are beneficial to children and adults with ADHD. These exercises help form connections between the neurons in the brain and increase focus and concentration.

Working Memory Training

Working memory, sometimes called short-term memory, helps us to remember what to do in order to complete a task. You use working memory when trying to remember a phone number or a task to be completed at work. As an adult with ADHD, you may have a terrible time with your working memory skills.

Two recent studies, one at Notre Dame University and one at Sweden's Karolinska Institute, reviewed a computerized program aimed at improving working memory in students with ADHD. Both studies (although small) showed this program to be promising in helping people of all ages. The study did indicate that the program helped some children more than others. Bradley Gibson, the lead author of the study conducted at Notre Dame, was not sure why some children showed more improvement than others.

The computerized program takes approximately five weeks to complete, working one hour per day, five days per week. The cost of the program is between $1,500 and $2,000 and is not covered by insurance. The program is not meant to replace traditional treatments, but instead is used as a complementary treatment.

Sunshine

A study conducted in 2007 confirmed what many adults with ADHD already knew, being outside and enjoying nature can help increase attention and focus. When you must spend an extended period of time concentrating, there is a reduction in certain chemicals in your brain. Being outside may replenish your brain, allowing you to recover from attention fatigue.

Types of Alternative Treatments

Alternative treatments include many different forms of treatments, including herbal remedies, chiropractic care, EEG neurotherapy, and vision therapy. Although some people may receive some relief from these types of treatments, there is no specific evidence of overall help. Some experts argue that the improvements of ADHD symptoms are a result of closely monitoring behaviors or adding behavioral modification strategies into daily life, rather than the treatment itself.

EEG Neurotherapy

EEG neurotherapy can also be referred to as EEG biofeedback. According to doctors using this technique, people with ADHD have an excess amount of theta waves and a deficit in the number of beta waves in the brain. EEG neurotherapy is supposed to train the brain to produce more beta waves.

Advocates of EEG neurotherapy point to a 60 percent success rate and indicate that some people using this treatment discontinue medication. Although this treatment shows promise, additional research is needed before considering this a viable treatment for ADHD.

> **The Lowdown**
>
> "Natural" is not a synonym for "safe." Herbal supplements can have side effects and can interfere with other medications. It is important to discuss all medications you may be taking, including herbal supplements and vitamins, with your doctor to avoid drug interactions.

It can take up to 60 sessions to achieve results and the cost of this treatment is extremely expensive. It can range from $3,000 to $6,000. It is not normally covered by medical insurance.

Herbal Supplements

Herbal supplements are readily available in any pharmacy. Because they are natural, most people assume they are safe. This, however, is not always true. St. John's Wort, for example, can cause or increase sensitivity to sunlight and should not be taken if you have allergies.

Supplements can cause side effects as well. Ginseng, a popular herbal supplement, can cause insomnia, nausea, nosebleeds, rapid heartbeat, and headaches. Ginseng is also a blood thinner and can be dangerous to people with bleeding disorders or who are on other medications.

At this time, the FDA does not regulate herbal supplements. Manufacturing of these products can vary, so one brand can be stronger or weaker than another brand (even the same brand, during different manufacturing runs, can vary in strength).

Be sure to talk with your doctor before taking any supplements to make sure there is no risk of interactions with other medications you are taking, or complications with other health conditions.

Vision Therapy

Vision therapy consists of eye and perceptual exercises, sometimes using colored lenses or prisms. This type of treatment is based on the belief that faulty eye movements cause behavioral problems.

The Lowdown

When evaluating alternative treatments, ask what scientific studies are available to back up claims of effectiveness. Customer testimonials are sometimes used to mask the fact that science does not back up a product or service.

Vision problems, however, can mimic some of the symptoms of ADHD (and learning disabilities), including inability to focus for extended periods of time, especially when doing detail work or reading. There is no scientific data to back up claims that vision therapy improves symptoms of ADHD.

Auditory Stimulation

Using auditory stimulation to help people with ADHD is based on a study completed by the Division of Child and Adolescent Psychiatry at Schneider Children's Hospital in New Hyde Park, New York. In this study children were divided into three groups (half had ADHD). All three groups were given math problems to complete. The first group listened to music, the second group had talking in the area, and the third group was in a silent area. The children without ADHD did relatively the same no matter which environment they were in. The children with ADHD performed better while listening to music.

This study may give you a good reason to listen to music while completing tasks, but it does not indicate this is an effective treatment for overall symptoms of ADHD.

Cerebellar Training

Cerebellar training is a combination of eye, balance, and sensory exercises. This type of alternative treatment is based on the belief that connections between the cerebellum and the cerebrum in the brain either work too slowly or are not working. The exercises are supposed to improve these connections and improve the functioning of the cerebellum. The entire exercise program takes between 12 and 15 months to complete.

Several years ago, the journal *Dyslexia* published a study on this program. However, it was later found out that one of the authors of the study was paid by the organization that offered the service.

Children and Adults with Attention Deficit/Hyperactivity Disorder (CHADD) lists this treatment as controversial and not backed by medical science.

Chiropractic Care

There is a belief within the chiropractic community that ADHD may be caused by trauma to the spine (occurring throughout our lives, beginning at birth) or a misalignment of the skull causing uneven pressure on certain parts of the brain. Chiropractors perform adjustments to realign the skeleton. Proponents of this treatment believe these realignments will improve symptoms of ADHD.

There has been one study of this treatment and, in an article entitled, "Attention Deficit Disorder," Dr. Joel Alcantara (a chiropractor) called the results of the study "inconclusive." Medical science and our current knowledge of anatomy do not agree with the theory behind this treatment.

ADHD and Diet

Eating healthy is a good thing. A well-balanced diet improves your overall health and lowers your risk for developing serious, chronic illnesses, such as heart disease. The Centers for Disease Control (CDC) provide nutritional and dietary guidelines to help in developing healthy eating habits.

Some people believe that your food intake can either cause or worsen ADHD symptoms. There are three main theories regarding ADHD: processed foods cause behavioral problems, *gluten* can cause ADHD symptoms, and sugar causes hyperactivity.

The most well-known diet for ADHD is the elimination diet created by Dr. Benjamin Feingold. This diet was based on the theory that artificial colorings, flavorings, and preservatives caused hyperactivity. Most scientific studies since that time have disproved this theory and found no proof that this diet decreases hyperactivity or improves symptoms of ADHD. Some experts believe any improvement in behaviors occurs because of the increased attention to behaviors, not because of the diet.

Elimination diets remove all foods containing preservatives and artificial colorings and flavoring. If you choose to try an elimination diet, please take the time to talk with your doctor to be sure you are not eliminating necessary nutrients from your diet.

The newest diet proposed for ADHD is the gluten-free diet. Gluten is a protein found in wheat, barley, and rye. People with celiac disease have a difficult time digesting this protein and may experience damage to their intestines from the protein. Symptoms of celiac disease include stomach pains, diarrhea, developmental delays, learning, and attention problems. These overlapping symptoms, according to some experts, are what cause the confusion in whether a gluten-free diet can help symptoms of ADHD. According to these experts, if a person's symptoms of ADHD improve after beginning a gluten-free diet, he or she may have been misdiagnosed with ADHD and may have had celiac disease all along.

def•i•ni•tion

Gluten is a protein found in rye, wheat, and barley. Gluten is found in most cereals and many breads. Gluten-free diets eliminate these foods from your diet. People with celiac disease have a difficult time digesting gluten.

The Scoop

Eating a well-balanced diet can decrease swings in mood and behavior caused by changes, surges, or drops in blood sugar.

Processed sugar and carbohydrates can cause an increase in blood glucose levels. This can create a temporary increase in activity. This activity level, however, is short-lived and decreases as soon as the glucose level drops.

Questions Before Using Alternative Treatments

Every day, countless people spend time, money, and resources searching for and buying products claiming to help or cure ADHD. Although some may not be harmful, they may be a waste of your money and your time. Others may prove harmful. Before going out and spending your money, ask yourself the following questions:

For herbal supplements:

◆ Are there instructions for proper use, including dosage (based on age and weight), how to use the product, whether to take with or without food, and what to do in case of accidental overdose?

◆ Are the ingredients listed on the package? This should include active and inactive ingredients.

◆ Are the side effects, warnings, and possible drug interactions, or interactions with other food products, listed on the package?

For all alternative treatments:

◆ What does the product or service claim it can do for you? Are words such as "miraculous," "amazing," or "cure" used in the ad or literature about the product/service? These types of ads should raise red flags.

◆ Does the product claim it will work for everyone? No treatment is effective for everyone—this should be a warning.

◆ What data does the company use to back up claims of effectiveness? Is there scientific data to support claims or does the company rely on testimonials of previous customers? Beware of any products relying on customer testimonials; this may indicate there is either no scientific data to support claims or the data does not agree with the testimonials.

◆ What scientific studies have been completed on the product or service? Have the studies been published in journals? If not, what documentation can the company provide you about the studies?

Were the studies completed with control groups? How many people participated in the studies? How many studies were completed?

♦ Does the company attack traditional medicine as a way of selling their product or service? Are they using "scare tactics" to sell you something, rather than selling on the merits of their product or service?

♦ Are there medical doctors backing up the treatment? Who are the medical doctors? Are the doctors reputable?

♦ Is the product or service marketed through infomercials, self-published books, or mail order?

♦ Has your doctor heard about this product or service? Does your doctor recommend trying this treatment? Will the treatment interfere with current medications or worsen symptoms of other medical conditions?

♦ Will your insurance company pay for this treatment?

Think It Over

When a company attacks traditional medication or uses scare tactics to try to get you to buy their product, they are probably hiding the lack of scientific information to back up their claims of effectiveness.

If, after answering these questions, you still have concerns about an alternative treatment, you can check the website for the U.S. Food and Drug Administration (www.fda.gov). The site provides copies of letters sent to companies that sell and promote products based on undocumented claims.

The Least You Need to Know

♦ Some complementary treatments, such as exercise and omega-3 are helpful at reducing symptoms of ADHD.

♦ Natural is not a synonym for safe, herbal supplements can have side effects and interfere with other medications.

♦ The Food and Drug Administration does not regulate alternative treatments. Consumers must be aware.

♦ Insurance companies rarely pay for alternative treatments.

Chapter **6**

Coaching

In This Chapter

- ◆ Coaches as partners to success
- ◆ Differences between coaching and therapy
- ◆ How to know if coaching is right for you
- ◆ Discovering where to find a coach

How many times have you promised yourself that today will be the day that you won't procrastinate, that you will accomplish your goals and you will not waste time? My guess is, if you are an adult with ADHD, the answer is just about every day of your life.

You are not alone. According to one recent study, adults with ADHD lose over 22 workdays per year being distracted. It's no wonder, then, that you always feel as if you are rushing to catch up with the rest of the world.

ADHD coaches, a relatively new concept, frequently work with clients to develop strategies for coping with and managing symptoms of ADHD. In this chapter, we will discuss how a coach is different from a therapist, how to figure out if coaching is right for you, and what to expect during the coaching process.

What Is a Coach?

What do you see when you think of a coach? As I was writing this and asked several people about their impression of a coach, one answer I received over and over was the image of a large man, standing on the sidelines, tension written all over his face, screaming at the athletes on the field. So when you envision an "ADHD coach," you may be wondering why you would want such a person in your life?

The ADHD world has its own set of coaches, and they are not loud or scary. They are people who, in most cases, have undergone training to help adults with ADHD manage life's obstacles. Coaching has been found to be very helpful for many people with ADHD. It is not considered a medical treatment but can be used in conjunction with traditional treatment, frequently with much success.

Coaching in the business world has been around for several decades. Executive coaches were sometimes hired by an organization to mentor or assist individuals who were talented but may need extra assistance to develop a higher level of management skills. Individuals wanting an extra advantage could hire a coach to help in achieving goals and climbing the corporate ladder.

Coaches helping individuals were mostly personal trainers, working one-on-one with athletes. In the past few decades, personal coaching has taken on a whole new meaning. Coaches became specialized and the industry exploded. Now we see life coaches, career coaches, academic, and personal development coaches. There are coaches specializing in women, in men, in college students. Most importantly, to us, there are specialized ADHD coaches.

> **The Scoop**
>
> Dr. Edward Hallowell and Dr. John Ratey first introduced the concept of ADHD coaching in 1994 in the book, *Driven to Distraction*.

In order to understand what coaching is, we also need to understand what coaching is not. Coaching is not therapy (more about that later). Coaching is not someone telling you what to do and how to do it. Coaching is not someone providing you with the answers to your troubles.

Coaching provides a unique relationship between coach and client. Coaches combine education, motivation, accountability, and direction to help you reach a goal or develop a skill. Coaches help identify goals and dreams by asking questions and listening not only to what you say, but what you may *not* say. A coach will then guide you, based on your answers, to find ways to achieve or work toward your goals.

The Lowdown

Be honest with your coach when discussing your progress and your setbacks. A coach can only work with the information he or she receives from you and if the information is inaccurate, the coaching will be, too. If you need to, ask a family member or friend to be with you during review sessions.

Coaching should be a process in which you help yourself find guidance and structure. When a coach is successful, you no longer need the coach. In other words, a successful coaching program makes the coach obsolete.

Coach Training and Certification

Hundreds of organizations offer training classes for coaches. Although some work with general personal coaching, others specialize in ADHD coaches. You can find coaching classes online, as independent study, as telecommunication courses, or in an actual classroom setting.

Each training program teaches specific information based on the school's philosophy, but there are also many similarities to what a coach is taught. Coach training programs help to develop skills in listening, asking questions, and guidance.

Some coaches choose to become *ADHD-certified coaches*, but no licensing or certification is required to practice coaching. Anyone can choose to become a coach and set up a coaching business, even if they have not received any education or training. Organizations such as the International Coaching Federation (ICF) are working hard to create standards, licensing, and certification requirements for the coaching industry.

def•i•ni•tion_____

ADHD-certified coaches have received specialized training and have worked with clients for at least 500 hours and must pass a written and oral test. Currently, the Institute of Advancement for AD/HD Coaching is the only organization specifically providing certification for ADHD coaches.

Coaching vs. Therapy

Coaching is different from therapy. A therapist works to analyze your thought processes and discover why these thought processes interfere with your daily life. The therapist works with patients to help resolve past issues to improve your future. Coaches help in more practical matters. A good coach guides without giving orders. A good coach helps you reach your potential and your goals through changing everyday behaviors. In other words, therapists work on "why," and coaches work on "what," "when," and "how."

Think It Over _____

Coaches cannot diagnose or treat mental illness. If you believe you may have undiagnosed comorbid conditions such as depression or anxiety, talk with your doctor or therapist before beginning coaching.

In therapy, patients work to increase self-understanding and acceptance, and heal emotional wounds from past events. Therapists help patients face feelings, delving into the subconscious to explore and find the root of problems.

Coaches, on the other hand, work to find practical solutions and help clients implement better choices. Together, the coach and the client map out specific actions to accomplish personal growth. Coaching focuses on the present and the future, creating plans of action to achieve goals.

Coaching and counseling are both important and both offer a specific service. Counseling or therapy works when a person needs to resolve a problem, while coaching works to improve a situation.

Coaching for Adults with ADHD

Adults with ADHD work best with structure and organization—but these are exactly the same areas that cause the most problems. Medication can help but can't take all the symptoms of ADHD away. And some people can't tolerate or prefer not to take stimulant medications. How then, can adults with ADHD introduce structure and organization into their lives in order to work toward their goals?

Coaches specializing in ADHD understand how symptoms impact daily life. Many times ADHD coaches will work with you on changing abstract goals into specific action plans, help you remain focused on goals, and work on implementing motivational strategies.

ADHD coaches understand the obstacles adults with ADHD face in the areas of time management and organization. Although coaches may offer recommendations and practical solutions, they will not order a client to follow instructions. A coach understands change must come from the client. Coaches will work, instead, with the client to come up with motivational strategies to implement each day.

Is Coaching Right for Me?

There have not been any studies to show whether coaching is beneficial in the treatment of ADHD. Many adults, however, have found coaching to be extremely helpful. Most coaches will tell you that in order for coaching to work, clients must be committed to change and willing to spend the necessary time to improve behavior.

Sometimes coaching is not the right answer, or should be delayed in order for other issues to be addressed:

♦ If you have comorbid mental-health issues, such as depression, bipolar disorder, anxiety, or substance abuse, these areas should be treated and managed before beginning coaching. Coaching is not a treatment and should not be used as such.

> **The Scoop**
>
> Most ADHD coaching for adults is done over the telephone and via e-mail. Coaching for children is normally more effective when done face-to-face.

◆ If you are going through extreme or stressful life events, such as divorce or separation, or the recent death of a loved one, you may want to work with a therapist to manage the high emotional turmoil before beginning coaching.

◆ If you have a chronic medical issue or have a serious physical illness, you may want or need to have that addressed and managed by your doctor first. Coaching is more effective when you have the physical ability to commit to behavior changes.

Coaching can bring about dramatic changes, but you must be committed to change. You must have the willingness and the ability to make changes, and take responsibility for your actions. You must be physically available to participate in coaching sessions. Coaching is not a magic bullet—it does not automatically guarantee success. You, as an active coaching participant, must bring about the change.

The Coaching Process

Generally, there is an initial meeting between the coach and the client. This meeting may take place over the telephone and is often longer than regular coaching sessions. This initial meeting may last between one and two hours. During this session, you and your coach should discuss your needs and expectations. At the end of the session you should understand:

◆ When coaching sessions are to take place, and how long each session will last.

◆ What options are available for follow-up in between sessions.

◆ How much the coaching program will cost.

◆ When payment is expected and how you will pay the coach.

◆ What arrangements can be made if you must miss a session due to an emergency, and what constitutes an emergency.

◆ What you can expect from the coach.

◆ What your responsibilities are.

◆ How often you and your coach will have sessions to review progress and reevaluate goals and coaching needs.

In addition to the practical matters, you should also have discussed some of the problems you are facing in your life, and have chosen one or two areas to begin to improve. As with all behavioral programs, it is imperative to isolate one or two areas to begin with. Trying to improve too many areas of your life at once will only overwhelm you.

Regular coaching sessions may occur weekly, bi-weekly, or monthly. Regular sessions can last anywhere from 30 minutes to one hour and during this time you will probably review goals, progress, and discuss any setbacks you may have experienced. Your coach may also help you understand ADHD, provide recommendations, and revise goals when needed. In between these sessions, you and your coach may have decided to communicate via e-mail or short telephone calls. These check-ins help develop accountability and motivation.

Your coach may also give you homework or assignments to complete between sessions, such as creating to-do lists, completing certain tasks, and setting goals. Since coaching is based on individual needs and is unique to each client, it would be impossible to list specific assignments you might receive.

> **Think It Over**
>
> If you miss a coaching session without giving your coach 24 hours notice, you will probably be charged the regular rate for the session. Be sure you know what your coach's policies are regarding missed appointments.

> **The Scoop**
>
> Some coaches may require an initial commitment of either three or six months to be sure you are committed to change.

There is no time limit for how long coaching lasts. Again, this depends on you. Some people may choose to use a coach for a specific reason, such as looking for a job. Once you have a job, the coaching ends. Other people may want to use a coach for longer periods. The length of your coaching relationship would be decided based on what you want to accomplish. There should be, however, set review dates. At these sessions, you and your coach should review progress and goals and make changes, as needed.

Will a Coach Tell Me What to Do?

If you are looking for someone to tell you what to do, a coach is not the answer. Coaches will not and should not make decisions for you. Coaches can provide structure, give you a sounding board, or offer a new perspective on a situation. Coaches can offer observations, make recommendations, or give feedback. Coaches, however, should always allow the client to do the decision making.

How Will Coaching Help Me Exactly?

Coaches can help with so many different aspects of a person's life that it is hard to list exactly how a coach can help. To give you an idea, coaches specializing in ADHD frequently work with their clients to add structure, set goals, establish organization, and increase time management. But coaches can do so much more:

♦ Help you change wishes into specific goals and identify the obstacles that may be standing in the way of reaching those goals.

♦ Identify where your talents are and what you are passionate about.

♦ Find your unique skills.

♦ Change thought processes from dwelling on weaknesses to focusing on strengths.

♦ Increase your understanding of ADHD traits and characteristics and see these as positive attributes (such as creative problem solving).

♦ Find your organizational and learning styles to add customized structure into your daily life.

♦ Teach you customized strategies for dealing with distraction, procrastination, time management, and perfectionism.

♦ Assist in developing strategies for specific areas such as academics, finances, social, relationships, or professional.

♦ Provide feedback, reminders, and encouragement.

Remember that coaching isn't meant to be a long-term commitment. The goal of coaching is to be able to manage on your own, to coach yourself through the tough moments and times of your life. A good coach understands that part of the coaching process is to work toward independence.

Finding a Coach

Because there are no current licensing or certification requirements for coaching by law, it is important to ask about education and previous experience. A few organizations do certify coaches; these may be a good place to start your search:

The Institute of Advancement for AD/HD Coaching (IAAC; www.adhdcoachinstitute.org) certifies coaches specializing in ADHD. Certification means a person has worked for at least two years in a coaching capacity and has spent at least 500 hours working with clients with ADHD.

The International Coach Federation (ICF; www.coachfederation.org) certifies life coaches, but does not certify coaches trained specifically in ADHD. You can, however, use the search on their site to narrow down your choices and find a coach with previous ADHD experience.

In addition to these directories, you can try contacting a support group in your area for referrals, especially if you prefer a coach within your locality.

> **The Lowdown**
>
> The ADHD Coaches Organization (ACO; www.adhdcoaches.org) does not provide certification for coaches but does offer a coach-referral service.

What to Look for in a Coach

Coaching is a partnership. You need to feel comfortable with the coach and you need to be confident the coach will be able to help you move forward. At the same time, the coach must feel sure you will be able to make a commitment and work toward change. For this reason, an initial consultation is a good idea. During this initial session, you and the coach should discuss:

◆ Your needs and expectations.

◆ The cost of the coaching sessions.

- How and when payment is expected.

- The coach's approach and philosophy of coaching.

- What the coach's confidentiality and privacy policies are.

- How the coach handles emergencies, both in rescheduling a session because of an emergency or holding an additional session if you are facing a crisis.

Coaching is a partnership and you must be comfortable with the coach. Think about whom you would best be able to work with. Some questions to consider include:

- Do you feel you would work better with a man or woman?

- Do you want a coach who specializes in ADHD plus something else, such as academic, entrepreneurship, business, and gender issues?

- Do you want someone who works specifically in one area, such as organization, time management, relationships?

- Do you want someone personable, funny, and outgoing?

> **Think It Over**
>
> When interviewing coaches, ask what ADHD conferences, if any, he or she has recently attended. Ask about the speakers and presentations from the conference. This will let you know whether the coach stays up to date on topics relating to ADHD.

Your decision on whether to work with a coach or not will be based on the information you gather from your initial conversation with the coach. Don't be shy or afraid to ask questions. Write down important information during the conversation so you can refer to it later, when you are making a final decision.

Coaching Across the Country

Most people think meeting with a coach each week involves a face-to-face meeting, as you would meet a therapist or a doctor. Coaches, however, frequently meet with clients by telephone and follow up can be through e-mail or telephone.

Coaches, therefore, do not need to be in your local area, but can be across the state or across the country. It is possible to work with a coach face-to-face, if you prefer, but this may limit your choice of coaches.

Is Coaching Covered Under Health Insurance?

Coaching is considered educational, more in tune with tutoring services than *medically necessary* services, and therefore is not usually covered by health insurance. Because coaching can be costly (an average of between $300 and $600 per month), roughly the same as what a therapist would cost, this is an important consideration for many people.

Before beginning coaching, you should contact your insurance company to find out what your policy covers. It is possible that some insurance companies will elect to cover coaching as part of an overall treatment plan.

def•i•ni•tion

Services considered **medically necessary** are those needed for the diagnosis or treatment of your medical condition. They are considered to be good medical practice and are not used for either your or your doctor's convenience.

The Least You Need to Know

◆ For coaching to be successful, you must be willing to make a commitment to change.

◆ Coaching is not normally covered by health insurance.

◆ A few organizations are working toward creating standards and licensing requirements for the coaching profession.

◆ Therapy and coaching are not the same. Therapists look to resolve problems in your past; coaching looks to find solutions for your future.

◆ Most coaching for adults is done over the phone or via e-mail. Coaching for children is usually done face-to-face.

ADHD and Relationships

ADHD impacts every part of your life and that includes your relationships. Spouses need to work together to find each partner's strengths and learn to work together. Understanding ADHD can help in overcoming some common problems.

Although marriage may be the most important relationship in our life, there are other relationships, with friends, relatives, and co-workers. In this part we discuss how to explain ADHD to those people in your life, and the importance of standing up for yourself when people you come in contact with don't believe in an ADHD diagnosis.

Finally, we explore some of the common problems adults with ADHD often have in communication, and offer tips to help you work through the difficulties.

Chapter 7

ADHD in Marriage

In This Chapter

- ◆ How inattention can be misunderstood to mean you don't care
- ◆ Why adults with ADHD often lack internal structure
- ◆ Just because it is important doesn't mean you will remember it
- ◆ Why both partners suffer when ADHD is not treated

Humorous. Creative. Spontaneous. Energetic. These are all qualities to describe adults with ADHD, and these very qualities may have been what caught your spouse's attention in the beginning of your relationship. But once the dating stage was over and it was time to get down to the boring routine of daily life, the qualities your spouse once loved seemed to disappear and be replaced with what seems like irresponsibility, inability to complete a task, laziness, and disorganization. What happened? Where did that fun, exciting person go?

Adults with ADHD often lack the internal structure, discipline, and organization needed to manage a household. They rely on external structures, such as the workplace, to help in accomplishing tasks. When you are floundering and feeling overwhelmed in a relationship, the natural instinct is to reach out for a life preserver. In most cases, you reach out for your spouse, counting on him or her to be the structure in your life. But the non-ADHD partner can end up feeling more like a parent, always nagging about chores that need to be completed, bills that need to be paid, tasks that need to be done. Harmony is replaced by resentment and frustration.

In this chapter we'll talk about all those things, but we'll also talk about why it doesn't need to be that way. By working together, building on each other's strengths, and managing symptoms of ADHD, you can work to create a strong and healthy relationship.

ADHD in Marriage

A good marriage requires dedication, hard work, and a strong emotional connection with another human being. Adults with ADHD often become bored and distracted, certainly not traits conducive to creating a long-term, intimate relationship. Even when you deeply love someone and feel ready to commit, the constant need for high-stimulus situations can interfere with your ability to sustain a long-term relationship.

But ADHD doesn't just impact you. Your partner also feels the inattention and the distractibility that overrun your life. Your partner can feel unimportant. Your partner can feel as if you don't listen or don't care. Imagine your spouse telling you something important that happened at work. You start out listening but as the story drags on, you start thinking you are hungry and you silently decide what you are going to cook for dinner; you spend a few minutes paying attention to the show on television; or you simply start looking around, distracted by everything else going on in the room.

Is it that you don't care about what happened to your husband? Or is it that this not a good time to discuss it? Inattention and distractibility are often misunderstood. These symptoms mistakenly reflect that you don't care.

Hyperfocus can also be a problem in intimate relationships, causing you to ignore the needs of your partner as you immerse yourself in whatever activity that currently holds your interest.

Forgetfulness, a common trait in adults with ADHD, can also appear as not caring, or more specifically, not caring enough to remember. The old myth, "If you care enough, you will remember," is just that, a myth. Not remembering to pick up the dry cleaning or stop at the grocery store doesn't really have anything to do with how you feel about your spouse. Unfortunately, sometimes the messages get mixed up, especially when forgotten items and events are more important than picking up the dry cleaning.

Impulsiveness frequently shows up in decision making. It is assumed in most relationships that decisions, especially financial decisions, are made together, as a team. Impulsive spending, not sticking to a budget or participating in activities such as gambling, can wreak havoc and chaos on a relationship. Impulsiveness is often seen as selfishness.

Think It Over

Hyperfocus can be used positively, allowing you to complete a project, but it can also be negative, making those around you feel ignored, forgotten, and unimportant.

After a number of failed relationships, it is easy to become discouraged. You may feel you are just not able to fulfill the demands of a relationship, that you are not capable of loving or being loved. Once this happens, you may find it impossible to remain in or even begin a relationship, since you are expecting disappointment. And of course, once you decide failure is the only possible outcome, success is almost impossible. You may decide that you don't "need" a relationship, that you are fine the way you are, or you prefer to be alone. You may choose to avoid relationships, withdrawing emotionally from the people in your life. This makes intimacy even more difficult.

You may understand how destructive your actions are but, without proper treatment, be unable or not know how to stop or change. The symptoms of ADHD, though, are not insurmountable and not all the symptoms are detrimental to a relationship. Many couples, with only one partner with ADHD or where both have ADHD, have happy and healthy marriages.

What ADHD Brings to the Relationship

As much as the symptoms of ADHD can hurt a relationship, they can also enhance it. Many people with ADHD are creative problem solvers, thinking outside the box to come up with unique ideas and solutions. The creativity, combined with impulsiveness, can add fun and adventure to your relationship. Because of the need for stimulus, adults with ADHD seek out fun, high-intensity activities. Many spouses of adults with ADHD enjoy the adventure and seeing the world from a new perspective. Life with ADHD is anything but dull!

The Lowdown

ADHD can be quite funny at times. Make sure you take the time to laugh at your mistakes or ADHD-isms with your spouse. Humor is always a better choice than anger.

Adults with ADHD can be highly intuitive. Although you may not always pay attention to the details around you, even during conversations, you may be in tune to the underlying emotions. You may understand the feelings beneath the words and be able to respond to how someone feels, rather than what he or she says.

Even the major symptoms can have a positive side to them. Hyperactivity provides endless energy and the ability to work longer hours means accomplishing more. Rather than sitting in front of the television, adults with hyperactivity will get up and do something. If you have hyperactivity, you may be outgoing and charismatic, easily making friends. You may be enthusiastic, ready to take on any new adventure.

Impulsiveness can add spontaneity to an otherwise structured lifestyle. Impulsive actions can add excitement, give us a different perspective on our problems, and foster creativity. If you are impulsive, you may be willing to take on new risks and try new things. Inattention and distractibility cause you to move from project to project, learning and experiencing many different things, allowing you to search for your passions in life.

Frequently, adults with ADHD are quick to forgive mistakes (when other people make them; you are usually much harder on yourself). You usually have a good sense of humor and often react to situations with compassion.

Relationships are give and take, you must accept the flaws and the good in another person. Living with ADHD in a relationship can be tough. It can be frustrating. But treatment can help to manage the symptoms that consistently interfere with the relationship so that the positive side of ADHD is able to shine through.

When Both Partners Have ADHD

The most important ingredient in a marriage when both partners have ADHD is, without a doubt, a good sense of humor. Life is sure to be one adventure after another and sometimes chaos will rule the household.

Since ADHD shows up differently in people, just because both of you have ADHD doesn't mean you will both have the same symptoms. You might be extremely disorganized and forgetful, while your spouse might be hyperactive and impulsive. You will probably both share some similar symptoms; for example, you may both have a hard time paying attention for extended periods of time, or may consistently leave tasks partially done. But, no matter the differences, you'll probably have a number of similarities as well.

> **The Scoop**
>
> Adults with ADHD often have a distorted sense of time, misjudging how long an activity will take, one of the causes of chronic tardiness.

Finding a balance when both spouses have ADHD is all about communication (which is so important we dedicated Chapter 9 to it) and developing systems that work for your situation. Start with deciding what is important. Create a list of what you feel is important to you as a couple. (You may be surprised to know that what is important to you is not necessarily important to your spouse.) Once you complete the list, you can narrow down areas that matter to both of you and begin to work together on improvements on those areas first.

There may be areas that matter to you, but not to your spouse (and vice versa). For example, if you work from home, you may want your office space to be kept a certain way. This, then, would be your responsibility.

Helping the Non-ADHD Partner

"Honey, I'm sorry I'm late. Again."

"I forgot."

"I didn't realize how much time had passed."

"I got caught up doing …"

How many times have these statements been repeated in your marriage? So many times the symptoms of ADHD are misunderstood. Forgetfulness, not paying attention, focusing on one task to the point of ignoring everything around you, disorganization, and poor time management are all ways in which symptoms appear in everyday life. Much of the confusion lies in the fact that these are traits everyone experiences at some time or another. But for adults with ADHD, these traits are an everyday occurrence. And many times they are attributed to laziness, selfishness, or not caring about the other person, instead of being understood as being part of ADHD.

When two people enter into a marriage, they want it to work. They want to have a successful, happy marriage. You don't get married intending for it to fall apart or for each day to be filled with resentment, anger, or frustration. Both people get married with the intention of spending their life together and working together toward mutual dreams.

Think It Over

Often what couples may dislike about each other is the same thing that attracted them in the first place. The one who was hard working and reliable becomes the "boring workaholic." The one who was free spirited and adventurous becomes the "air-headed, unreliable flake." It helps to remember that the person you married is still the same and that you can learn to love the same trait by seeing it differently.

In order for that to happen, the non-ADHD spouse needs to understand ADHD and all of the quirks that come along with it. Forgetfulness, disorganization, and poor time management are not symptoms of selfishness or laziness. Chances are, the ADHD sufferer wants to remember and his frustration grows each time he doesn't. Before resentment builds on both sides of the marriage, take charge, learn strategies that work for you, and create your own unique and loving relationship.

Educating Your Partner

In order to create strategies that will work in your marriage, both you and your spouse need to understand ADHD. The more you know the better off you will be. Although ADHD is somewhat different in each person, adults with ADHD also have core symptoms and patterns of behaviors. Understanding these can help you come up with strategies that will work for you and your spouse.

You can begin to learn about adult ADHD in a number of different places:

♦ There are lots of great books on adult ADHD (including this one) that you can read together.

♦ A number of websites offer accurate information on ADHD (the resource section in the back of this book provides a listing of reputable websites).

♦ Support groups are available, not only for adults with ADHD but also for spouses and family members.

♦ Your spouse can join you at the doctor to learn more about what to expect and how problems can be solved.

Choosing to learn about ADHD is the first step toward developing a strong, healthy relationship. Ignoring problems never seems to work. Acknowledging, accepting, and looking for solutions will help both you and your spouse understand one another and work together to create your future.

The Lowdown

National organizations, such as Children and Adults with Attention Deficit/Hyperactivity Disorder (CHADD) and Attention Deficit Disorder Association (ADDA) have a large network of support groups to help adults with ADHD and their families.

Some Common Problems

ADHD in a marriage not only impacts the life of the person with ADHD, but the spouse as well. Their career, finances, or social life may suffer because of problems at home. Understanding your non-ADHD spouse is just as important as him or her understanding your ADHD. Seeing your marriage from his or her perspective can help you decide which areas of your marriage you need to work on first.

Your spouse's career may not be what she envisioned. The spouse with ADHD may move from job to job, leaving the non-ADHD spouse to remain at an unsatisfying job, for the steady pay as well as for the benefits. She may stay at a job she doesn't like because the household needs the stability. Or she may enjoy her job but underperform because of worries at home. She may be constantly working to correct situations or put out fires started by her spouse instead of focusing on her job.

Many times non-ADHD spouses will end up feeling like single parents. The spouse with ADHD may have a difficult time parenting. Emotional outbursts, indecisiveness, lack of organization, and poor time management are just a few of the areas that may suffer. Non-ADHD spouses may be the ones who coordinate homework, meet with teachers, and keep track of the kids' activities. They may feel they need to field complaints or intervene in arguments between their spouse and children, especially if their spouse is prone to emotional outbursts.

Finances are a weak spot for many adults with ADHD. That leaves this responsibility to the non-ADHD spouse. He or she needs to budget and plan, not only for today but also for the future. Impulsive spending, a common trait in adults with ADHD, can wreak havoc on the household finances, causing even more stress.

The non-ADHD spouse can also have self-esteem issues. Adults with ADHD can be self-absorbed, moving from one project to another, or simply distracted and not paying attention to their spouse. The non-ADHD spouse can begin to feel invisible and not important.

Distraction and hyperfocus interfere with sex and intimacy. When you become distracted and ignore the needs of your partner, you are sending the message that he or she is not important. In the same way, when you hyperfocus on an activity, your spouse and your family may get pushed to the background, left to feel as if they are playing second fiddle to whatever you may be interested in at the moment. Because adults with ADHD have a difficult time sitting still for long periods of time, cuddling is not always a shared activity.

It is important, then, for you to find other ways to let your spouse know how you feel. At the other end of the spectrum, some non-ADHD partners are expected to be ready for sex at all times, even without romance or foreplay. Lastly, medications can cause sexual side effects, cutting down on your desire for sex. Your partner's desires, however, are still there.

When one partner pulls more than his share of the weight, taking care of the daily chores, resentment and anger may build. The non-ADHD partner may feel overwhelmed and taken advantage of. If ADHD has only recently been diagnosed, years of frustration must be dealt with.

> **The Scoop**
>
> Antidepressant medications, sometimes used in the treatment of adults with ADHD, can cause sexual side effects. Know the possible side effects and talk with your doctor and your spouse about what you should expect from these medications.

Enabling vs. Supporting

There is a difference between *enabling* someone and helping or being supportive. Sometimes the non-ADHD spouse can, in the name of helping someone, create a cycle of enabling.

In a marriage when one partner has ADHD, and has problems with completing daily tasks around the house, it is easy to fall into the trap of the non-ADHD partner simply completing the tasks. But this is not helping, it is enabling.

> **def•i•ni•tion**
>
> **Enabling** is doing things for someone who has the physical and mental capacity to do it himself or herself.

Being supportive, or helping someone, is finding a solution or creating a system in which the person can complete the task independently. For example, if one of the chores for the partner with ADHD is to do the food shopping, but he or she continually forgets items needed, making a list would be the supportive way. Enabling would be simply going to the store to make sure everything needed is purchased.

In relationships where one partner has ADHD, enabling frequently ends with resentment and anger in both partners. The non-ADHD partner becomes resentful, feeling as if he or she is the sole responsible adult. The ADHD partner can be angry and resentful, feeling as if he or she is being treated like a child. Helping, or being supportive, leads to a more healthy relationship.

Overcoming Problems

Whether one or both partners have ADHD, you will need to create systems to overcome daily struggles and problems within the relationship. Below are some tips for both partners when learning to work together:

◆ Remind your partner that ADHD behaviors are not malicious and do not mean you do not care.

◆ Seek treatment for ADHD. Medication can help, but you must also have tools to help change behaviors.

◆ Ask your partner to use supportive measures rather than enabling behaviors.

◆ Accept that you have been living with ADHD for many years, possibly undiagnosed, and have developed certain habits. Ask your partner to be patient.

◆ Use tools, such as lists, to help accomplish tasks.

◆ Ask your partner to be specific in what he or she wants, but be open to how it gets done.

◆ Make sure expectations are realistic for both partners.

◆ Acknowledge strengths and efforts often. Let your partner know how much you appreciate him or her.

If you have recently been diagnosed and are working to change behaviors, understand and accept that there may be setbacks. You and your spouse should communicate through this process. It may be easy for your spouse to take these setbacks personally. Be patient, caring, and understanding. Find new solutions.

Household Chores

Household chores are one of the biggest problems in couples where one or both have ADHD. Household chores are boring. For most people they are not fun and if given a choice, they will be put off until ... never. But, they need to be done. So how do you work through the large list of household chores, especially when one or both of you have a problem finishing or completing chores?

Traditional Male vs. Female Roles

In most households, men and women continue to take on traditional male and female roles. Women may be responsible for the cooking and the childcare, while men are responsible for lawn care and taking care of finances. But these traditional roles may not fit your household and you and your partner's individual strengths. Let's face it, most household chores are boring, and boring is hard for those with ADHD. But if you choose those chores that you can manage, there is a better chance of the chores getting completed.

> **The Lowdown**
>
> People with ADHD often work better with visual cues. When completing household chores, use a white board to check off tasks as they are completed to give a sense of accomplishment.

Imagine a couple, the woman has ADHD and the man is the non-ADHD partner. She finds doing laundry to be extremely boring and many weeks will start the laundry only to leave it sitting in the washing machine. She forgets about it until someone in the household looks for a clean shirt and finds the washer filled with wet (and possibly mildewed) clothes.

Her husband mows the lawn each week and absolutely detests the job. He sees it as useless and, if he had the choice, would pave over the entire lawn. On the other hand, he does not mind doing the laundry.

He can sit with the clean clothes, watch sports on television and get all the clothes folded. To him, it is the ultimate chore because he can do his favorite thing—watch sports—and feel productive at the same time (and not feel guilty for watching television).

His wife, however, likes mowing the lawn—she likes being outside, enjoys the smell of fresh cut grass, and can do it without being bored because of the movement and exercise. To her, this is the ultimate chore, one that provides exercise and movement. Instead of bowing to traditional roles, this couple can simply switch chores. Tasks will get done based on individual needs rather than both hating what they are doing.

Working Together

There are always enough household chores to go around. The work never seems to end. There will always be chores no one wants to do. Some couples find it helpful to make a list of all the chores that must be done to keep the household running. This can include running errands, going grocery shopping, as well as cleaning and laundry. Once a list is completed, chores are divided into three categories: mine, yours, and ones no one wants to do. "Mine" and "yours" should be divided based on strengths and abilities. "No one wants to do" can be rotated each week. You may find it easier to complete a task if you know you don't have to do it next week.

Some couples find hiring outside help to complete some chores helpful. You can hire a local high school student to take care of yard work. There are services that will do your grocery shopping, clean your house, or do odd jobs. The money spent on these services can be well worth the decrease in daily stress.

Explanations vs. Excuses

ADHD is not an *excuse* for poor behavior (for example, consistently running late) but it can be an *explanation* (you may have time distortion, especially when hyperfocusing or you may have a hard time with time management and are not able to judge how long things will take).

Instead of dwelling on the lateness or the excuse, both partners
should try to understand why
it happens and what steps both
can take to make sure it doesn't
continue to occur. ADHD then
becomes an explanation, rather
than an excuse.

def•i•ni•tion

An **explanation** is a clarifica-
tion or an attempt to create
understanding. An **excuse** is
an attempt to remove blame.

The non-ADHD partner needs to understand symptoms of ADHD are
not a reflection on how the ADHD partner feels about him or her, but
a reflection of not effectively managing ADHD symptoms.

The Least You Need to Know

◆ ADHD in a marriage impacts both spouses, even if they don't
both have ADHD.

◆ Many couples with ADHD forego traditional gender roles to find
unique ways to work together.

◆ Inattention and hyperfocus can leave your partner feeling unimportant and neglected.

◆ Supportive behaviors include tools to help the spouse with ADHD
complete a task independently.

◆ ADHD symptoms are not a reflection of feelings but a reflection
of not effectively managing ADHD.

Chapter 8

Other Relationships

In This Chapter

- ◆ Explaining ADHD to your family
- ◆ Coping with nonbelievers in your family
- ◆ Getting along with co-workers
- ◆ Creating a support network of friends

Humans are social creatures. We desire and crave human contact, not only in romantic relationships but also through family, friends, and co-workers. Being accepted and loved is what we all want. This may be more than just emotion. Friendship, for example, has been shown to increase our happiness and relieve stress.

In this chapter, many types of relationships are explored. From the do's and don'ts of talking to your family about your ADHD to learning to get along better with co-workers, we will provide tips to help you create and maintain relationships and friendships.

Parents, Siblings, and Family

Chances are, you weren't diagnosed with ADHD until you were an adult. Some of you may still remember when it was called minimal brain dysfunction or listed as a childhood disorder. And yet here you are with a diagnosis of adult ADHD. The diagnosis may bring you relief and understanding, the great "Ah-ha" moment when all of the behaviors, from your school days up until now, suddenly make sense. It seems natural that you would want to share this newfound understanding with your family, friends, and co-workers.

Talking to Family About ADHD

If you are the first person in your family to be diagnosed with ADHD, or at least the first adult, it may be hard to broach the subject. There are so many misconceptions in the media and the general public about ADHD, and many of these are so ingrained it is sometimes difficult to overcome what people "think" ADHD is and replace those ideas with the reality of ADHD.

Although every family is different, the following are some general do's and don'ts for talking with your family about your diagnosis of ADHD:

♦ Don't call a large family meeting or make an announcement at a family gathering if you are not sure what reactions you will be receiving.

♦ Do start with one or two family members whom you believe will be supportive. Explain ADHD to them, and use their reactions to help you prepare for telling other family members. You may want to enlist their support when telling other family members.

♦ Do make a list of how ADHD has impacted your life. This can include major experiences, such as your career, as well as how it interferes with your daily life.

♦ Don't feel obligated to share the entire list with your family. Use this list to help you talk about your ADHD. Your family need only know what you choose to share.

♦ Do look for a one to two page informational article or fact sheet on adult ADHD. The doctor who diagnosed you may have some info to help explain the major symptoms of ADHD.

♦ Don't come laden with several books on the subject. That might be overwhelming. A simple fact sheet works best in the beginning.

♦ Do have book titles or additional information available for family members who are interested in finding out more about ADHD.

♦ Don't insist your family members read several books on ADHD.

♦ Do ask your family what they believe about ADHD and be prepared to talk calmly about the myths and misconceptions versus the reality of ADHD.

> **The Scoop**
>
> Approximately 76 percent of all cases of ADHD are due to genetics. If you have ADHD there is a high chance either your mother or father have it as well.

♦ Don't become emotional or defensive when discussing the myths. A calm and confident discussion is better.

♦ Do assume this is an ongoing discussion. Allow family members to slowly digest information you presented and come back later with additional questions.

♦ Don't create a marathon informational session that can seem more like a classroom lecture.

♦ Do be prepared for many different reactions. Each family member will have his own opinion of ADHD based on his own experiences. Preparing for different reactions ahead of time will help you stay focused on your answers.

♦ Don't assume every family member will offer his or her support and encouragement.

♦ Do have information, including where to go for a diagnosis, for other family members who may wonder if they have ADHD as well.

♦ Don't try to diagnose other family members based on your experiences.

When Family Doesn't Agree with Your Diagnosis

Every family's dynamics are different. Although we would like to think that family members—parents, sisters, and brothers—are supportive no matter what, that is not always the case.

Sometimes, parents (even when their children are grown) become defensive when faced with a diagnosis of ADHD. They may see the diagnosis as an affront against them, implying they did something wrong. They may become offended. When parents are confronted with the pain their child went through during childhood, they may react defensively because they think they should have known or think the child is accusing them of something they did or failed to do.

Parents may not want to believe anything is wrong with their child, or they may believe many of the myths surrounding ADHD. They may even believe you are making up the diagnosis for sympathy or to get out of adult responsibilities.

Siblings can react in much the same way. Some will be supportive and others will see this as one more way you are making excuses for childish behaviors.

Think It Over

ADHD is hereditary. Some family members may be coping with undiagnosed ADHD. Accepting your behaviors as ADHD may force them to confront their own symptoms.

In these cases, it will be up to you to decide whether or not to share your diagnosis. Remember, you received your diagnosis to help improve your life; the diagnosis is for you, not for your family members. If your family cannot be supportive, it may be better to keep the diagnosis to yourself and learn to cope with and manage symptoms of ADHD on your own.

Standing Up for Yourself and Your Needs

Standing up for yourself may, sometimes, mean backing down and being silent. Your family does not need to be aware of your treatment or your diagnosis. Standing up for yourself can mean not telling them what you are doing.

Undiagnosed adult ADHD frequently means you have gone through years of struggles, gone from job to job, had financial problems and relationship problems. You may have spent years hearing family members say, "You could if you tried harder," or, "Just grow up." These hurtful comments have probably done a number on your self-esteem, and right about now you are probably looking for your family's support. Maybe you went to your family to share the diagnosis as a way of explaining many of your past behaviors and as a way to look positively into the future. But instead, you were greeted with, "Oh, another excuse."

> **The Lowdown**
>
> If you are feeling angry about your family's reaction but don't want to lose your cool, write a fake letter to family members letting them know how you feel. Then rip up the letter or throw it away.

If that is the case, think about why you went to the doctor and what changes you would like to see happen in your life:

- ◆ What areas of your life did you want to change?

- ◆ How can you spend your time around more supportive people?

- ◆ What family events do you need to be at? Are you there because you feel guilty, or because you enjoy being around your family?

- ◆ Can you find times to spend with those family members who are understanding and supportive without being around those who are not?

All of us need to know we are loved and accepted the way we are. When your family doesn't offer you the support you need, reach out to friends and find support groups where you can be yourself, without feeling judged.

Co-Workers

How satisfied you are with your job can depend largely on how well you get along with your co-workers. When you are at odds with the people you work with every day, just getting up and going to work is a chore. But when you get along, work is more enjoyable and may not even seem like work.

Every business has a collection of many different personalities. Businesses do not hire based on common interests or compatible personalities. Companies hire, instead, on your experience and your ability to do the job. Therefore, you must have the ability to get along with a large number of people.

Acceptance

It can be daunting to be placed in a room with so many different personalities. From the young, recent high school graduate to the elderly gentlemen who's been with the company forever, each person will have his own view and perspective of the world, his own experiences, and his own opinions. You may not agree with your co-workers about any number of subjects. These may be people you have nothing in common with, or people you would not socialize with, under normal circumstances. But somehow, you must all get along in order to complete your job.

> **Think It Over**
>
> Office politics can be an easy downfall. Avoid gossip, even when the talk is about someone you don't like. Your words may come back to haunt you. The best recourse is not to say anything.

Some traits of ADHD may help you. You may be outgoing, you may enjoy learning about new people and new things. This natural curiosity can help you accept each of your co-workers for who they are. But you might also have a fear of being accepted. Because of past experiences, you may have built a wall around yourself. You may be afraid that if people get to know you, they won't like you; they may misunderstand your ADHD traits like your forgetfulness or your impulsiveness. Accepting your co-workers for their individuality is the first step to being accepted for yours.

Workplace Etiquette

Being open and accepting of your co-workers doesn't mean you should inquire into their personal lives or share details of your own. A professional relationship is best. This means you find a balance between being friendly and being guarded.

Some symptoms of ADHD, such as impulsiveness, can interfere with your relationships with your co-workers. You may blurt out inappropriate remarks, send the wrong e-mail, or otherwise disrupt the workplace. The following are some tips to managing professional relationships:

◆ If you have an issue or conflict with a co-worker, wait before addressing it. To avoid rushing to judgment or insulting someone, get in the habit of taking the night to think it over.

◆ Avoid being defensive. There may be times you will be told about something you did wrong or completed incorrectly. Rather than becoming defensive and lashing out, listen to what your boss or co-worker has to say.

◆ Keep your cool. Situations at work may sometimes make you mad. Avoid overreacting.

◆ Find ways to manage your emotions at work, such as using a stress ball, taking a walk during breaks, or using relaxation techniques at your desk. Wait until you get home to vent your irritation or anger at something a co-worker did. Use the evening to decide the best way to handle the situation.

◆ Keep separate e-mail accounts for business and personal use. Avoid using your personal e-mail for business purposes or your business e-mail for personal reasons. By keeping the accounts separate you can avoid accidentally e-mailing someone something you would rather they don't see.

◆ Remember social networking sites are often visible to the general public. Many different people may see information you post. Be careful what information you put out on the Internet.

◆ Be considerate and respectful of all of your co-workers.

Most of the time, the relationships you develop with your co-workers will be "strictly work," in which you only share information about the work-related tasks. Sometimes you will develop deeper friendships with co-workers, but be careful not to share personal information at the workplace where other co-workers can overhear conversations.

> **The Scoop**
>
> Companies with good co-worker relationships have lower turnover rates and higher productivity levels. Making an effort to get along with your co-workers can actually increase your chances of staying at your job.

All of the different types of relationships matter to your success at your job. The ability to communicate and form relationships with your co-workers reduces stress and increases job satisfaction.

Being Late, Missing Deadlines, and Making Apologies

How many times are you embarrassed at work over your actions? Or how many times do you feel the need to apologize for your behaviors?

The workplace is different because those relationships are not your choice. You and your co-workers are together based on your employer's choice, rather than your own. Because of this, certain behaviors are not as easily forgiven. In friendships outside of work, ADHD mishaps can be overlooked or laughed about.

In a work relationship, these same mishaps may be seen as detrimental. A co-worker may see your actions as interfering with their ability to get ahead because, so often, tasks are intermingled and dependent on each other. For example, suppose Mary must complete a task and then give the finished paperwork to Bob. Bob needs Mary's portion of the task in order to complete his project. If Mary's work is delayed, then Bob's job suffers. Relationships at work are based, at least in part, not only on how well you complete your own work, but also on your ability to be part of a team and contribute to your co-worker's success.

> **The Lowdown**
>
> If you make a mistake at work, take responsibility and offer a plan to fix it. Above all, never blame another co-worker for your mistake.

Co-workers may become resentful or will highlight your mistakes in order to be sure they are not blamed or seen as incompetent. Over time, disorganization, poor time management, and other symptoms of ADHD can interfere not only with your job, but with the ability of your co-workers to complete their work. You may feel as though you are spending much of your time apologizing for blunders, lapses, and oversights. Your co-workers may roll their eyes, sigh, and then try to make sure their next project does not include you.

All of this takes a toll on your self-esteem. Sooner or later, if your relationships with your co-workers deteriorate, your dissatisfaction with your job grows. The following tips can help you create positive relationships with your co-workers:

♦ Be sure you are receiving treatment for your ADHD.

♦ Use technology to help you remember appointments, deadlines, and meetings.

♦ Use a coach to help you develop better interpersonal skills.

♦ Don't use your co-workers as therapists; keep your personal problems personal.

♦ Focus on your work rather than worrying about what other people are doing or saying.

♦ Make sure you don't use work time to complete personal tasks.

♦ Take an interest in your co-workers' work and how your jobs work together. Understanding the processes might help you create ways to better work as a team.

♦ Determine where your weaknesses are and what areas might most impact your co-workers. Take time to create strategies to improve those areas first.

♦ Educate your co-workers about ADHD and how it impacts your job. Let them know the mistakes you make are not intentional but are caused by symptoms of ADHD.

We spend a great deal of our time at work and when these hours are enjoyable it helps to make the rest of our time enjoyable as well. When we don't get along with co-workers we can feel stress, not only at work but at home, as well. Therefore, creating strong relationships (not necessarily friendships, but good working relationships) with our co-workers helps to improve all aspects of our life.

When Accommodations Make You "Different"

Deciding whether to let your co-workers know about your ADHD is entirely up to you. You are not required to share this type of information. Many adults with ADHD choose not to explain about ADHD because of past bad experiences, afraid co-workers may see it as a weakness or an excuse. Some adults with ADHD, however, prefer to have a diagnosis of ADHD out in the open, to let co-workers know and give them a chance to understand.

Sometimes, adults with ADHD are given *accommodations* in the workplace. These can be simple modifications, such as being allowed to wear a headset to block out distractions or having a flexible schedule. Sometimes these accommodations may make you feel different, make you stand out, and your co-workers can come to resent you, feeling as if you are getting special treatment. In these cases, you might choose to explain your diagnosis and why your accommodations help you to better do your job.

def•i•ni•tion

> **Accommodations** are modifications to duties or extra assistance provided to you to help you perform the essential functions of your job. An example may be to provide you with organizational software.

How much you tell your co-workers will depend on the relationship you have already developed. You may choose to explain more to some co-workers; comfortable they will understand and be supportive and encouraging. With other co-workers, you may simply want to state you have a disability and the accommodations are there to help you do your job better.

Friendships

Friendships are important to our happiness. Friends give us a sense of belonging and add purpose to our lives. Friendships have been shown to …

- ◆ Relieve stress.

- ◆ Improve self-esteem and feelings of self-worth.

- ◆ Increase happiness.

- ◆ Help you in times of upheaval or unhappiness.

- ◆ Support you in making positive changes in your life.

- ◆ Share your successes and times of joy.

- ◆ Decrease your chance of developing either a physical or mental illness.

When friends are in our lives we live happier, more fulfilled lives and live longer.

Sorry I Forgot Your Birthday (Again)!

Just as you like to feel appreciated and loved by your friends, other people feel the same way. When birthdays and special events are forgotten, friends feel as if they are not appreciated, or that they are taken advantage of. This can happen when you have nothing but good intentions and simply forget, or are feeling overwhelmed and anything not urgent gets pushed to the back burner. When you remember, or get around to it, you are embarrassed at having forgotten and then ignore the situation rather than confronting it.

Remembering names, places, and events may also be a problem. What are the names of your friend's children? How about her husband's name? Forgetfulness can be embarrassing and sometimes it is easier to avoid the situation than admit you forgot such essential information.

The Lowdown

If you often forget names, try to repeat the name several times in your conversation and create a visual connection with the name and the face. Incorporating several methods can help increase the chance of remembering the name.

Feeling Judged vs. Feeling Loved

One of the best parts of friendship is the ability to be with people who accept you for exactly who you are. You don't have to pretend. When friends are not willing to accept your shortcomings, you can end up feeling judged.

Many adults with ADHD say that social situations are emotionally draining. You may constantly worry about saying something wrong or talking too much. The belief that you are going to be judged can be overwhelming. Being in situations where you must meet new people is even worse. Difficulties with conversation, interrupting, blurting out, and inappropriate comments can make people shy away from you. People with ADHD have been judged, unfairly, over and over. Because of this, a wall goes up to shield you from further accusations. It is easy to just opt out of social situations, finding the stress too much to handle. But we all know that is not the right answer. Having friends is too important to our well-being.

Many people, however, will not judge you; they will accept you, shortcomings and all. You want to seek out those people to be and spend time with.

Finding Friends Who Are Supportive

When we were young, school offered a number of different activities. After-school clubs and structured social activities gave us numerous opportunities to be with other people. But as adults, where can you find social outlets? The following list provides some ideas:

- ◆ Join the local YMCA/YWCA and enroll in classes that are interesting to you. This might be exercise classes, relaxation classes (such as yoga), or learning a new subject, such as photography.

- ◆ Join a local sports league. Most towns and cities have various leagues, such as bowling, basketball, or baseball leagues for adults.

- ◆ Check out the adult education opportunities offered by your local high school. Some community colleges also offer noncredit adult education classes.

- Take music or art lessons. Art stores or galleries may offer classes. Music stores also offer a variety of music classes.

- Join a book club. Libraries many times have a variety of book clubs.

- Join a group at your church.

- Volunteer at a nonprofit organization.

- Join an adult ADHD support group.

> **The Scoop**
>
> Children and Adults with Attention Deficit/Hyperactivity Disorder (CHADD) offers support groups throughout the United States. If there is not a support group in your area, they can supply information and help you start a group.

Usually, when you find an area you are interested in, you will be more relaxed. The initial moment of meeting someone is always the scariest. Remember, you do not need to instantly share a connection; having a shared interest can be enough to begin a relationship.

Maintaining Friendships

Once you have made some friends and feel comfortable, you need to maintain the friendships. This step can also be difficult for adults with ADHD. You may be overwhelmed by daily activities and ignore the needs of your friends, forgetting a lunch date or to call a friend back. But making a little effort can pay off in helping you to maintain friendships.

- Do activities you enjoy and ask friends to join you. This can be as simple as going for a walk in the evening or going to yard sales on a weekend morning. When it is an activity you enjoy, you are more apt to feel comfortable and enjoy the time spent with a friend.

- When meeting a friend for dinner, opt for the buffet. This helps by giving you an opportunity to walk around (if you need to move) or break up awkward moments.

- Choose sports activities. Meet for a game of tennis, racquetball, or aerobics class. This limits the conversations but allows you to spend time with someone.

- When inviting friends to your home, make it a potluck dinner, limiting the preparations you need to make.

- Invite friends to your home for a movie and dessert rather than for dinner.

- Set aside one hour per week to answer phone calls or send e-mails to friends. Make this part of your weekly schedule. This small amount of time will help let friends know you are thinking of them.

Just as you want to know your friends are thinking of you, your friends also appreciate the effort you make to keep in touch with them. The benefits you receive from having friends in your life are immense.

The Least You Need to Know

- Your family may be resistant to hearing about your diagnosis of ADHD.

- Even though you are an adult, your parents may feel they did something to cause your ADHD symptoms.

- Accommodations can help you do your job better, but they can also make you feel different.

- You are not required to disclose your ADHD to co-workers if you feel uncomfortable doing so.

- Inviting friends to share activities you enjoy can help you relax and enjoy the time you spend with friends.

Chapter 9

Communication

In This Chapter

- ◆ Exploring obstacles to communication
- ◆ How distractibility breaks down communication
- ◆ Overcoming forgetfulness during conversations
- ◆ Learning ways not to monopolize conversations

A conversation is so much more than just two (or more) people talking. A conversation also includes nonverbal cues, such as facial expressions, tone of voice, and hand gestures. During a conversation it is important to keep track of tones, movements, and words. But adults with ADHD may also be experiencing fear or nervousness, dealing with insecurities, trying to form what they will say next, and trying to anticipate where the conversation is going. In other words, you may be trying so hard to focus, you lose track of the actual conversation.

Symptoms of ADHD can be barriers to effective communication. Hyperactivity can lead to monopolizing the conversation and impulsivity can lead to interrupting while others are talking. In this chapter, we will discuss some of the most common obstacles with communication in adults with ADHD and give you some tips and suggestions to help you work through the different areas.

Problems with Communication

Communication is an exchange of ideas, thoughts, or perceptions. It is essential in every area of life. Relationships are built upon good communication. Our jobs are dependent upon communicating with bosses and co-workers. No matter where we go in life or what we choose to do, we must communicate with others. We use communication to express our joys, our expectations, our sorrows, our wants, and our needs.

Even though we learn to communicate from the time we are born, we don't always have effective communication skills. Communication is so much more than simply speaking words. It involves conveying emotion to another person. It involves listening to what someone is saying with words—and what they are *not* saying. It involves being an active listener. It involves a give and take, actively listening to another person and waiting for your turn to speak.

> **The Scoop**
>
> Only about 40 percent of communication in a face-to-face conversation is verbal. The balance is based on non-verbal cues, such as facial expressions.

Luckily, communication skills can be learned, no matter what your age and no matter when you were diagnosed with ADHD. Remember, practice makes perfect and communication is no exception to this rule.

Different Perceptions

We each view the world a little differently and our communication is a result of our prior experiences. Unfortunately many people, both with and without ADHD, believe their perception is the "right" one simply because it is the only one they know. He or she may believe that everyone else sees things exactly as they do. They are so wrong.

Imagine two individuals. One is non-ADHD and a very organized thinker. He truly believes and lives "a place for everything and everything in its place." In his house, there is nothing out of place and it is always clean. He sees the universe as an extremely organized system of living things. Each morning he completes a to-do list and, by the end of the day, almost every item is checked off. His day runs like clockwork because he cannot imagine it any other way.

The second person is an adult with ADHD and a very conceptual thinker. He sees the big picture and can mentally figure out the end result of any problem. The details and the steps to bring about the big picture are difficult for him to manage and he usually leaves that up to someone else to figure out. His house is pile after pile of papers but he seems to know where to find something when he needs it. (He would be lost if someone came and cleaned for him!) He sees the universe as a beautiful playground, filled with wonders to stop and examine. He never bothers to create, let alone complete, a to-do list; he knows that too many interesting things may happen during the day and he doesn't want to miss any of them. Whatever gets done—great; whatever doesn't—well, there's always tomorrow.

I'm sure that each of us knows someone similar to the two people described here.

On a rainy day, the first person may review his situation, think about his roof and whether it might leak, check the basement for dampness, and walk out the door with umbrella in hand, raincoat on, fully prepared for his day. The other person may miss the sunshine and the birds singing, and may also visit his basement, but not because of dampness but in search of an umbrella that he knows is around somewhere, unless he left it at a friend's house the last time it rained. He may need to gather up some towels because he forgot to roll up the car windows and now the seats are wet. With the extra chores of searching (in vain) for the umbrella and gathering towels, he is late and rushing around. He runs out the door, completely prepared for the rest of his day to be more of the same.

> **Think It Over**
>
> When we look at something from only our own perspective, we see just one part of the situation. We must see things from different perspectives to understand a situation wholly.

Each of our characters would discuss the weather differently. The first would not understand why rain would cause a delay, since your umbrella should be in the hall closet and you should never leave your car unlocked, never mind with the windows down. He cannot possibly understand how a rainy morning would change anything. The second person cannot understand the first perception. He views the world as chaotic because his life is always in motion, never organized, and rarely simple. He can't imagine opening a closet and having his umbrella just hanging there waiting for him!

Neither perception in this example is right, and neither is wrong. Each person views every experience in their life according to their own perception. Although this example is an exaggeration, it shows how the very same thing can appear so differently to people. True communication can only occur if we allow ourselves to view the world through someone else's perception for a little while.

Both our perfectionist and our adult with ADHD must take the time to look at the world differently if they wish to understand each other. Otherwise, they are simply speaking two different languages.

Effective communication is all about an exchange of ideas. It is impossible to exchange ideas if you are not willing to look through someone else's eyes. A few minutes spent trying to see the world as the other person does can help you not only better communicate but to make a much deeper connection.

Tips and Suggestions

 ◆ Understand ADHD. Use it as an explanation for behaviors, not an excuse.

 ◆ Help to educate those around you about how you view the world. Don't judge them if they don't understand immediately. Take the time to see their world as well.

 ◆ Play a game with your partner. For 10 minutes, have your partner (or friend) describe exactly what he or she sees and feels about their surroundings. The next 10 minutes, it is your turn to explain how you view the world. Don't judge, just listen to the different perceptions.

Distractibility

It has been said by some experts that ADHD is not a disorder of distraction, but is the inability to filter out stimuli in order to pay attention and focus on one thing. During a conversation, the person with ADHD may be listening, but also may be watching the bird on the windowsill, the cat crouching in the grass, and the car passing by. Each thing will take attention from the other so that no one thing gets his undivided attention. The conversation, although it may be important, is just one stimulus of many going on at the same time.

For the person with ADHD, it is frustrating to realize that you are no longer following the conversation. Now you have to figure out what you missed as well as try to follow what is currently being said. You may feel embarrassment or stress over trying to follow a conversation that has continued long past your attention. In group settings, the amount of distractions increase, making it even more difficult to follow a single conversation.

The Lowdown

Use several of your senses during a conversation. The more senses you use, the more you will stay interested in the conversation.

To the other people in the conversation, inattention/distractibility can seem like lack of caring or indifference. Some people may become irritated about having to repeat themselves, or impatient with having the same conversation over again. In turn, their irritation may cause anxiety in the person with ADHD, who will now spend more energy trying to follow the conversation. They may focus so much on the act of following the conversation that they may not follow the content of it at all. Irritation and anxiety build, and communication has broken down.

Tips and Suggestions

◆ For important conversations, make appointments to speak with someone privately. Find a time and place that will have the least amount of distractions to help you follow the conversation.

- Take notes during the conversation. This might help you to keep focused.

- Ask questions. Keeping the conversation interactive will help you stay involved and interested.

- Consider having the conversation during an activity, such as talking while taking a walk.

Emotional Outbursts

ADHD is often accompanied by other disorders, such as depression, bipolar, anxiety, or mood disorders. Even without accompanying mood disorders, emotions can change quickly in an individual with ADHD. The frustration of not being understood or of forgetting what you want to say can lead to anger. In a conversation, it may seem as if this anger is directed at the other person or persons in the conversation, but it's not.

def•i•ni•tion

Social anxiety disorder is the intense and irrational fear of being scrutinized or judged by other people causing someone to withdraw from social situations or interaction with other people.

If you have not been diagnosed until adulthood and spent years trying to overcome symptoms of ADHD, without any understanding, you may harbor feelings of anger and guilt or feel insecure. These emotions can erupt with intensity if you perceive you are being misunderstood, being judged as "stupid," or are being placed in an embarrassing situation. Some may develop *social anxiety disorder.*

Conversations, especially group conversations, can be extremely difficult. Not only can these conversations be hard to follow, they also create much anxiety. You may have spent most of your life feeling as if you did not fit in with your peers. This loss of confidence does not go away with a diagnosis; it can take years to overcome insecurities and feel comfortable talking with others—especially people you have just met.

As with children, emotions can appear in many ways. Some may react to their anger by lashing out, becoming insulting, loud, or violent. Others may become extremely withdrawn, shutting down as a defense mechanism. Still others may react to their intense emotions by reverting to being "the class clown" and acting silly or attempting to become the center of attention. This can be construed as being selfish and self-centered by those who do not understand.

Tips and Suggestions

♦ If you suffer from social anxiety and feel very stressed when presented with crowd situations, take some time to practice your communication skills. Begin with small groups of maybe two or three people. Begin with people you know and trust and, as you gain confidence, add more people to your practice circle.

♦ For those with intense emotions that can erupt without warning, talk with your doctor about the possibility of comorbid conditions.

♦ Learn to understand your emotions and what may trigger them. Try to keep a diary of what situations caused anger, withdrawing, or other intense emotions. By understanding your emotions, you may be better able to cope with situations or conversations that cause you pain or anger.

Finding the Right Words

Just as a person with ADHD can have a difficult time organizing her home or workplace, she can also have a difficult time organizing her thoughts and her brain storage system.

Being able to clearly articulate what you mean requires you to delve into your brain to find the right word or phrase. It also requires the ability to quickly organize thoughts into sentences.

The ADHD brain cannot always retrieve the data it needs. The perfect descriptive word is in their brain but is not readily accessible. We have all known something that we can't

The Scoop

Word-retrieval problems can be a problem in conversation, causing misunderstanding when the wrong word is chosen. One research study showed that phonetic clues, rather than context clues, can help a person retrieve a word from their memory.

remember or have said that something is "on the tip of our tongue." Somewhere in our brain the knowledge exists, but at the moment we do not have the ability to locate it.

So it is with an ADHD brain. With thoughts constantly moving and distractions taking attention away, it can be hard to locate the piece of information within the vast storage of the brain. Therefore, the correct words or phrases do not always come when needed. You may become frustrated because you know what you want to convey, you can feel it—and sometimes even think you have conveyed it—but somehow it has been misconstrued or misunderstood. People who don't understand ADHD may feel lost in the conversation and get annoyed or just look at you with amusement or noncomprehension. Again, communication breaks down.

When someone has a word-retrieval problem they usually can remember the concept surrounding a word but can't recall the specific word. A study released in 2000 showed phonetic clues may help someone retrieve a word from their memory.

Tips and Suggestions

◆ Take your time in trying to explain something. If the right words do not come immediately, get back to the person with an explanation later.

◆ Remove yourself from the situation for a moment to take a few deep breaths and calm the thoughts running through your mind.

◆ Ask your conversation partner to repeat back what you said so that you are sure they understood you correctly.

Forgetfulness

Forgetfulness in conversations can create a number of different obstacles:

◆ You may forget what the other person said shortly after they said it.

◆ You may forget what you wanted to say.

◆ You can concentrate so much on remembering what you want to say that you miss part of the conversation and end up answering a question that is no longer relevant.

◆ You may interrupt while others are speaking in order to say what you wanted before you forget it.

No matter how forgetfulness ends up interfering in conversations, it is difficult for everyone. Consistent interruptions are seen as rude, no matter the reason. The frustrations can build on both sides, creating stress in relationships.

Many people without ADHD believe that if it is important enough to you, you will remember it. But that is not so with ADHD. Many individuals with ADHD report that the opposite is often true. The more important the item, the harder it is to remember. For those of you who have forgotten to pick up your children, arrived at work without dropping the children off, or left a spouse waiting far too often, it is obvious that importance has nothing to do with the ability to remember.

Think It Over

Could your forgetfulness signal something more serious? If you are beginning to forget things more often than you have in the past, you may want to talk with your doctor. If your forgetfulness is consistent and not worsening, it is probably a symptom of ADHD.

Tips and Suggestions

◆ Take notes during the conversation in order to follow along. You may find you don't actually need the notes, but having written something as well as listened to it may help you to remember it.

◆ Create an environment that will reduce distractions and increase your ability to focus on the conversation.

◆ Surround yourself with people that understand ADHD.

◆ Tape a conversation if you believe you will need the information later.

◆ Don't feel guilty asking people to repeat what they have said. Don't apologize for ADHD, and don't allow others to make you feel inferior because you can't remember.

Impulsiveness

Impulsiveness, like forgetfulness, can appear in several different ways. It can show up as blurting out answers to questions or interrupting the speaker. It can be the "foot in your mouth" when something came out without you meaning to say it. Maybe your thought instantly slipped from your mouth when you had intended to keep it to yourself. It can be jumping into a conversation you only heard a snippet of, and saying something totally off topic.

Impulsiveness can seem rude, inconsiderate, and offensive. It can drive acquaintances away and frustrate friends and family. People may wonder what you are going to say next and shy away from conversations with you. Impulsiveness in communication can create animosity at the job. Though sometimes an impulsive remark may be true, it may be uncalled for or inappropriate at the time.

The Lowdown

Educate those you speak with frequently about how your ADHD affects your ability to communicate and ask their assistance in repeating without judging or becoming annoyed.

Impulsiveness frequently becomes more apparent in high stimulus areas. The person with ADHD may become overexcited or hyperactive, creating the opportunity to speak loudly, out of turn, and sometimes inappropriately.

Tips and Suggestions

♦ During office functions or meetings, find someone you work with who understands ADHD or accepts you for yourself. Ask them to be your "buddy," giving silent reminders to slow down and listen first.

♦ Wear a watch with a timer, set to vibrate every 15 minutes or so, and remind yourself to take a few deep breaths and relax before entering another conversation.

♦ Remove yourself from high-stimulus events for a few minutes each half hour or hour to calm yourself. Take a few minutes to meditate or close your eyes and slow your brain and thinking.

◆ Try changing your comments to questions to show your interest in the subject.

Nonverbal Cues

Several studies have shown that individuals with ADHD have a harder time reading the expressions of others. Face-to-face communication often requires a person to understand the feeling behind the words. This is often accomplished by seeing facial expressions and watching body language as well as hearing the words. Words can be misinterpreted or misunderstood if taken in the wrong context. For example, if someone is joking and laughing but their words indicate differently, you may receive mixed messages about the meaning of the words.

In addition, individuals with ADHD do not always understand the reaction they have caused in others by their words. They do not always know if they have hurt someone's feelings or made them angry and so they continue the conversation. They appear to be unfeeling or uncaring about the feelings of others.

When misunderstandings, hurt feelings, and anger occur, it is easy for others to create a distance between themselves and the person with ADHD. It is easy for the person with ADHD to become wary of conversation, wary of groups, and shy of situations where they may meet new people. Practicing can help you to better understand the nonverbal portion of conversations.

Think It Over

Body language can add to a conversation but can also be misinterpreted. Body language that points to mood is often read correctly, but deeper meanings, such as whether someone is lying is not so easy to read and often misinterpreted.

Tips and Suggestions

◆ Visit a high-traffic area, such as a mall or train station. Sit quietly and unobtrusively on a bench and watch people as they walk by. Study their faces and expressions and try to determine the feelings behind those expressions. Watch their body language to see how different reactions are similar in certain situations.

- Ask a few friends or relatives to practice with you and, during conversations with them, ask them occasionally what they are feeling so that you can associate expressions with feelings.

- At a family gathering, watch as people hug to say hello and good-bye. If you watch carefully, you can tell which people tolerate others and which have genuine love for each other. Their body language while hugging will tell you much about their inner emotions.

- Talk with your partner about your difficulty and ask him or her to be conscious of it during conversations. Have them talk about how they feel as well as show it.

The Hyperactive Mind

Having a mind that goes a mile a minute can be helpful in many situations. It can allow you to come up with innovative solutions. It can allow you to see a situation from many different perspectives. But in a conversation, a hyperactive mind can sometimes cause you to become lost in your own thoughts and lose track of the conversation.

Let's imagine Margie, an adult with ADHD. Last week, Margie was talking with her sister on the phone. Her sister asked if she wanted to meet for lunch the following Tuesday. Immediately, Margie began a mental process to determine if she was free that day. Her thoughts went: "Tuesday … I think I am free Tuesday; I know I have to go on Samantha's field trip next week, but that's Wednesday—or is it Thursday? I need to find that permission slip—did I return it to school yet? I wonder where I might have put it. Maybe it's in the cabinet, or over with the mail. I really need to look for that. Does Samantha have the right clothes to wear? I need to do the wash to make sure; I wonder what would be best for her to wear? I wonder what the weather will be like that day?"

At this point, her sister interrupted her thoughts and asked again about next Tuesday. Margie, totally engrossed in her new train of thought, said, "Tuesday? What's happening next Tuesday?" Her sister, not understanding, said, "Forget it." And hung up the phone. Margie had no idea what had just happened and did not know why her sister was mad.

Many individuals with ADHD indicate that this is more apt to happen when talking on the phone, without the benefit of a face-to-face conversation. However, it can often happen face-to-face as well. One woman told me that she has gotten up in the middle of her husband talking, completely forgetting he was there, and moved on to whatever she might be thinking at the moment. Her husband, used to this after many years, would follow her to the next room and begin again.

Hyperactivity sometimes lessens in adulthood but it can still cause you to become bored and restless, making it difficult to follow a conversation for extended periods.

Tips and Suggestions

- ◆ Keep a pad and pen near the phone to take notes during conversations, so that you always have reminders of what is being discussed.

- ◆ Use ADHD as an explanation rather than an excuse, and explain to your family and friends what you need during a conversation to keep on track. Let them know that if you ask them to repeat something, it does not mean that you feel what they have to say is unimportant.

Monopolizing the Conversation

So now you have entered a conversation and are interested in the subject matter. You may just start talking and not stop, interrupting others when they begin to speak. The hyperactive mind at work again.

You may just want to make sure you get your point out. Maybe in the past you have found it difficult to find the right words and so you have learned to repeat yourself, several times, in several ways, to make sure others understand. Or maybe your surroundings have overstimulated you, making it difficult for you to control your hyperactivity and so you talk, and talk, and talk. Or maybe you have forgotten the point you were trying to make and you think that if you keep talking, you will eventually remember it and then tie it all together.

Grabbing the attention of others can be a great and wonderful thing; it can help you make friends, find others with similar interests, or teach others what you know. But it can also be detrimental if you continue to demand their attention without giving attention back. It also stops being a conversation and starts being a monologue. No matter what the reason, *monopolizing* a conversation is a sure way to make the people around you slowly begin to move away. A conversation is an organized situation. You must talk and listen, give and take.

def•i•ni•tion

To **monopolize** is to have possession of or own, exclusively. Therefore, monopolizing a conversation is when you are the only one talking and you do not allow other people to contribute to the conversation.

Tips and Suggestions

◆ Train yourself to ask questions after every few sentences you speak and to listen to the answers. By asking questions, you are letting the people you are speaking with know that you value their input.

◆ Many people with ADHD find it stimulating and exciting to be in a crowd without being an active participant. By sitting back and watching, you can learn much about the people you are with. Watch their expressions and body language and enjoy the activity around you.

◆ If you often find yourself monopolizing conversations, wear a watch with a vibrating alarm that you can set to go off every five minutes. The vibration should remind you to stop talking and listen to what others have to say.

◆ Remind yourself that you can learn a lot by being quiet and listening to the experiences and the knowledge of others.

The Least You Need to Know

◆ Adults with ADHD may have a hard time finding the right word or phrase to explain what they mean.

◆ Sometimes adults with ADHD interrupt others during a conversation because they don't want to forget what they were going to say.

◆ Impulsiveness can cause you to interrupt others or blurt out an inappropriate response.

◆ Nonverbal cues can account for almost one half of the communication in a conversation. Adults with ADHD sometimes have a hard time reading nonverbal cues.

◆ Hyperactivity can cause you to monopolize the conversation or make it difficult to follow the thought process of the conversation.

Part 4

ADHD at Work

ADHD is most apparent at work for many adults. Disorganization and difficulty with time management are only some of the major obstacles adults with ADHD face. In this part we offer lots of suggestions and tips to help compensate for the symptoms of ADHD.

We also give you information on the laws that help to protect workers with disabilities. You will learn who is eligible under the law and what types of accommodations you can request.

For adults with ADHD, finding the right job can make all the difference in their life. We'll explore different options, such as working with a career counselor, using options such as flextime, or whether self-employment may be a good option.

Chapter 10

Managing Symptoms in the Workplace

In This Chapter

- ◆ How symptoms of ADHD decrease productivity
- ◆ Finding ways to compensate for impulsiveness
- ◆ Overcoming inattention on the job
- ◆ Disorganization interferes with work performance

Some characteristics of ADHD—taking risks, high energy level, and creative problem solving—can enhance your job performance. But symptoms of ADHD can also interfere with your job. Problems with organization and time management, difficulties with remembering details or information, and trouble prioritizing, all point to poor work habits. One recent study indicated that adults with ADHD lose over 22 workdays per year because of inattention, and are absent from work, on average, 8 more days per year than non-ADHD adults.

In this chapter we'll discuss how symptoms of ADHD may interfere with your job, as well as strategies you can use to help boost your performance.

Hyperactivity

Hyperactivity is a "high level of activity that interferes with the ability to concentrate or interact with other people." (*American Heritage Science Dictionary*, 2002) Many people with hyperactivity choose jobs that include movement throughout the day, such as sales positions. For those who work in more sedentary jobs, restlessness and fidgeting can appear to co-workers and bosses as lack of interest, boredom, or lack of motivation. Strategies to help cope with hyperactivity become important.

Working in an Office

Office or "white-collar" jobs pay better than blue-collar jobs. The U.S. Department of Labor reports white-collar workers make, on average, 45 percent more than blue-collar workers. White-collar jobs usually require sitting at a desk for a good portion, if not the majority, of the day. While office jobs may be more desirable, they may be undesirable for people who have trouble sitting still. If you need constant movement, consider carefully whether the job you are considering is right for you. Ending up restless and looking for a new job a few months down the road may only add to your frustration—and it isn't going to help your resumé.

> **The Scoop**
>
> A recent study indicated that employees with ADHD (in the United States) cost companies approximately $4,336 in lost productivity each year.

Hyperactivity doesn't have to interfere with your ability to do your job. Many jobs allow for movement throughout the day, or provide enough stimulation to keep your interest up. However, it may take some trial and error to find the right job for you.

Tips and Suggestions

♦ If your job entails talking on the phone, use a long cord or a headset that allows you to get up and walk around while talking.

♦ Are there tasks that require walking around, such as making copies, faxing information, or delivering paperwork or information to other people and departments? Use these tasks to break up your

day and provide you with a way to get up and move around once
in a while.

♦ Bring your lunch to work and eat at your desk, then use your
lunch break to go outside and take a walk. The exercise will use
up excess energy and help you focus better when you return to
work.

♦ During meetings, take notes. This will show your interest, help
keep you focused, and give you something to do.

♦ Take the stairs instead of the elevator.

♦ Ask for flexible hours to plan your day around your peak hours or
to vary your schedule and add variety to your workweek.

Working in a Boring Job

Adults with ADHD tend to get bored easily. Completing tedious tasks
can seem like torture. Boredom is one reason for frequent job changes.
A new job can hold your focus and attention for a period of time. Once
you learn and master a job, it becomes boring and you begin to look for
something new and exciting.

Other jobs are just plain boring from the beginning. Although no one
likes to be bored, adults with ADHD can find boring jobs excruciat-
ing: the need for movement and stimulation becomes overwhelming.
It is important to choose a career path that you are very interested in,
although even a great job can sometimes get boring.

Sometimes you just have to put up with the boring parts of your job.
Adding interesting and stimulating activities outside of work can help
to alleviate the frustration levels felt during the workday.

Tips and Suggestions

♦ Use a timer to keep you focused: set it to go off every 15 minutes
to remind you to pay attention to your task.

♦ Break projects into chunks and take a short break in between
tasks. Get up and walk around, or stand up and stretch.

Think It Over

Volunteer for stimulating projects and tasks that may come up—but be careful not to volunteer too quickly and overcommit yourself.

♦ Plan your day so that you complete the boring tasks during your energy peaks. If you wait until you are tired, it will be even more difficult to complete the tasks.

♦ If possible, delegate or trade the boring parts of your job.

Impulsiveness

Impulsiveness—acting without thinking—can create many different problems at work. You may jump into projects without thinking them through and end up not being able to finish them, or handing in a low-quality project. Impulsiveness shows up as not caring. Impulsiveness can also cause emotional outbursts or even getting up and quitting when you are frustrated—even when you don't have another job waiting.

Taking on More Than You Can Handle

Often adults with ADHD have a hard time saying "no," when a boss or co-worker asks for assistance on a project. You may be the first one to jump up and volunteer even though you are having a hard time managing the work you currently have. Chances are you will end up overwhelmed, and all of your work will suffer.

Impulsiveness does not always need to be a negative. It can help you to make quick decisions and think on your feet. It can help you in emergency situations. Finding a balance helps use impulsiveness to your advantage at work.

Tips and Suggestions

♦ Get in the habit of saying, "Let me think about it and get back to you later." Even if you are sure you will end up taking on the extra responsibility, take some time to plan out what you can do and how you can do it.

♦ Team up with another co-worker. Maybe you can volunteer to take on the extra project with the assistance of someone else—possibly someone good at organization and planning.

♦ If impulsiveness continues to cause you problems, consider working with a coach or therapist to come up with ways to internally monitor your impulsive actions.

The Lowdown

Impulsiveness can increase when you have a strong emotional reaction to someone or something. Understanding triggers to impulsive behaviors can help you get them under control.

Emotional Outbursts

Being able to do your job well is not enough. Employers want people who respond rationally and intelligently to every situation. Strong emotional responses signal an inability to handle stress.

If emotional meltdowns are a matter of course for you, keep a diary of what caused the outburst. Learning to understand your triggers can help you to manage your emotions. Certain situations may require you to take a step back or remove yourself temporarily in order to cope with emotional overload. Keeping track will not only help you but will provide you with information to better work with a therapist or coach on developing specific strategies.

Tips and Suggestions

♦ Enlist a venting partner you can call to complain or vent to without being judged or having your tirades interfere with your relationships with your co-workers.

♦ Use relaxation techniques, such as deep-breathing exercises.

♦ Eat properly; bring a healthy lunch to work and take a walk during lunch to let off excess energy and frustrations.

♦ If you have frequent emotional outbursts, consider looking for a position that allows you to work alone.

- If emotional outbursts generally lead to quitting your job, promise yourself you will talk with a friend or relative about the situation before quitting.

- Give yourself overnight to think about leaving your job. Sometimes just taking some time to calm down will give you a new perspective.

Inattention and Distractibility

Inattention is the inability to focus for extended periods of time. It can appear as if you are not paying attention, have trouble following directions, or simply that you do not care about your job. Both your bosses and co-workers may become frustrated with your forgetfulness or missing deadlines.

Pay Attention to Your Boss

How many times does your boss tell you about a new project or have meetings to update the staff on company expectations? Do you pay attention, or does your attention wander, and later you wonder what it was he or she said?

Your boss and co-workers may get the impression you are deliberately ignoring requests if you miss important parts of conversations. Their frustration may lead to strained relationships at work. Many adults with ADHD keep a notebook with them at all times to write down important information or instructions, giving them a reference to look back at later.

Tips and Suggestions

- Take notes when in meetings or talking with your boss to help keep you focused on the conversation.

- Write down ideas you want to contribute to the conversation. This will help you avoid blurting out or interrupting discussions because you worry you will forget what you want to say.

- Tape record important meetings so you can listen again later.

Focus on Your Work

Have you ever sat at your desk intending to complete a project only to have trouble staying focused? Each part of the task seems to take hours as you pay more attention to what co-workers are talking about or what is going on outside your window. Your mind just doesn't stay focused for more than a few minutes before wandering off again.

Many people with ADHD find taking a quick break and walking outside helps to increase their focus. If this is impossible, getting up, doing some stretches at your desk, or taking a walk around your office may help. Experiment to find out what works best for you.

> ### The Scoop
>
> Making careless mistakes, difficulty prioritizing tasks, problems getting started, and losing track of things are all signs of inattention in adults with ADHD.

Tips and Suggestions

◆ Use your computer to set reminders for you to pay attention while working at your desk.

◆ Take advantage of e-mail and send yourself a message to remind yourself of work that needs to be completed or deadlines you must remember.

◆ Review your week ahead each Monday morning. If necessary, ask your boss to sit down with you once a week to review your priority projects.

Loss of Productivity

A common complaint of many adults with ADHD is the many distractions at work, causing them to waste hours trying to complete a simple task. The phone ringing or the co-worker stopping by to chat will cause you to stop what you are doing. When it is time to get back to work, you might not remember what you were doing, or may have a hard time transitioning back to your task at hand. A task that should have taken an hour to complete may take you several hours.

One of the dangers of constant distraction is difficulty in transitioning from one activity to another. Once you move away from a task, it will take you much longer to refocus your attention. Minimizing distractions therefore can help to increase productivity.

We can't avoid distractions when working in a large office. Phones ring, co-workers stop to talk, or your boss wants you to drop everything to complete a project. Every distraction can send you into a tailspin, causing you to lose track of what you were doing.

Tips and Suggestions

- Have phone calls go directly to your voice mail and set aside a specific time each day to answer phone calls.

- Request a cubicle or office in a quiet area to minimize distractions.

- Use headphones to listen to music or *white noise* to block out distractions.

def•i•ni•tion

White noise is created by combining all frequencies of sound together. The sound is comparable to gentle sounds of nature such as rainfall or ocean waves. Many adults with ADHD find white noise calming.

- Ask for flextime and work at times of the day when there are not as many people in the office.

- Work at home for part of the day.

- Keep a notebook on your desk. Anytime you get disrupted, write down what you are doing so that, when you get back to work, you will know exactly where you left off.

- Create a daily schedule and complete the same tasks at the same time each day to minimize distractions.

- Complete one task before beginning another.

- Write down thoughts that are taking you off-task and then get back to work knowing you will remember your ideas.

- Keep a white board in your office or cubicle with a list of tasks to complete. Erase each as you complete it. Write the most important items in red.

◆ Keep clutter on your desk to a minimum, so other projects don't distract you from what you are currently working on.

Disorganization and Time-Management Problems

Disorganization can appear to your boss and your co-workers like carelessness. Some experts believe chronic disorganization is one of the most debilitating traits for adults with ADHD. Important papers get lost, tasks remain undone or unfinished. Jobs may be lost based solely on the lack of organizational skills.

Dealing with Paperwork

Desktops can become a "black hole." Piles of paperwork may be everywhere. Searching through the papers to find what you need can look disorganized, scattered, and incompetent.

In order for an organizational system to work, it must be designed around your specific needs. Many adults with ADHD fight the idea of adding structure and routine, believing it will stifle creativity, but a more structured and organized environment may allow you to better express your creativity because the clutter of your disorganization does not surround and distract you.

Tips and Suggestions

◆ Use your computer as much as possible by scanning documents or using word-processing software rather than keeping track of paperwork. You can always print out information if someone else needs a copy.

◆ Develop a simple filing system that works for you, then structure your day to include time for filing.

> **The Lowdown**
>
> Complete paperwork first thing in the morning before you are tired or faced with additional frustrations of the day.

◆ Admit when you are overwhelmed with papers and ask someone for help before your mountain of paper becomes an avalanche.

Chronic Lateness

The costs of being chronically late can be devastating. Many people have lost jobs because they can't seem to arrive on time. Being late can be embarrassing and can cause resentment in your co-workers; after all, somehow they manage to get to work on time each morning.

You probably are not late because you are trying to annoy your co-workers or you think you are better than them (although that may be what they think). Probably, your time perception is off or you subconsciously like being late, enjoying the adrenaline rush of trying to make it on time. But lateness can cause resentment and can impact your employer's profits.

Tips and Suggestions

◆ Plan to be early.

◆ Set an alarm on your cell phone to ring each morning when it is time to leave for work.

◆ Keep track of everything you do for a week, noting the time it takes to get ready in the morning, to get to work, to go out and buy lunch at your favorite restaurant. This information can help you better plan your day.

◆ Avoid what causes you to be late. If you get caught up checking e-mail each morning, don't turn your computer on until after work.

"You Wanted This When?" Working with Deadlines

Managing projects over several days or weeks may be one of the hardest organizational challenges. This type of project takes skills including managing paperwork, tracking progress, time management, and communication. All of these skills are problem areas for adults with ADHD.

Procrastination also plays a major role in missing deadlines or rushing through the end stages of a project in order to complete it on time. Handing in sloppy or late work shows employers you are irresponsible and unprofessional. Developing effective strategies may be essential to getting ahead in your job.

Tips and Suggestions

◆ Create deadlines for portions of large projects.

◆ Team up with a co-worker who is good at time management and planning.

◆ Make allowances for procrastination and distraction when determining a timetable for completing the project.

◆ Keep a schedule of the project posted by your desk.

◆ Use alarms, timers, and schedulers to help keep you on track.

> **The Scoop**
>
> Putting off tasks or projects not only impacts your job, but your health as well. Procrastination can increase stress and anxiety and lower self-esteem.

◆ Create daily to-do lists based on the project and due dates.

The Least You Need to Know

◆ There are no right or wrong jobs for adults with ADHD. It is important to take your specific symptoms into account and find a job that will work for you.

◆ Making sure you participate in activities you are interested in outside of work can help you cope with a boring job.

◆ Minimizing distractions can help you to limit the number of times you must transition from one task to another.

◆ Being organized at work can free you to allow your creativity to flow.

◆ Being chronically late can cost you your job or create resentment in your co-workers.

Chapter 11

Protecting Yourself at Work

In This Chapter

- ◆ What laws protect you at work
- ◆ How protections differ in a small company
- ◆ How to be your own advocate
- ◆ Possible accommodations

There are a few laws made to prevent discrimination of individuals with disabilities in the workplace. For some with ADHD, these laws may apply. Not everyone who has ADHD is eligible for protection; there needs to be substantial impairment in order to be considered disabled.

In this chapter we'll talk about the different laws, how they may apply to you, and what you will need to do in order to be eligible for protection under these laws. Beyond these laws, however, individuals with ADHD can take positive steps in the workplace to help create a successful environment. We'll explore some ideas on how to approach your boss, what types of accommodations are considered reasonable, and what you can do to help create a successful work environment.

The Rehabilitation Act of 1973

The Rehabilitation Act (RA) of 1973 prohibits discrimination of people with disabilities by the federal government, employers contracted by the federal government, and those institutions receiving federal funds (such as schools and colleges). You may have heard of the RA referred to as Section 504. It is often referred to this way when discussing accommodations in schools for children with ADHD.

The Americans with Disabilities Act

The Americans with Disabilities Act (ADA) offers the same protections of nondiscrimination in the private sector. Discrimination cannot occur within the application process, hiring, firing, job training, promotion, or advancement. In addition, any privileges of employment must not be discriminatory.

Many private enterprises and businesses must comply with the ADA. This includes:

- All state and local governments.

- Private employers with 15 or more employees.

- "Places of public accommodation" (this would include most private schools and colleges).

In addition, employees must disclose the disability to the employer in order to be eligible for protection under the law.

The Scoop
Companies with less than 15 employees are excluded from the Americans with Disabilities Act (ADA).

Who Is Eligible for Protections Under RA and ADA?

In order for someone to be protected under these laws, four conditions must be met:

♦ The person must be considered disabled under the law.

♦ The person must be qualified for the job, with or without reasonable accommodations.

♦ The person is being excluded from employment or otherwise discriminated against (for example, not receiving a promotion) specifically and solely because of their disability.

♦ They must be covered under one of the above laws.

According to the law, a person with a disability is "any individual who has a physical or mental impairment which substantially limits one or more of such person's *major life activities*, has a record of such impairment, or is regarded as having such an impairment." Mental impairment can include emotional or psychological disorders, cognitive impairment, and learning disabilities. ADHD is not specifically listed; however, it has been recognized by the courts as a mental or psychological disorder and would, therefore, be a covered disability.

def•i•ni•tion

A **major life activity** includes self-care activities, manual tasks, hearing, speaking, breathing, walking, learning, and work.

A diagnosis of ADHD does not guarantee eligibility for accommodations under either the RA or the ADA. The impairment must be substantial and significant. This means that a person is not able to perform at least one major life activity as compared to the average person in the general public.

If treatment (medication, psychological or behavioral interventions) helps to increase the ability to function to the level of the general public, this is taken into consideration and the person would no longer be eligible for protection. In other words, if a person is benefiting from treatment, these laws may no longer apply to their situation.

Employees must be able to show documentation for their diagnosis to receive protection under these laws. Some of the paperwork that may be needed includes:

◆ A written diagnosis, preferably including a diagnosis from the *Diagnostic and Statistical Manual* (DSM-IV-TR).

◆ A description of the specific impairment and the effect of treatment (including medication), both positive and negative, on the impairment.

◆ A comparison of the person's ability to an average person in the general public to complete the same major life activity.

◆ An indication that the person is qualified for the position.

◆ A list of recommended reasonable accommodations and why the accommodations are necessary.

The Lowdown

An indication of your diagnosis is not enough to provide protection under either the RA or the ADA. You must provide written documentation from your doctor indicating your symptoms are severe enough to cause you to be disabled.

This report should be completed by a qualified mental-health provider and submitted to the employer when requesting accommodations or protections under the RA or ADA.

Requests for accommodations must be specific and reasonable. It is impossible to define reasonable, as it depends upon the requirements of the job.

Working for a Small Company

Companies with less than 15 people are not required to abide by either the RA or ADA laws. If you work for a small company, you may still be protected against discrimination based on local or state laws. Check with your municipal government and state labor department.

In some ways, working for a small company can be easier. Some small employers are more flexible and may be more willing to provide accommodations, as long as there are no detrimental effects on other employees or on profit.

You probably know all of the employees on a much more personal level, including those in management. Talk with your boss about what you feel you need to better do your job. Rather than discuss laws and discrimination, make it a positive conversation. Approach your boss with suggestions about how implementing these suggestions can help the company achieve its goals.

Small companies are often more informal than large corporations. This type of environment may suit you better. But small companies can also be less structured. You may find you work better in a large, structured organization. Think about how you work best. This can help determine whether you would be better off working for a small company or a large organization.

Talking with Your Boss

You are the best judge of whether you should tell your employer about your ADHD and request accommodations. Many adults with ADHD choose to manage symptoms on their own, through behavior modification and medication, due to fear of the reaction from bosses and co-workers. Discrimination might begin after you have disclosed your diagnosis. On the other hand, in order for you to be eligible for protections under both RA and ADA, your employer must be aware of your disability.

If you are doing well in your job and don't need accommodations, you probably don't need to say anything. If you are worried about losing your job because your job performance is suffering based on your symptoms of ADHD, it might be time to talk with your employer.

> **Think It Over**
>
> When approaching your boss about your ADHD, be prepared with only one or two accommodations and reasons why these will help you do a better job. Whenever possible, use documentation and numbers to back up your information.

What Do You Want from Your Boss?

Before you approach your boss to request accommodations, decide what you want. As you go about your work, write down what tasks you struggle with and what you feel may help you to better do your job. Keep in mind that, although companies may be required to provide accommodations, they must be reasonable and not cause *"undue hardship."*

Companies are also not required to supply personal items such as eyeglasses or hearing aids. You must also be able to demonstrate that you can perform your job with these accommodations in place.

The more specific you can be, the better chance you have. Rather than requesting "items to help me learn new tasks," you may want to ask for "laminated sheets with detailed instructions for completing new tasks." With the first request, your employer may deny you, or provide you with an accommodation that ends up not helping you. The second request, which is reasonable, doesn't cost very much, is specific, and may be easier to get approved. In other words, help your employer to help you.

def•i•ni•tion

Undue hardship is when an accommodation requires a significant expense, will lower productivity, or decrease quality.

Starting the Conversation

Using a proactive approach usually works better than demanding accommodations or threatening your employer. The following examples can help you in framing your requests.

Instead of:

"I have ADHD and you must provide me with a quiet, distraction-free place to do my work."

Try:

"I have many strengths which make me a good fit for this job. If I would be able to use the conference room to review my notes before making presentations, I think I would be able to do a much better job."

Instead of:

"The Americans with Disabilities Act says you must give me accommodations. I want a white board in my office."

Try:

"I am sure I can complete this project. If I could have a white board in my office to keep track of my progress, it would help me stay on deadline."

You can make your request for accommodations either verbally or in writing. Many people like to start the process informally, by just talking with their boss. You can follow up with an e-mail or written statement summarizing the conversation if you want to keep track of your requests and how your employer has responded.

Advocating for Yourself

Whether you choose to disclose your ADHD or manage symptoms on your own, you can help improve your chances of success in the workplace. The first step to being your own best advocate is to understand the company you work for. Usually, you will receive a handbook when you begin work. Although it is tempting to flip through the pages and disregard the information, read over the policies and procedures listed in the handbook and keep it in your desk to refer to later. Should you decide to request accommodations, it might contain information you need. Even if you don't want to ask for accommodations, knowing and being able to refer to company policies on tardiness or grievances is extremely helpful.

Besides the company handbook, keep a notebook in your desk to write down information such as your boss's name, names of your co-workers, phone numbers, when payday is, how you report being late or missing work, policies for vacation time, and any other information you may need. Having this information available can save embarrassing moments of asking the same questions again and again.

Control What You Can

Pay attention to situations and circumstances you can control. Make sure you dress neatly and appropriately for your position. Be on time, offer to stay late or work overtime when needed, and keep conversations with co-workers job related. In addition, put forth your best effort, no matter what the task may be. If your boss asks you to pitch in and work on something that is not in your job description, do your best to help out.

The Lowdown

Keep an eye out for classes and seminars that will update your skills. After attending, share information with your co-workers. This helps you to remain a valuable employee.

When you excel in the areas you can control, you will develop a reputation of being dependable and your boss will look upon you as an asset to your department and to the company. This will help you should you require accommodations—or should you occasionally mess up.

Pay Attention to Your Own Accomplishments

Your boss isn't always going to notice what you have done right; after all, you are expected to do your job correctly. That doesn't mean you can't keep track of your accomplishments. Keep a file on your desk of completed projects, achievements, and times when you were complimented on your work. Even if you don't have written documentation, write down what the project or task was, who noticed your hard work, and what he or she said. Be as specific as possible, including dates and any other information you can think of.

When working on a project or task, discuss the outcome, show your interest and keep your boss apprised of the status. You don't want to overdo it, boasting about your skills, but you can point out your successes. Make sure, however, you always give credit to others when they have contributed to your success on a project.

Think It Over

It is hard for us to toot our own horn because we feel uncomfortable bragging or boasting about our achievements. Write down three accomplishments you are proud of and limit your self-promotion to these to avoid sounding as if you are bragging.

The information you gather can help during reviews and can document your ability to do the job. This is especially important if you are requesting accommodations and need to show you are qualified but need some assistance in certain areas.

Accommodations

If you do choose to ask for accommodations, keep accurate records. Keep copies of all documentation you provided your employer. Create a log of what accommodations you requested, whom you spoke with, the date you spoke with him or her, and the outcome. Make notations on how the accommodation worked for you. If the accommodations were denied, note in your log when you received notice and why it was denied.

Should you receive accommodations, don't flaunt them in front of your co-workers. Use the accommodations to improve your work performance. Some co-workers may ask questions about why you are receiving extra services. It is not necessary for you to discuss any extra assistance with your co-workers. This would be your decision based on your relationship with your co-workers. You may want to talk with your boss first, asking his or her opinion to be sure there are no misunderstandings and to show your professionalism.

> ### The Scoop
>
> You can request accommodations either formally or informally. A conversation with your boss is considered a request and must be addressed by the company. Requests do not need to be in writing.

What accommodations you may need will depend on the severity of your ADHD symptoms and your current job. Not everyone with ADHD will need accommodations. Some may need only a few accommodations and others may need several. Before you request accommodations you will want to decide what you need to do your job properly, and what, how, and why you want your employer to provide assistance.

Determining What Accommodations Could Help You

The first step would be listing all of your job responsibilities. Divide the list, making one column for the responsibilities you currently do well without extra assistance. Another column should include those responsibilities you feel you need accommodations for. The third column should list which symptoms of ADHD interfere with your ability to do the job. This should not be a generic list of ADHD symptoms, but should be specific to you. The last column should indicate the accommodations you think would help you and why they would help you.

Examples of Accommodations

Some examples of workplace accommodations for adults with ADHD may include …

◆ Providing a checklist for large projects.

◆ Organizational software.

◆ A handheld organizer.

◆ A large wall calendar.

◆ Additional time to learn new tasks.

◆ Laminated instruction sheets detailing new tasks.

◆ A noise-canceling headset.

◆ A white noise machine.

◆ Relocating office or cubicle to area with less distractions.

◆ Making use of flextime.

◆ Organizational assistant to help with filing and other paperwork.

◆ Developing color-coded filing system.

◆ Use of a professional organizer or coach.

◆ Creating a cheat sheet of important company or project information.

◆ Sensitivity training classes for all employees.

◆ Allow working from home, even if part time from home, part time from office.

◆ Use different communication methods, such as verbal, e-mail, voice mail, written memos based on employee's strengths.

◆ Allow for breaks throughout the day.

◆ Create flow charts of projects, tasks, or daily routines.

◆ Provide daily or weekly feedback.

- Create clear and concise performance standards and requirements.

- Use electronic files when possible to reduce paperwork.

This list is not all-inclusive but is meant to give an idea on what types of accommodations could be considered reasonable and would help with some of the common workplace problems adults with ADHD face. You should adapt a list of accommodations specific to your needs.

The Lowdown

Check your employee handbook to see if your employer has a procedure for requesting accommodations. If so, you will want to follow the steps outlined in the handbook.

What If Your Company Denies Accommodations?

Unfortunately, some companies deny or ignore a person's request for accommodations even if they are reasonable, well thought-out, and well documented. If this happens to you, you have the right to file a complaint with the U.S. Equal Employment Opportunity Commission (EEOC). This is the federal agency that enforces the ADA. The employee should contact the EEOC within 45 days of the alleged discrimination. The employee will work with a counselor to determine if a complaint should be filed. If so, the EEOC will investigate the claim and make a determination.

The Least You Need to Know

- Most employees with disabilities are protected under the Americans with Disabilities Act.

- Employees must disclose ADHD in order to be protected under the ADA.

- When requesting accommodations, it may be best to approach your boss with one or two requests and reasons why they will help you.

- Keep a file of your accomplishments at work to help you when requesting accommodations and during a review.

- Accommodations can be requested orally or in writing.

Chapter 12

Finding the Right Job

In This Chapter

- ◆ Deciding what type of job would be best
- ◆ Using your strengths to find the right job
- ◆ Modifying jobs to suit your needs
- ◆ Is self-employment right for you?

You know it must be out there: that perfect job. A job that works for someone who's full of energy and ready to take risks; a job where it doesn't matter if you arrive late and you don't have very much paperwork to keep track of. The problem is, you haven't found it yet—and in the meantime, you keep moving from job to job.

The fact is, there is no perfect ADHD job, because everyone is unique and has a different combination and severity of symptoms. But just as you have symptoms that may interfere with your ability to perform some jobs, you also have your own unique set of strengths.

In this chapter, we'll talk about how you go about determining what type of job is right for you, some ideas on finding a job, and whether self-employment is a good choice for you.

Finding the Right Job

Every industry offers a large array of different jobs. Take the advertising industry; you can work in sales, as a graphic artist, in ad layout, or as an administrator. No matter what your interests and passions are, there are bound to be a number of different jobs that incorporate your passions and skills. It is a matter of figuring out where you fit in.

Working with a Career Counselor

Career counselors work with individuals to assess education, experience, skills, abilities, personality, and interests, and match them with a career. Often, a career counselor will have you complete assessments and skill inventories then use this information to provide you with different options.

The Lowdown

Before working with a career counselor, take the time to check out references. Ask for 10 names of prior clients and contact at least 4 on the list.

Once you narrow your choices down, the career counselor will work with you to create a plan of action. Career counselors help you complete applications, prepare resumés, and practice for interviews. They may also have specific knowledge on further education or training to help you reach your goals. Some career counselors may have a network of contacts within the community.

Do Your Research

If you are looking into moving into a new career or a new industry, or don't know what you want to do, do some research first. You might want to know what types of jobs are available in a specific industry and what the typical responsibilities of those jobs are. You might want to know how satisfied other people are with their jobs.

Ideas for researching different types of jobs:

◆ Use job sites such as CareerBuilder.com or Monster.com to read descriptions of many different types of positions. Use a keyword search to put in your interests and skills to see what types of jobs come up.

◆ Search for journals or maga-
zines specific to the industry
or type of job you are looking
into. These can give you some
insider information on different
aspects of the job you may not
have thought about.

◆ Search for blogs or message
boards about the industry or
job type to read what people
within the industry are saying.

> **The Scoop**
>
> A career choice doesn't
> need to be forever. The U.S.
> Bureau of Labor Statistics
> estimates that people hold an
> average of 14 different jobs
> before the age of 40. If you
> choose a career, and find
> you don't like it, you can start
> the process over.

◆ Join a professional association for the industry you are planning to
enter. Many of these associations offer networking opportunities
or, at least, can offer you insider tips to help you with interviewing
for these specific jobs.

◆ Read your local newspaper to find information about local
companies.

It can seem overwhelming and time consuming to spend so much time
researching but it can pay off in the end. During the interview process,
you will be well informed and understand the job opportunity, the
industry, and the specific company you are applying to. This may give
you an advantage over other job applicants.

Using Networking

Networking can be scary. Adults with ADHD often have trouble with
social skills and are worried their weaknesses in that area can negate
any good that may come from networking.

Here are a few tips to help you network better:

◆ Decide what your goal is before you start talking with people. Are
you looking for information on a career or a specific company?
Are you looking to get an interview or an "in" at a certain company? Knowing exactly what you want can help you tailor your
conversations.

def•i•ni•tion

Networking is using personal and business contacts to build additional connections for the purpose of looking for a job or business opportunities.

- ◆ Practice your introduction. Write down how you plan to introduce yourself, then practice in front of a mirror or with friends and relatives.

- ◆ Most people like to talk about themselves; ask questions to learn more about the person and listen carefully to the answers.

- ◆ Write down questions you want to ask. Keep them on an index card in your pocket so you can review if you forget.

Although networking can be hard, it can offer many benefits. You may be nervous, but if you remain outgoing and friendly, your networking efforts could open up opportunities for you.

Build on Your Strengths

What are you passionate about? What brings a smile to your face? What do you enjoy learning about? Chances are, whatever it is, there is a job that utilizes your skills and your interests. If you have been struggling in job after job, you may be working in positions that have nothing to do with your interests. Sometimes this requires changing careers, starting over, or making a major move.

Take an Inventory of Job Skills

No matter how many jobs you have had, you probably have built up a number of skills. Think about every job you have had and make a list of all your responsibilities. Be as detailed as possible. If you have done volunteer work, include duties from these as well. For example, someone who has worked in numerous offices may have the following list:

- ◆ Filing

- ◆ Answering phones

- ◆ Customer service

- Typing

- Proofreading

- Data entry

- Computer skills (list software you are familiar with)

It doesn't matter how experienced you are; your list should include all job functions you are familiar with.

Personal Characteristics That Make You an Asset

As important as specific job skills are, personality traits and life skills are just as important. Make a list of personal characteristics that help you at work. This list should include traits such as:

- Creative

- Good at working independently

- Good at working as part of a team

- Outgoing

- Hard-working

- Dedicated

- Like fast-paced jobs

- Prefer jobs with lots of structure and routine

Think It Over _____

Personal satisfaction and growth opportunities are two of the top 10 reasons people stay at a job. Keep this in mind when looking for a new career.

You may want to place a star next to the traits you feel are your best since those are the ones you will want to incorporate in a job. You should now have a listing of the skills you can bring to a new job.

Working with Your Interests

Now it is time to decide on an industry. When we are first choosing a career, during our late teen or early adult years, we have only limited life experiences. As we grow and experience more, our interests may change. Our first choice of a career may no longer be the best for us.

Think about what you would do if you didn't need to worry about failing. What would you do if you could make up the perfect job? What would your job look like? What would the responsibilities include? Although you may not find a job that fits exactly, this is where you should begin.

Make a list of the hobbies and activities you enjoy. What do you like to spend your time doing? Do you enjoy working with children? Are you good at art? At photography? Do you enjoy reading? This will become the list of industries you should consider.

Putting It All Together

You should now have lists of your skills and characteristics, and a list of industries. Choose a few of the industries. Research each industry to see what types of jobs are available and match those jobs with your skills and characteristics. Once you complete this step, you should have a list of several jobs that you may be good at. These positions have a good chance of holding your attention because you chose them based on your passions in life.

What Training Would You Need?

Once you have created or found your perfect job, think about what type of training you already have and what additional training you would need. Is this a job you would need to go to college for? Are training programs available? Do you need to work in an entry-level position to gather some experience? This job is your goal. Set up a plan of action, outlining the steps you need to complete, in order to reach your goal.

Flextime and Other Options

It is possible to make adjustments to a current position, working around the ADHD symptoms that are most interfering with your abilities to effectively do your job.

Flextime

Flextime offers the ability to create your own schedule, as long as you meet certain conditions. These conditions vary from job to job and company to company. The basis of flextime is you will be required to work a forty-hour week. You may be able to set your schedule, working four ten-hour days or coming in later in the morning and working until the evening. Some flextime jobs can also include split shifts, working some hours in the morning and coming back to work in the evening. Flex hours are usually meant to accommodate the needs of the employee.

Flextime allows you to work at off-times, when the office is empty and there are fewer distractions. If you understand when your peak efficiency is each day, flextime allows you to schedule your workday for when you are most efficient.

Sharing a Job

Sharing a job works when two people choose to both work one job. You can each work twenty hours per week (or whatever split is best for the two employees) or you can work certain days of the week and the other person can work the other days. This type of arrangement may help in relieving work-related stress. In order for this to work, both people must work with the same effort and efficiency; resentment may build up if one person feels he or she is working harder and carrying the bulk of the responsibility.

Working from Home

Some jobs may be easily accomplished from home, especially with the ability to access data over the Internet. This can help if you become easily distracted by the activity at the office. You must have the self-discipline to get work accomplished in your home. For some jobs, you can work part-time from home and part-time from the office, providing you with the best of both worlds.

There are some pitfalls, however, for the person with ADHD who chooses to work from home. You must be committed to setting up a strong structure for yourself. You

The Lowdown

When working from home, stick to your normal routine. Wake up at the same time, take a shower, eat breakfast. Staying on a normal workday schedule can help you to be more productive.

need to work set hours every day. You also need to set up a "distraction-free zone," meaning a separate space to work, personal phone turned off, and an agreement with your family not to disturb you during work time except for truly urgent matters. The better you plan out working from home, the more likely you are to succeed.

Is Self-Employment a Good Option?

Many entrepreneurs have ADHD, or share many of the characteristics of adults with ADHD. This could be because some of the positive characteristics of ADHD are also conducive to owning your own business. For example, adults with ADHD often have several projects going on at one time, juggle many responsibilities, and are creative thinkers and risk takers.

The Scoop
According to the U.S. Census Bureau, over 2000 people start their own business every day. In one study, the rate of self-employment for people over the age of 50 continued to grow, with over one third of the male workforce, aged 50+, being self-employed. (Boston College Department of Education, 2008) Self-employment is a good option for many adults with ADHD.

The Benefits of Creating Your Own Work Environment

Many people see self-employment as the ideal work situation. You can set your own hours and be your own boss. No one else can tell you when or how to work. For adults with ADHD, self-employment can also have the following benefits:

♦ You have control over how much work you complete each day.

♦ You can develop a business based on your individual strengths and skills.

♦ As you develop your business, you can hire someone to take care of the details you are not so good at.

♦ You can have a sense of accomplishment by owning your own business.

- You add variety and stimulation to your workday. Since you are in charge of everything, you are involved in all aspects of the business; every day can be different.

- Your success is not dependent on other people; you control your own success.

- Your salary is not dependent upon a paycheck; you control how much money you can make.

- You have more flexibility for sick days or doctor's appointments.

- You can avoid rush-hour traffic by working on a different schedule or working from home.

- You get to make the rules rather than following someone else's rules.

- You can develop your own ideas rather than having them approved by someone else.

- You can forget the job interviews, worry about layoffs or losing your job.

- You can create your own work environment and organizational systems based on your individual needs.

- You can wear what you want (unless you are visiting clients).

- You can choose what you want to do, what industry you want to work in, and whom you work with.

As you can see, there are many benefits from owning your own business. After years of trying different jobs and working for different companies, self-employment can offer the opportunity of no longer feeling as if you don't fit in or are not right for your job. With self-employment, you design your own position.

The Downside: Organization and Administrative Duties

Just as there are benefits, there are also drawbacks to owning your own business. Being responsible for all aspects of the business can give you variety and make every day different, but it also means you might be responsible for duties you aren't good at or don't like, such as filing, bookkeeping, and other administrative duties. The following is a list of potential downsides to being a self-employed adult with ADHD:

- ◆ You must be organized, able to create and execute your plan.

- ◆ Generally, starting your own business requires long hours, especially in the beginning.

- ◆ You may not be able to afford office support, meaning you are responsible for all paperwork and administrative duties.

- ◆ You are responsible for all mistakes, and for following up and making all corrections—even apologizing to clients.

- ◆ Self-employment requires self-discipline and internal motivation.

- ◆ You won't have the support of co-workers or bosses to help you through problems.

- ◆ You may not have anyone to bounce ideas off of.

- ◆ You may miss the social contact of going to work each day.

- ◆ If you are working from home, you never leave work. You may find it difficult to transition from working to relaxing, or vice versa.

The Lowdown

Working with an accountant is a good business move, especially for adults with ADHD. Finances, tax regulations, and paperwork are not usually strong points for those with ADHD—and not having your paperwork filed correctly can land your new business in hot water.

Some of these disadvantages are the result of working from home, although not all self-employed people will do so. Some will have financial backing or partners. You will need to look at your particular situation to determine what your advantages and disadvantages are.

Weigh the Pros and Cons

There are a number of benefits that are disadvantages as well. You will need to look at your personality to decide if you are better off self-employed or working for someone else.

- While it is true you don't have a boss to answer to and you are on your own, this can also be a terrifying prospect. You will usually have a number of clients to whom you provide a product or service; these clients become your boss. If they aren't happy, or you are delayed on meeting a deadline, you might not get paid.

- While it is true you won't have the distraction caused by a busy office or workplace, distractions can happen at home, maybe even more so. The television calls out to you, the lawn you didn't get mowed last night is looking scraggly, and lunch becomes a project in itself.

- While it is true you can create your own job description and no one can tell you what to do, paperwork is extremely important. You need to pay your bills, keep track of expenses, and follow up on any paperwork from your clients. Organization and administrative duties fall upon your shoulders—there isn't any getting around it.

- While it is true you have more flexibility and are not limited in developing creative ideas, self-employment normally requires an initial investment as well as ongoing financial considerations. You may need to get health insurance or plan for your retirement—and those paid vacations are no longer paid.

On the one hand, self-employment requires an enormous commitment; on the other hand, you can pass off many duties to a professional or an employee. And, sometimes, self-employment includes a partner or someone who is willing to provide the administrative part while you get to work on creative ideas. Both working as an employee and being self-employed have benefits and downfalls. Take your time deciding and use resources available to you if you want to take the step toward becoming self-employed.

The Least You Need to Know

- Career counselors can help match your interests and skills to a job.

- Finding a job that uses your strengths can help increase your chances of success.

◆ Options, such as flextime, can help make a job more conducive to your ADHD.

◆ Self-employment offers both advantages and disadvantages.

Part 5

Managing ADHD in Daily Life

This part offers plenty of tips and suggestions for adults with ADHD, focusing on many of the areas that are most difficult. Running late, setting goals, procrastination, and money management are a few of the areas addressed here.

Emotional outbursts and mood swings can be common in adults with ADHD. These can be the result of becoming easily overwhelmed or having a hard time managing stress. We offer suggestions for helping to manage your emotions on a daily basis.

Chapter 13

Time Management and Procrastination

In This Chapter

- ◆ Exploring reasons for chronic tardiness
- ◆ Finding ways to focus on what is important
- ◆ The five categories for prioritizing
- ◆ Procrastination can hurt your job, your health, and your relationships

Time management is frequently a big problem for adults with ADHD. Chronic tardiness can create problems at work and in your personal life. Friends and family may feel you are being rude when you continually keep them waiting. They may believe you don't value their time, that you believe what you are doing is so much more important than their activities. Usually, this isn't true at all—you simply lost track of time.

Being consistently late is a sign that you aren't managing symptoms of ADHD very well. You may need to simplify your life or better manage the distractions constantly taking your attention from the task at hand. In this chapter, we will discuss reasons for chronic tardiness, as well as ways to improve by setting goals, minimizing distractions, prioritizing tasks, and using technology to manage your time, and your life, better.

Always Running Late

Being late is one of the biggest complaints of adults with ADHD. Beyond embarrassment, you can lose your job because of chronic tardiness. Friendships and family relationships can be strained if you consistently show up late for get-togethers. Worse is the guilt you feel when running late to pick up your children. You may constantly promise yourself you won't be late again, but it happens anyway.

The Lowdown

Some people enjoy the adrenaline rush of running late. They may enjoy driving fast and trying to beat the clock, trying to be on time even after leaving the house late. You might want to find more outlets in your life to provide you with high-stimulus activities and feed the need for adrenaline rushes.

There are many strategies to help you be on time. Some adults with ADHD will use timers, or alarms on their cell phones, or set clocks and watches ahead, all to no avail. Trying to change your habits without taking into account the reason behind the behavior doesn't often work. There are some common reasons adults with ADHD are always running late. Changes should address these issues, rather than just addressing the tardiness.

Avoidance: I'm Not Interested

When something holds no interest for you, you have no motivation to be involved, not to mention be on time. Adults with ADHD are often drawn to high-stimulus, high-energy activities. When your job, family gatherings, or wherever you need to get to, offers no interest, chances are you will avoid going and allow other things to take your attention, causing you to be late.

Changing your perspective can help you to be on time. Find something good about your job; instead of telling yourself you don't want to go, tell yourself why you want to go, even if it is simply to get it over with. Finish your obligation and then do something you are interested in.

Hyperfocus: I'll Just Be One More Minute ...

Hyperfocus is when you pay so much attention to one thing you ignore everything else around you. Many adults with ADHD find hyperfocus helps at work, making it easier to complete tasks.

Hyperfocus can cause problems when you need to be somewhere but forget to pay attention to the time. When you are engrossed in a task, you may feel as if only ten minutes have passed when, actually, half an hour has passed and now you are running late! Some adults with ADHD find using timers helps to manage hyperfocus. If you need to move on to the next task in fifteen minutes, set a timer for ten minutes to remind you it is time to wrap up the current task.

Think It Over

Hyperfocus is sometimes a defense mechanism when you are feeling overwhelmed and need to separate yourself from your surroundings.

Time Distortion

Many adults with ADHD have a distorted sense of time. You are not able to judge accurately how much time something will take. For example, you may misjudge how long it will take to drive from your home to school to pick up your children. Or, you have one more task to complete and judge that it will only take a few minutes to complete, forty-five minutes later you are still working on it. Without judging time accurately, you will consistently run late.

Simplify Your Life

The typical adult with ADHD may have several projects going on at one time, in addition to work, taking care of their home, running the kids around, and any volunteer activities. Feeling overwhelmed can paralyze you.

The following five tips will help simplify your life and decrease your feelings of being overwhelmed:

♦ Only agree to one volunteer activity at a time. This could be helping at school or volunteering at your church. No matter what it is, accept only one and decline all other offers until the first is completed.

◆ Use resources to help make your life easier, such as online bill payment services.

◆ Prioritize what is important in your life. Decide what direction you want your life to take and what steps you need to take to get there. Set goals. Make sure activities you participate in are helping you reach your goals.

◆ Make a list of all weekly chores. Decide which chores you can delegate. You may consider hiring a high school student to come to your house once a week to complete some of the chores.

◆ Limit the time you watch television. Choose a few shows per week you enjoy rather than automatically turning on the television and spending hours watching shows you have no interest in. You may add hours of free time a day this way.

Simplifying your life also means accepting where you are in life. Wherever you are, it's okay. You may not have accomplished all you wanted to and may have goals that you haven't yet reached. Accept where you are and move forward, instead of looking backward.

The Importance of To-Do Lists

To-do lists are essential to good time-management skills. These lists provide a guideline for what items are to be completed within a given amount of time. You may want to create a list weekly or daily. Either way, to-do lists help you remember what you need to do.

> **The Scoop**
>
> About 75 percent of Americans keep some type of a to-do list. These lists can help you with everything from what to buy at the store to what you need to do to improve your career.

Completing a list each day can help you see how much you have gotten done. Place a mark next to high-priority items so you know at a glance what you should devote your time to first.

Setting Goals the Right Way

So many times we set goals but it doesn't seem to make any difference. We still don't accomplish what we set out to accomplish. This could be because of how we set goals. We don't create a plan of action. The following are steps to improving our chances of following through and reaching goals:

1. Choose just one goal at a time.

2. Make sure your goal is realistic.

3. Write down your goal.

4. Break down the goal into smaller goals.

5. Remind yourself of your goal. Use e-mail reminder systems, send yourself a postcard or use an online calendar or PDA to give yourself reminders of what your goal is and why it is important to you.

6. Reward yourself for following your plan of action.

Goals have little chance of being successful until we create a plan on how to reach the goal. Remember, however, that goals may change as your situation changes. Remain flexible so you can adjust your goals if necessary.

 The Lowdown

Accept that you may have setbacks but commit to continuing to reach your goal, despite the setbacks.

Manage Distractions and Disruptions

Distractions are a part of life. Generally, when someone is interrupted in the middle of a task, he or she will temporarily shift his or her attention to the new item, complete it, and then move back to the original task. This isn't so easy for adults with ADHD. Transitioning between activities is difficult. Getting back on track is hard or sometimes the original task is forgotten and the adult with ADHD moves on to whatever took their attention.

The following are tips to helping minimize distractions:

♦ Turn off your phone when you are at home. Let the answering machine pick up calls. If you're driving or running errands, keep your cell phone on vibrate or silent and keep it in your glove compartment so you are not tempted to answer it every time it rings.

♦ Set aside a specific time to answer phone calls rather than stopping what you are doing to talk on the phone.

♦ Turn off the television. If you need background noise, consider music instead, but make sure the music is upbeat and will keep you moving, rather than put you to sleep.

♦ If you must get something accomplished, consider hiring a babysitter to keep your children occupied while you complete your chores.

♦ Turn off your computer. It is tempting to check e-mail or get caught up in social networking sites. If the computer is off, you will not be as tempted to sit down "just for a few minutes."

♦ Create routines. Having daily routines can help you avoid giving in to distractions. You will know what you are supposed to do and when you are supposed to do it. Once you get in the habit, you can avoid distractions.

 Think It Over

Make sure you eat right. Eat plenty of fresh fruits and vegetables and drink plenty of water. Hunger or dehydration can increase inattention, making you more susceptible to giving in to distractions.

If you find that, no matter what you do, you are still easily distracted, take a short break and take a walk outside for ten minutes. The fresh air and exercise will help you focus better when you return to your tasks.

Prioritize Tasks

ADHD causes problems with executive functioning, which helps us plan and prioritize our tasks. Because of this, adults with ADHD have a jumble of ideas, tasks, and projects—but no plan for getting it all done. How do you prioritize your tasks? How do you manage to complete everything, even those things you don't really want to do?

Imagine you've written each task you have to do on separate pieces of paper and thrown them into a big jar. Your idea of prioritizing is to reach in and grab one task. If you want to do it, you do it; if you don't, you either throw it away or put it back in the jar. You have no clear path to finishing all of the tasks, so you never empty the jar and you feel as if you never accomplish anything.

In order to prioritize tasks, you have to clearly understand your "priority categories." For example, how do you categorize something you have to do today to make it stand out from something that must be done by next week? The first step is to come up with categories to help you decide what tasks should be done first. Your categories might look something like this:

1. **Absolutely Urgent:** These must be done right away or by a deadline and are important to your job, your family, or to you personally.

2. **Urgent:** These are important to you, your family, or your job, but don't have a deadline.

3. **Chores:** These are things you don't necessarily *want* to do but have to do anyway.

4. **Maybe:** These are things you would like to do, but they aren't especially important and it doesn't matter if you do them today, tomorrow, or next week.

5. **Dreams, Wishes, and Ideas:** These are things you might like to do but have no immediate importance in your life.

Once you can categorize all of the tasks you need to complete, it is easier to begin to accomplish tasks. You are no longer floundering, wondering what to do: you have a specific order of what to do and when to do it.

The Lowdown

Always remember, your list should be flexible enough to take into account changes in your situation. Your list is a tool to help you stay organized, but it should not control you.

Using categories such as these may be confusing at first, but, as you continue to work with them, you will start automatically assigning categories as soon as you receive a task. Once you do that, you can determine when something should be done and whether you need to give immediate attention to it or whether it can wait.

Just as important as categorizing your tasks, is finding a way for you to manage the list. Task lists are ever changing and evolving. New tasks are added, some tasks are completed, others are no longer important. The sheer number of tasks on the list can be overwhelming, but the following ideas may help you:

- If you are a visual person, you might want to have a white board with tasks listed in order of importance.

- You can use the jar approach, with five separate jars, one for each category of importance.

- Task-management software is available for your laptop computer or for handheld electronics such as iPhones or BlackBerries.

- A notebook that allows for a continuous list can help, especially if you like to see the items that have been crossed out to help build a sense of accomplishment.

No matter which method you choose, prioritizing tasks is a must for managing deficits in executive functioning. Creating a system that works for you can also help in managing distractions and inattention.

Using Gizmos and Gadgets

Forgetfulness, hyperfocus, executive functioning deficits—all these cause problems with organizing and managing your day-to-day activities. Sometimes, you need external help. The following are gizmos and gadgets to help you keep track of what you need to do:

- Locator devices: These gadgets have small, radio-controlled patches you place on items you frequently use, such as your keys or your wallet. There is a base monitor. Press a button on the monitor and your lost item will beep. These come as stationary monitors to keep on a counter at home for commonly misplaced items in the house or portable monitors to attach to your belt, making sure you don't leave your keys or wallet at the store.

♦ Portable USB drives: If you need to keep computer data with you and don't want to carry your laptop or paper files, you can attach a portable USB memory drive to your keys and have it with you at all times (provided you can find your keys).

♦ Alarm watches: A number of different watches allow you to program different alarms and alerts. Some watches have preprogrammed text messages (such as "Take medicine"), or may allow you to program your own message to remind you of appointments or other tasks to complete.

♦ Task manager software: Online calendars and task managers can help you to keep your to-do list prioritized and up to date. Many offer programmable reminder services and generate an alarm if you choose.

♦ Many cell phones, personal music players, and PDAs can hold your complete calendar, be programmed to sound an alarm, and sync with your computer to keep your calendar up to date.

♦ Alarm clocks and kitchen timers: When you are worried about hyperfocusing and forgetting an upcoming task, set your kitchen timer or alarm clock to let you know when it is time to move on to the next task.

♦ Wake-up services: There are services that will call you when it is time to wake up, just like in a hotel.

♦ Alarm clocks to turn on lamps or music: You can attach an alarm clock to a lamp to brighten your room, making it more difficult to stay asleep or alarm clocks that work directly with your iPod, waking you up with the music you enjoy.

♦ Online budget calculators: There are many online programs to help you budget your money and create a monthly budget or long-term financial plan.

Electronic devices are forever changing and improving. This list offers some basic suggestions but many of the above can be customized to fit your exact situation and circumstances.

The Scoop
There are a number of free, online reminder services. You can send yourself an e-mail to remember one appointment or have an e-mail sent on a recurring basis.

Procrastination

It's easy to *procrastinate*. You can choose to do anything except what you should be doing. There are a number of different reasons why people procrastinate:

◆ **Fear:** You may be afraid of failure so, rather than chance not doing something well, it is easier not to do it at all.

◆ **Lack of motivation:** It may be a task or project that you have no interest in or do not want to do.

◆ **Lack of priority:** You just don't see the job as a high priority, or there are too many other tasks that are higher on your list.

◆ **Lack of knowledge:** You don't know how to do the task and it seems easier to avoid doing it than trying to figure out how to do it.

◆ **Overwhelm:** You don't know how to start. You are intimidated by the task and just don't know how to get started.

Procrastination itself is not the problem, it's the underlying problem you have to deal with. Once that has been sufficiently resolved, the procrastination will go away on its own. Many people, however, try to change the actual procrastination, telling themselves, "just do it" rather than determining what is causing the procrastination. This would be similar to telling someone who needs eyeglasses to "just see," instead of trying to find out why they can't see correctly.

def•i•ni•tion

Procrastination is avoiding or delaying doing something.

The Cost of Procrastination

Certainly, the financial cost of procrastination can be felt. If you don't complete the project for work within the deadline, you could lose your job. If you don't pay your bills on time, you add late fees to the bills.

Relationships can suffer due to your procrastination. Imagine the spouse who comes home from work to no electricity because you never got around to paying the bill. Or the co-worker who ended up staying late all week because you never got around to finishing a project. Resentment builds quickly when friends, relatives, and co-workers feel they must step in to complete what you did not. They know you are capable of completing the task, they know you had the time to complete the task, they also know you just didn't do it and left it up to them to finish for you. Procrastination creates a "me" environment rather than an "us" environment.

Think It Over

People who procrastinate have more problems sleeping, more stomach problems, and more colds and flus than people who don't procrastinate.

Tips for Overcoming Procrastination

Procrastination is a learned response, a way of avoiding what is unpleasant or not understood. It is a cover-up for an underlying problem. Once we determine what is causing the procrastination, we can work on specific strategies for overcoming it.

The following are tips for managing your procrastination:

◆ Break projects or tasks down into small chunks. Concentrate on only the first part of the task. Don't even think about the rest of the task until the first part is complete.

◆ For time-consuming tasks, use a timed goal rather than a performance goal. For example, "I will work on this project for 30 minutes today." It might be easier to get started if you know you only have to get through the next 30 minutes, and then you can move on to something more enjoyable.

- Write down your plan on how to tackle the task. Break your plan into steps and concentrate on one step at a time. (Allow yourself only a certain amount of time to create your plan or you may end up procrastinating by overplanning.)

- Reward yourself for completing a task by doing something you enjoy. Alternate between fun activities and boring activities.

- Accept "good" as an acceptable outcome. Sometimes perfectionism causes procrastination; if you can't do it perfectly, you would rather not even try. Try giving yourself a time limit for your project (when the time is up, you're done), rather than working until it is perfect.

- Use your normal distractions as rewards. For example, do you procrastinate by checking your e-mail? Tell yourself you will work for 30 minutes, then you can take a break and check e-mail.

- Work with a partner. Your partner can be one who adds accountability or someone who makes the project more fun.

Procrastination can wreak havoc on your relationships, your finances, and your job. Although often seen as a time-management problem, it is not. It usually has more to do with being overwhelmed. Although there are many different strategies for dealing with procrastination, breaking down tasks into smaller ones is frequently the best strategy to employ.

The Least You Need to Know

- Traditional methods to improve chronic tardiness, such as setting alarms or using timers, don't work long term unless you find the underlying reason for consistently being late.

- Choose one volunteer activity at a time and don't agree to another one until your commitment is over.

- Limit yourself to a specific time each day to answer e-mails rather than checking it repeatedly throughout the day.

- A number of technological gadgets exist to help you find misplaced keys or keep track of your to-do lists.

- When you consistently procrastinate, friends and relatives may get the idea that you feel your needs are more important than theirs.

Chapter 14

Tackling Hypersensitivities, Budgets, and Clutter

In This Chapter

- Examining the relationship between ADHD and hypersensitivities
- Creating a household budget
- Learning to declutter your surroundings
- Hoarding as an executive functioning deficit

Although the main symptoms of ADHD are inattention, distractibility, and impulsiveness, a number of its characteristics can interfere with daily life. Many people with ADHD have various hypersensitivities. These could range from feeling uncomfortable because of a tag in your shirt, to not being able to sleep because of the ticking of the clock. Disorganization and lack of planning skills impacts finances, budgeting, and managing a household.

Many people see ADHD as a disability interfering with learning and other activities requiring focus, but it is so much more and impacts virtually every aspect of a person's life. In this chapter we provide lots of practical tips you can use every day to help compensate for some of the more bothersome traits of ADHD.

Hypersensitivities

Hypersensitivity, also called sensory defensiveness, is an unusual reaction or sensitivity to stimuli taken in through one, or more, of the five senses (touch, taste, smell, hearing, and vision). Some research has shown people with ADHD are hypersensitive, especially girls. Sensory defensiveness has also been associated with autism, some learning disabilities, and Fragile X syndrome.

> **The Scoop**
>
> Some research indicates up to 20 percent of the population has some type of sensory sensitivity. It may be they are not necessarily sensitive, but instead notice so many more sensory events, and feel them more intensely, leading to feeling continuous "sensory overload."

Hypersensitivities can make normal, daily activities unbearable or, at the very least, extremely distracting. Scratchy clothing, strong smells, or even the tag inside your shirt can cause you to lose concentration. Sensitivity to touch often interferes with intimate relationships.

Noise Sensitivities

Some people may be overly sensitive to certain sounds or frequencies. Motors running, the sound of the refrigerator, or even the sound made by electricity, can seem irritatingly loud and bothersome. Sounds other people may not even consciously hear, such as the ticking of a clock, can cause enormous discomfort. Certain sounds can cause irritability.

Many people with sound sensitivity have problems with the volume of the television or radio or may not be able to attend movies because of the loud volume.

Some strategies that adults with ADHD can use to help manage auditory sensitivities:

- Use white noise, such as a fan, to help you sleep or when focusing on a task.

- Use noise-canceling headphones or listen to music through headphones.

- Use flextime at your job to increase the time you can work when there is less noise.

- Use pads or carpeting under appliances in order to reduce the noise.

- Use foam ear plugs to eliminate or reduce distracting noise.

Even the slightest sounds can interfere with sleep, causing additional problems. It helps for you to become aware of how and what sounds most affect you, so you can better manage this condition.

Oral Defensiveness

With oral defensiveness, food needs to be the right temperature. It needs to have the right taste. People with oral defensiveness may like very spicy foods or may not be able to tolerate any spices. Most people with oral defensiveness are extremely picky. They may eat only a few foods. Oral defensiveness also causes sensitivity to textures, if foods are not the right texture, you may not be able to tolerate them. You also may gag easily.

Some strategies for coping with oral defensiveness:

- Add vitamin supplements to your diet, if your oral defensiveness stops you from eating a balanced diet.

- Find nutritious supplements for foods you can't tolerate.

- Use smaller toothbrushes, which may be easier to use.

- Chew gum, which will help calm you.

- Have a glass of water with your meals if you gag easily. Drinking water can help you swallow your food without choking or gagging.

Oral defensiveness can interfere with social situations. You may feel uncomfortable going to other people's homes or some people may see fussiness with food as you acting "like a baby" or being spoiled. Talk to your family and friends and let them know how different foods affect you.

Olfactory Sensitivity

Some people are so sensitive to certain smells, called *olfactory* sensitivity, they have a difficult time focusing on anything other than the smell. Common smells that cause a problem may be perfumes, burnt foods, car fumes, and cigarette smoke. But a smell doesn't need to be a commonly bothersome smell. It could be the mint toothpaste for one person and the smell of tuna fish for another.

def•i•ni•tion

Olfactory refers to anything having to do with the sense of smell.

Tips to help in coping with olfactory sensitivity:

- Use unscented soaps.
- Use products without added perfumes.
- Fill your home with scents you enjoy by burning candles or incense.
- Use an air purifier or have plenty of houseplants.
- Keep a handkerchief with a favorite scent with you to mask odors outside of your home.

To the person with smell sensitivity, an irritating smell can interfere with your ability to complete tasks. You may not be able to think of anything but the offensive smell.

Tactile Defensiveness

Tactile defensiveness is sensitivity to touch. Clothing, such as tags, tight-fitting clothes, and new or stiff fabrics, may bother people with tactile defensiveness. They may be bothered by someone touching them and may avoid crowded areas in order to avoid someone accidentally touching them. Some may be either under or overly sensitive to pain. Having dirty hands or feet may be very bothersome.

Some strategies for tactile defensiveness:

◆ Wear comfortable, loose-fitting clothes.

◆ Avoid clothes with elastic waistbands.

◆ Wear cotton or loose knit clothing; avoid clothes made from wool.

◆ Wrap your blanket around you like a cocoon.

◆ Buy socks without seams, shirts without tags, or cut tags out.

In addition, many people with tactile defensiveness have a difficult time being touched. Let people know how you feel and use other methods to show your affection. Talk to your partner if this impacts your intimate relationship. Together you can find ways to compensate for your difficulties with touch.

Money Management

Managing family and personal finances takes planning and organization, both difficult areas for adults with ADHD. Without these skills, bills go unpaid or get paid late, adding late fees on top of the original bill. From making sure deposits are made to keeping track of every check written, when you are working with the family budget, details are important. Missing just one step can cause you to lose track of your money.

The Lowdown

Sixty-seven percent of adults with ADHD have trouble managing money and 47 percent are more likely to have trouble saving money to pay bills according to a study completed by the University of Massachusetts.

Identify Problems

If your finances are a mess and you haven't a clue where to start or what to do, begin with identifying the main problems. Once this is done, you can work on one area at a time. Some of the problems adults with ADHD might have are …

♦ Paying bills late or not at all.

♦ Bouncing checks.

♦ Not keeping track of checks written.

♦ Not depositing money.

♦ Balances too high on credit cards.

♦ Not saving money for emergencies or the future.

♦ Having expenses higher than your income.

For some problems, such as back taxes, you may want to consult an accountant. Although it's easier to ignore some issues, sooner or later they will demand attention and often by that time they have snowballed to the point of catastrophe. Tackling financial issues, one at a time, is a much better approach.

Tracking Expenses

Sometimes, you spend more money than you take in, but frequently, adults with ADHD just don't know where their money goes. Tracking all of your expenses for one month will provide you with the answers you need to create a budget.

When tracking expenses, every little purchase counts, whether you could spend $1.50 on a doughnut, $1 on a candy bar, or $100 on a new pair of shoes. Keep track of every single purchase. If you have trouble keeping a log, take one month to use your debit card for every purchase you make, then use your checking account statement to track your purchases.

Think It Over

If you spend $6 per day on lunch when you are working, excluding weekends and two weeks for vacation, you will spend $1,500 annually.

At the end of the month, add up what you spend on different types of purchases. How much do you spend for gas and car expenses? For food shopping? For entertainment? You may be surprised at how much money you spend, and what you spend it on. For example, let's take the doughnut for $1.50. If you purchase a doughnut every day, by the end of the month you will have spent a minimum of $45 just for doughnuts; if you add in juice or coffee each morning, you may be spending over $100 per month—on a breakfast that isn't even very healthy. What else could you do with $100 each month?

Creating a Budget

After you determine where your money is going, the next step is to decide where you want your money to go. What are the necessities in your life? Are the doughnut and coffee essential, or can you make your own coffee each morning and save yourself $100 a month?

The Lowdown

If you feel you are not able to successfully budget your money, there are numerous bookkeeping services that may be a great help. Services generally are between $20 and $50 per hour and may well pay for itself by saving you late fees and giving you better control of your money.

A simple budget takes into account income and expenses:

1. List your major expenses, include items such as rent or mortgage, utilities, car payments, and any other regular monthly payments.

2. Based on your expense-tracking month, add in entertainment, food shopping, and other recurring expenses.

3. List all sources of income.

4. Hopefully, your income is more than your expenses. If it is not, you will need to review your expenses to decide what needs to be cut. If your income is more than your expenses, you might want to consider creating an automatic savings plan with the balance you have at the end of every month.

Impulsive Spending

Sometimes impulsive spending railroads the best budget. Television ads continuously sell products you don't need but look great. The Internet makes it easy to purchase goods, 24 hours a day. Spending has never been easier. For adults with ADHD, all of this can lead to impulsive spending and larger debt. There are some simple steps you can take to curb your spending:

◆ Always pay with cash, based on your budget. Leave your checkbook and debit card at home. Limit your purchases to the cash you have on hand.

◆ If you must have a credit card, keep only one and leave it at home, in a safe place. It's for emergencies.

◆ When shopping, use a calculator to stay within your budget.

◆ Throw away all catalogs that come in the mail. The longer they sit on your coffee table, the more tempted you will be to order something.

◆ Always wait 24 hours before making a major purchase. The next day it may not seem so important (or interesting).

◆ If you have a partner, make a pact to discuss all purchases over a set amount of money.

◆ Make lists before going shopping and limit your purchases to what is on the list.

Besides ruining your budget, impulsive spending can make you feel guilty. Learn to change "I must have …" to "I would like to have …." You can then look over your budget and decide when and if the purchase is a good idea.

Setting Goals

Another potential problem with financial plans is the inability to visualize your future. When you are saving money for a purchase, or for the future, it is hard to "see" what you are going to get for your money. The item you want today is clearly visible.

Some tips for helping to create a fund for the future:

◆ Set specific goals. Create three types of goals: immediate, mid-term, and long-term goals. Decide how much of your budget will go toward each goal.

◆ Use visual cues to help motivate you to save money. For example, if one of your immediate goals is to buy a new sofa, cut out a picture of the couch you want and tape it somewhere you will see it. This can help remind you why you are saving your money. For midterm and long-term goals, create a collage of pictures based on the lifestyle you want.

Every family is different and each household has individual needs and wants. You may want to make an appointment to talk with a financial advisor to help you create a plan based on the lifestyle you want to maintain.

> **The Scoop**
>
> You are more apt to achieve goals when they are written down. Even so, only about 2 percent of Americans take the time to write down their goals.

Financial Organization

The final step in creating a workable financial program for your household is organization. Find a spot in your house to keep all of your financial information. This can be a file cabinet, a drawer, or a desk.

What you want to keep:

◆ All bills you receive in the mail

◆ Checks to be deposited

◆ Copy of your budget

◆ Paid bills

◆ Bank statements

◆ Receipts

◆ Insurance policies

◆ Supplies: pens, calculator, envelopes, stamps

How you organize your special area is entirely up to you. The organization system needs to work for you and be one that you will use on a regular basis.

Clutter

For adults with ADHD, clutter has a way of taking over your home, sometimes to the point you stop asking people to visit and cringe if you receive an unexpected guest. Clutter can also spill over into other areas of your life. When your surroundings are disorganized, you may feel as if your whole life is chaos. On the other hand, if your surroundings are neat and tidy, you can feel as if your life is ordered and controlled.

The problem with clutter is that it never ends. Throughout our lives we continuously get new things; mail arrives every day, we go to the store and buy new items, and children come home with papers. When our homes are already filled, all of the new stuff needs to go somewhere. Unless there is space to put it, or you are willing to let go of other things, the new stuff tends to go beside or on top of the stuff that's already there. The result is clutter.

Clutter happens for several reasons. For the adult with ADHD, the lack of organizational skills and procrastination may leave a house full of piles of things. *Hoarding* is another problem. The fear of getting rid of anything leads to an immense amount of junk, sometimes leaving little or no space to even sit and relax.

def•i•ni•tion

Hoarding is the accumulating and storing of a large amount of items for future use, and the inability to discard items.

Piles and Piles

Look around your house. What is your clutter made up of? Do you have papers, old mail, items bought but never put away? Chances are, you need some of your clutter, things you use and will use again, but it's not put in the proper place. Other pieces of clutter, however, are probably things that should have been thrown out long ago.

The problem with clutter is that when it is "not too bad," you don't do much about it, putting off clearing the piles for more important tasks. As the clutter begins to take over your home, it becomes overwhelming. Not knowing where to start, or viewing the project of clearing the clutter as insurmountable, you just ignore it, and the piles grow larger and larger.

If you have clutter on top of your clutter, it may be time to make a clean sweep. Not all of the following suggestions will work for you, but choose one or two tips that you feel would work in your house.

♦ Set a goal to work for 15 minutes per day. Set a timer for 15 minutes and work as hard as you can putting things away or throwing them away. When the timer goes off, you are done until tomorrow.

♦ Break down the project into manageable tasks. Try decluttering only one room, or one area of a room, at a time. Even an area of only a few square feet may be what it takes to keep you from becoming overwhelmed. It may not seem so overwhelming if you focus on one small area.

♦ Use a basket or designate one specific area for all incoming papers. Instead of putting papers down in different places, such as the counter or the kitchen table, have one set spot to collect all pieces of paper. Go through the in-box weekly to throw out papers you don't need.

♦ Pick up five items and put them away. The trick with this tip is, if you don't have a designated spot for one of the items, you must find one immediately. Once you pick up an item, you can't put it back down and pick up something else. Once you have put away five items, you are done.

◆ Use a "maybe" box. If you have papers or items you aren't sure if you should get rid of, put it all in one box. Close the box and mark the date on the top of the box. Put it away in the basement or in a closet. If you haven't opened the box one year later, throw it away (without opening it). Make sure you don't put anything important, such as tax forms, in the box.

◆ Make decluttering a family activity. Take ten minutes in the evening, turn on some music, and have everyone pick a room to straighten up (if your family argues, put the name of each room on a piece of paper and have each person choose one, without seeing what is written on it).

◆ Walk around the house with a trash bag and throw out all the trash first. Next, fill a laundry basket with other clutter and give every family member one hour to take his or her things from the laundry basket and put them away. Anything left gets thrown away.

◆ Whenever you bring a new item into the house, throw one away. (Some people prefer "one in, two out.")

◆ Pass along items when you are done with them. For example, as soon as you are finished with a book, pass it on to someone else to read.

◆ Designate one spot to be your clutter area. This can be a drawer or a box. Put all your clutter into this one area. Once it is full, go through and put things away.

Sometimes, once you begin to declutter your living area, you will be motivated to continue. Experiment with different methods to find what works best for your family.

Hoarding

Hoarding is different than clutter. Hoarding is the inability to throw anything away. It can be a symptom of the executive functioning deficits that are so common among individuals with ADHD. Creating structure among disarray requires the ability to categorize, sort, and plan, all executive functions.

Hoarding can cause embarrassment and isolation. You may stop inviting friends or relatives to your home, not wanting anyone to see the piles of things you have around your house or you may no longer be able to offer someone a place to sit down. All of your chairs may be covered with "stuff."

Hoarding also can cause anxiety. Disarray in our homes can lead to feeling overwhelmed. You may feel guilty or ashamed, thereby creating anxiety.

The Scoop
Disposophobia is the clinical name for the fear of throwing things away.

Some tips to help with hoarding:

◆ Hoarding can be a sign of an anxiety disorder, specifically obsessive-compulsive disorder (OCD). If you are a hoarder, you may want to seek professional help to determine if you have OCD and if you need medical treatment.

◆ Sort through items before throwing any away. It may be difficult to throw one thing away, but if you are throwing away five out of ten old papers and keeping five, it may be easier.

◆ Start small. Start with trying to clear one small area.

◆ Use a professional organizer. If you have been hoarding items and are completely overwhelmed, it may be best to hire a professional organizer to help get you started. Make sure the organizer has had experience working with hoarders and will not be judgmental.

◆ Ask a friend or relative to help you organize, preferably someone who will help you throw away the items you are hesitating about throwing away, and will not be judgmental.

◆ Get rid of "tossed" things immediately, before you change your mind.

◆ You may want to donate unused items. Go through your house room by room and decide which items you are no longer using. Pack them up and donate to a local thrift shop. It is sometimes easier to donate an item than to throw it away.

Think It Over

Hoarding, in it's worst form, is dangerous. Too much stuff can create a fire hazard in your home. Not only that, but in the case of fire or other emergencies, piles of things or falling items can block possible escape routes. The Collyer Brothers, infamous recluses in New York City, saved everything. They had tunnels complete with booby traps in mountains of books, papers, and junk. They were found dead in their brownstone in 1947. One of them had been crushed to death by a paper tunnel cave in, while the other, who was disabled, starved to death!

If hoarding is interfering with your daily life and has been diagnosed as part of an anxiety disorder, there is treatment available. This treatment can be combined with treatment for ADHD.

The Least You Need to Know

- Girls with ADHD have been found to have more hypersensitivities than boys.

- Sensory sensitivities can be extremely distracting and decrease your ability to pay attention or focus.

- Money management requires organization and planning, both areas adults with ADHD have difficulty with.

- Clutter can be the result of disorganization, procrastination, and inability to deal with feeling overwhelmed.

- Managing hoarding tendencies requires executive functioning.

Chapter 15

Managing Emotions

In This Chapter

- ◆ Coping with anger problems
- ◆ Managing frustration in daily life
- ◆ Watching for mood swings, a characteristic of adult ADHD
- ◆ Minimizing overwhelm
- ◆ Reducing stress

Adults with ADHD can have problems with irritability, difficulties in managing frustration, and be overly sensitive to criticism. These emotions can take over, making you unable to think about anything else. You can completely lose focus, and many adults may find it difficult to put their emotions in perspective or return to the task they were doing.

In this chapter, we will discuss some of the major emotional concerns, such as anger, frustration, and overwhelm. We'll also go over practical suggestions on how to manage mood swings.

Anger

Anger is a normal human emotion. We all experience anger from time to time. Sometimes getting mad can even help us, by spurring us into action and helping us solve problems. It can give us energy when faced with a threat and help protect us from danger.

Sometimes, though, anger is seen, and used, as a harmful emotion because:

◆ Anger is frequently associated with aggression and violence, especially if you've seen it expressed that way growing up.

◆ We fear anger.

◆ We are taught that anger is wrong and feel guilty after becoming angry.

◆ We may take out anger on the wrong people, repressing it during a stressful situation and then lashing out later.

◆ We may hold our anger in, creating physical problems. We may experience headaches or stomachaches, or long-term problems such as high blood pressure and heart disease can develop.

Many people have never been taught *anger management*, or how to deal with the intense emotions that develop when we are mad, causing anger to turn into rage.

Adults with ADHD often find that impulsivity combined with anger results in hurtful remarks and unchecked rages. Some indicate they have a hard time controlling anger once it has begun, feeling as if the emotion must "play itself out" before they can move on.

Anger is often the result of an unresolved issue that may have nothing to do with the current situation. For example, feelings of inadequacy from your childhood may make you highly sensitive to criticism. A criticism at

def•i•ni•tion

Anger management is a process to help individuals reduce the emotional and physical response to situations or people that cause rage or infuriation. Anger cannot be erased completely, but we can control our response to it through practice.

work or from a spouse, even a perceived criticism, can bring anger to the surface. This anger is often misdirected, taken out on those people around us now, even though the anger stems from unfair criticisms in the past.

If you have difficulty with anger, there are some steps you can take:

◆ Pay attention to your feelings, notice when you begin to feel angry.

◆ Keep a log to help you better understand your emotions.

◆ Write down times you get angry, what was going on at the time, who you were with, what you were feeling, and what you said or did.

◆ Use your log to figure out what your anger triggers are.

> **Think It Over**
>
> Some signs you should seek psychological counseling for anger include: when you spend most of your time angry, when anger stops you from doing your job, when it interferes with relationships, or when it turns violent.

◆ Find more productive ways to cope with the underlying issues and the intense emotion you feel. Can you use your anger to find solutions rather than lashing out?

When you don't effectively deal with your anger, relationships can be ruined. Anger can create emotional distances between you and those closest to you. In order to avoid emotional outbursts, people may avoid you. Besides relationship issues, other disruptive and antisocial behaviors can develop if you choose not to find constructive and proactive ways of dealing with the intense emotions of anger.

Frustration

Frustration is the emotion we feel when we have an unresolved problem or project. Often the feeling of frustration is accompanied by anger, anxiety, or depression. Adults with ADHD often have a low level of frustration tolerance, meaning they become frustrated more easily and sooner than those with a higher level of frustration.

Frustration is usually accompanied by a feeling of being stuck, that no matter how hard you may try, whatever you are working on will never get completed. Many times, the result of frustration is to give up and stop trying.

Some steps to take when feeling frustrated.

1. **Look for what is going right.** When feeling frustrated, whether over a household project, your job, or your entire life, it is easy to fall into thinking nothing is going right. Usually this is simply not true. Almost always, something is going right, it is just hard to see through the frustration. Find the part of your problem that is working. Focus on the small part that is working. This may give you a different perspective and a different way of viewing the situation. It may point you in the right direction.

> **The Lowdown**
>
> Counting to 10 when you are frustrated really can help. Count slowly, take a deep breath with each count and you may be able to diffuse some of your frustration and look at the situation in a new light.

2. **Focus on the end result.** How do you want this situation or project to work out? What does your final result look like? Sometimes we become focused on one problem and forget it is just one part of a larger picture. Usually, there is more than one way to solve a problem or reach a goal. It could be you need to look at the problem differently or find a different way to reach your goal.

3. **Ask for help.** Listening to other people's perspectives can give us more options and different solutions we may not have thought about.

4. **Take a break.** Walking away for a short period of time may allow you to think about the situation differently and come up with different options on how to solve your problem.

5. **Accept that not all problems will work out the way we think they should.** Some problems never will. Is perfectionism getting in the way of completing a project? You may need to lower your expectations and be more realistic. You may be surprised with the outcome. Sometimes, the "silver lining" will appear out of a project or situation that didn't turn out as expected.

Frustrations are always higher when you don't take care of yourself. Proper sleep and nutrition as well as regular exercise can help you cope better with frustrations as they come up.

Mood Swings

Although *mood swings* are not indicative of adult ADD/ADHD, some physicians do include emotional outbursts or mood swings as a characteristic of adult ADD/ADHD.

Most people experience some form of mood swings each day, however, adults with ADD/ADHD often have changes in mood with more frequency and more intensity. Many adults talk about periods when they feel highly energized and positive about life, at other times they may feel depressed, and yet other times irritable. All of this can happen within the same day, or within a period of a few hours. The mood swings of ADHD are different than those of bipolar disorder. Bipolar disorder is characterized by extreme moods that persist for weeks or months.

def•i•ni•tion

> **Mood swings** are when one feels "up" one moment and "down" the next. Periods of elation can be followed by periods of feeling despair.

Mood swings are difficult for the people experiencing them; they never know how they are going to feel and may even avoid social situations in anticipation of changes in mood. Activities that they once enjoyed may be put aside or avoided. Mood swings are also difficult on family and friends. Some can feel as if they are "walking on eggshells," never knowing which mood they will encounter.

Everyone experiences mood swings to some degree. For most people, mood swings are a small part of life; however, if mood swings begin to dominate your life, or if you begin avoiding situations, you may want to seek professional help. Treatment can include:

- Medication
- Cognitive behavioral therapy
- Talk therapy
- Behavioral interventions

The Scoop

Women experience mood swings twice as often as men do. Mood swings may increase during pregnancy, post-partum, and menopause.

In addition to this type of treatment, if you are experiencing mood swings, making sure you get enough sleep, eating well, and adding exercise to your daily routine may help. Some people find creating and sticking to a daily routine helps. Knowing what you will be doing and what to expect next can decrease the amount of mood swings.

Managing Overwhelm

Overwhelm is a sense that you are running around in circles but you're not accomplishing anything. Overwhelm can also create a feeling of "brain-freeze," where you are so overextended you can't discuss your problems and you can't solve your problems; you can't move forward and you can't move back. In other words, you are stuck.

When you become overwhelmed, you might feel panicked or guilty because you have not accomplished everything that needs to be done. You may feel tired and irritable, but can't manage to switch off the thoughts and find it hard to rest.

But overwhelm doesn't only happen when you have too much to do. Sometimes you can feel overwhelmed due to the situation you are in rather than the things you need to do. For example, you may be dealing with being out of work or someone in your family might be ill. The high emotion may lead to overwhelm.

Think It Over

Overwhelm can make symptoms of ADHD, such as inability to pay attention or to focus, worsen. It can also cause symptoms similar to depression, such as lack of motivation, tiredness, and withdrawal from activities.

Women with ADHD today are susceptible to overwhelm. Working full time (outside the home), keeping up with housekeeping and child care, and running around to kids' activities can take their toll. The fast pace of life never seems to slow down and emotions can buckle under the stress of trying to do it all, and do it well.

Some ideas to help in managing overwhelm:

- Look at the different areas of your life and see what is out of balance. What is most important? Are you spending time working on those items or is most of your time spent on things that are not important? What can you do to bring some balance back into your life?

- Eliminate some of your activities and responsibilities in order to slow your pace of life. Schedule some time each day for relaxation.

- Avoid taking on new responsibilities. Let people know you are at your limit and, at least for now, will not be able to add any more to your schedule.

- Separate how you feel about yourself from what you need to accomplish. Your self-worth does not depend on whether you get everything on your to-do list completed. Remind yourself of your good qualities.

- Start somewhere. Many times overwhelm will send you into non-action mode. Getting started can help you to get out of overwhelm. When you finish one thing, even if it is the smallest item on your to-do list, you get one step closer to your goal. Break big projects up into small chunks. Respect your attention span.

Pay attention to your personal signs of overwhelm. Once you can recognize that overwhelm is about to happen, take a step back and try to stop it before it begins. Take some steps to change your environment, enlist help, and review your priorities. Make sure what you are trying to accomplish works to further what is important to you.

Managing Stress

Symptoms of ADHD can cause stress. Not meeting deadlines, forgetting your spouse's birthday, difficulty with social situations—all of these things can create stress in your life. But stress can also increase symptoms of inattention, distractibility, and impulsiveness. Eliminating stress is impossible. All of our lives include situations that may cause us worry and distress.

Other mental disorders, such as depression or anxiety, are also commonly seen in adults with ADHD. Both of these conditions can include or increase feelings of stress.

> ### The Scoop
>
> More than 75 percent of the general population feel some level of stress at least once every two weeks, according to the National Health Interview Survey.

Some adults with ADHD use stress as a way to motivate themselves. They may wait until the last minute to complete a project, thriving on the rush of trying to get something complete in a short amount of time.

But stress is not healthy. Physical illnesses, such as heart disease and high blood pressure, can be worsened by stress. Other conditions such as Tourette's syndrome can also worsen during stressful times. Here are some tips to help manage stress:

- Use deep breathing exercises. Incorporating deep breathing into your daily routine can help reduce stress. Inhale for a full five seconds and then exhale slowly. Continue to do this for two minutes. Complete as often as necessary throughout the day.

- Keep a funny stories journal. Laughter is a great stress reliever. Keep a journal of the funny things that happen and, when feeling down, read it. This can help you keep a more positive perspective on the current situation.

- Take a walk. Fresh air and being outside in nature has a calming effect. Even 5 to 10 minutes outside can make you feel refreshed.

- Vent to someone. Ask someone (a close friend or relative) to be your venting partner. Let him or her know you are not asking for advice but simply need someone to listen from time to time.

- Keep a stress-relief object with you. This could be a stress ball, a picture from a vacation, a seashell, or some other memento. Take a few minutes to look at the item, remembering a pleasant time. This is especially effective if you combine it with deep breathing.

- Roll your neck and head. Stretching the neck muscles can help relieve stress. Roll your head five complete circles to help relieve tension in the muscles of your neck.

- Do stretching exercises. Stand up and stretch for a few minutes. The movement will help to release tension.

- Practice meditation. Meditation can be done in just a few minutes. Practice at home at first. Once you are able to meditate, you can take 5 or 10 minutes to sit back, close your eyes, and relax.

The Lowdown

The scent of lavender is considered relaxing. At home you can use lavender candles or other aromatherapy. When away from home, put a few drops of lavender oil on a handkerchief and carry it with you. When feeling particularly stressed, take it out and enjoy a few minutes of relaxation.

ADHD can bring on much stress. For many adults, living with undiagnosed ADHD for many years has added to their feelings of failure, creating more stress. As you learn and understand about ADHD, incorporating stress-reducing strategies into your everyday life helps you to manage symptoms.

The Least You Need to Know

- Anger combined with impulsivity can cause hurtful remarks and out-of-control rages.

- Frustration can result in feeling stuck, as if your task will never get completed.

- Mood swings in adults with ADHD are different than those of bipolar disorder.

- Overwhelm can make symptoms of ADHD such as inattention worse, and can cause symptoms similar to depression.

- Living with adult ADHD can cause stress, which can worsen symptoms of ADHD.

Part **6**

ADHD Through Different Stages of Life

It is now known that ADHD isn't just a kid's disorder, it affects people throughout their lives, and the different stages of life can bring unique challenges and situations. In this part we'll address some of the times of life.

One such time is during the college years. Adults with ADHD need to be able to navigate the laws that offer protection during this time and work with professors and college administrators to make the college years successful.

In addition to college, women and men both have unique needs as adults with ADHD. Women may have an increase of symptoms during certain times of life, caused by hormonal fluctuations and men may have a more difficult time accepting and working with a diagnosis of ADHD.

During the later stage of life, other concerns, such as the high incidence rate of anxiety and depression in the elderly, and interactions between medications, must be taken into consideration while developing an effective treatment plan.

Chapter 16

ADHD in College

In This Chapter

- ◆ Considerations when choosing a college
- ◆ Laws to help protect you in college
- ◆ Resources for students
- ◆ Recognizing academic problems

College is frequently the entrance into adulthood. Choosing a college, although often with the help of parents, is one of the first adult decisions you may make. If you decide to live away from home, the next several years will be about learning to take care of yourself.

In this chapter, we cover a lot of information to help college students with ADHD, from discussing some of the things you want to consider when choosing a college, to learning about the laws that protect individuals with disabilities. We will also talk about how to recognize problems before they become major obstacles and what resources are available to help you succeed.

Choosing a College

Choosing a college requires research. Each college offers different programs. Sometimes, it may be as easy as choosing a college close to home, but other times you may need to visit colleges and decide which school will best meet your individual needs.

Before deciding on a college, first you need to understand yourself and your specific needs. What is going to help you succeed? Some questions you may want to consider are:

♦ Do you want to attend a small college or a large college? What was the size of your high school? If you attended a small high school, are you prepared for a school that is so much larger? If you feel you will need extra, more personal assistance from professors, a small college, with smaller class sizes may better fit your needs.

♦ What type of setting do you prefer? Some colleges are in rural areas, with few activities other than those on the college campus. Other colleges may be in the heart of the city, with constant activity all around. Will the constant activity be a distraction or do you need the hustle and bustle to provide outlets for hyperactivity?

♦ What types of support did you receive in high school? Chances are you probably will need some of the same supports in college. Make a list of resources, supports, and services you feel you may need to be successful. Once you begin looking at colleges, you can eliminate those that are not able to provide those services.

♦ Have you decided on a major? Many students entering college do not yet know what they want to do. In that case, choosing a liberal arts major provides you with the core classes you will need, no matter what your major, and gives you extra time to think about what direction you would like to take. At most schools, it is not necessary to state a major until your junior year; find out the requirements for the college you plan to attend. You may also want to take an assessment/interest inventory. This will help you see where your strengths lie.

The Lowdown

Some colleges, such as Landmark College in Vermont, have programs specifically designed to meet the needs of students with ADHD or learning disabilities.

You may have personal ideas of what you are looking for in a college, such as the types of activities the school offers and what the students are like. You might be able to get an idea by checking out posters of upcoming events in the dormitories, cafeteria, or student center.

Another consideration may be the dormitory rooms. If you have trouble sleeping, having several people in one room might cause you problems. You may need to look into whether the college offers single rooms.

Before visiting colleges, you may want to create a chart to help you sort out the information you gather.

Laws That Protect Students with ADHD

During elementary and high school, students are protected under two different laws, the Individuals with Disabilities Education Act (IDEA) and the Rehabilitation Act (Section 504). IDEA is meant to ensure the success of a child with a disability in school.

In postsecondary education, students can still be protected from discrimination; however, the laws governing colleges provide "access and opportunity" but do not guarantee success. Success in college is dependent upon the individual.

There are two laws that provide protection from discrimination in college. Section 508 is also part of the Rehabilitation Act, but is a different subsection of the law. It requires all people to have access to electronic and information technology provided by the federal government. The Americans with Disabilities Act (ADA) and the amendments added to this law in 2008, provides for equal access and opportunity and protects individuals with disabilities from discrimination.

In postsecondary education, responsibility for requesting accommodations falls to the individual as opposed to IDEA, which requires schools to identify children with disabilities. In elementary and high school, school personnel would be responsible for determining what services are

The Lowdown

In most cases, it's a good idea to let your parents have access to information on your grades and progress, since it's very possible that you won't realize things are going downhill until it's too late to stop it.

needed, administration of the services, as well as follow-up. In college, you must do all of this yourself. Colleges may also not supply information to parents on academic progress, unless the student specifically requests that information be released to parents.

The student is also responsible for providing the college with documentation of the disability. Information from the high school on accommodations received can help in deciding on eligibility for services, but is not adequate documentation on its own. You should speak to the disability office at your college to find out what documentation they require.

Think It Over

If you wait until the last minute to let your doctor or therapist know about an accommodation letter, there's a good chance you won't get it when you need it. Make sure you provide medical professionals plenty of notice on what documentation you will need and when you will need it.

The Disability Support Services Office

The *Disability Support Services Office* (may also be called Office for Student Disability Services or Support, or Learning Support Services) can tell you what types of accommodations are available and what type of documentation you will be required to submit in order to be eligible for special services. Before visiting a college, contact the support office ahead of time and set up an appointment.

def•i•ni•tion

The **Disability Support Services Office** works with students with disabilities to make sure all individuals with disabilities are assured an equal opportunity to participate in, contribute to, and benefit from all classes, programs, services, and activities.

Questions you should ask include:

◆ What types of services are available?

◆ What documentation is needed?

- What are the procedures for applying for special services?

- How quickly can you receive services (in case you choose not to apply until you absolutely need to)?

- How long has the college offered services for students with ADHD?

- How many students with ADHD are registered with the disability office?

- Is there a fee for extra services?

You may also want to discuss the faculty's attitude toward accommodations. Do some members of the faculty resist in providing special services? Some departments within the college may be more receptive to making accommodations, such as liberal arts, education, psychology, or social services. Other departments, such as business, may be more resistant to providing extra services to students. The disability support office can usually help with resistant faculty to assure your accommodations are carried out.

Examples of Accommodations

Although your needs will be specific to the difficulties you have experienced in school, the following are some examples of accommodations that may be offered:

- Calculators for science and math or the ability to use calculators during tests

- Course substitutions

- Extended time for taking tests or ability to take tests in quiet areas

- Tests given orally or computerized tests

- Note takers or printed notes provided by the teacher

- The ability to tape lectures

- Classrooms with minimum distractions

- Electronic organizer

◆ Providing instructions for projects/assignments in writing

◆ Coaching or mentoring programs

You may also be able to receive accommodations during the registration process and be able to either register early or register online.

The Scoop
Lots of people with ADHD actually never sign up for support services until they are already floundering and it's too late. If you go to the support center, you'll be surprised at how many classmates are in line with you!

Additional Services Offered by the College

Besides specific services to help you in the classroom, many colleges provide additional services to help students. Here are some services that may help you:

◆ Tutoring

◆ Computer labs

◆ Writing labs

◆ Math labs

◆ Counseling

◆ Mentoring

Some courses may also be offered as web-based classes. Lectures can be viewed over and over, and notes may be available online. In addition, some colleges offer courses in social skills, note taking, learning strategies, or communication skills.

Besides academic considerations, be sure to ask about counselors and support groups for students with ADHD.

Staying Home vs. Living in a Dorm

Living away from home, in a dorm, is both scary and exciting. You will no longer have parents telling you what to do and when to do it. You will be able to stay up late and sleep in (as long as your class schedule allows) and do homework on your time. But with this freedom also comes responsibilities. You will no longer have someone prodding you to finish your work or get to class on time. For some students, living away from home helps to strengthen *independent living skills.* For others, the lack of structure is overwhelming.

def•i•ni•tion

Independent living skills are those skills needed to perform everyday tasks. This can include time management, planning, scheduling, personal hygiene, laundry, nutrition, and budgeting money.

Some of the areas you need to be responsible for when living away at school include:

◆ Monitoring your health care. You will need to have a doctor available to provide prescriptions if you take medication for ADHD. Sometimes your doctor from home can arrange phone meetings or even video meetings, on services like Skype, to check your progress and arrange to have prescriptions sent to you. You will need to contact the doctor when your prescription is running low.

◆ Making sure you eat correctly. College students are notorious for eating fast food and junk food instead of healthy food. But to keep your ADHD under control, proper nutrition is important. It will be up to you to make sure you eat a well-balanced diet.

◆ Getting the proper rest. Many individuals with ADHD have trouble sleeping, sometimes because you become so involved in a task that you lose track of time. You won't have parents reminding you to stop and get some sleep. It will be your responsibility to keep track of time and get the rest you need each night, and to contact your doctor or therapist for help if lack of sleep is interfering with your daily functioning.

◆ Daily needs. Chances are your parents purchased items such as toothpaste, shampoo, and soap with their shopping. It was always at home and always available. At college, you will need to keep track of these items and go to the store when you are running low. You will also need to do your laundry.

◆ Budgeting money. You may have your own money from a summer job, may be working part time during college, or may be on a monthly budget. No matter where the money comes from, you will need to budget your money to make sure you have enough left to cover your needs.

◆ Getting to class. No one at college monitors your attendance. It is your responsibility to make it to class each day, to take notes, and to prepare for tests.

The Lowdown

Individuals with ADHD are often not good self-observers. You're prone to see things as you hope they'll be, rather than how they are. That's why you need a mirror. It can be a parent, a therapist, or anyone who will tell you the truth. Many an ADHDer thinks they're doing just fine until they get their grades and see, as Dean Wormer said in *Animal House*, "Zero point zero."

Once you have mastered independent living skills, living away at school can have many benefits. It is a wonderful experience to meet new people and develop friendships. Colleges also offer numerous opportunities and activities for you to explore your interests.

College also offers unending parties and social events. It can be hard to stay away from the party life and buckle down and study. The freedom you have can help you grow or it can cause you problems. It may be too easy to attend the party rather than studying for the test you have, and to fool yourself into thinking you'll pull it out at the last minute, just like in high school. Odds are, you won't. This is college; more is expected.

You will need to decide if you are ready to live away from home. Your chance of success at college depends on your readiness. If you don't feel you are ready to live away from home, you might want to consider attending a local college. Some students choose to do this for one to two years and then go away to college. The extra time spent at home helps them to adjust to college classes and requirements without the extra pressure of independent living.

Recognizing Potential Academic Problems

In high school, teachers make you aware of falling grades. They may talk to you after class or contact your parents, and offer extra assistance or provide you with a list of missing assignments. In college, however, you don't have anyone that monitors your grades on a daily basis. Individuals with ADHD may have problems linking events that happen today with events not happening for several months. Because of this, the test you failed today may not be associated with a poor grade for the entire class. You may have a poor sense of time, believing you have lots of time left to make up the grade and suddenly, you are placed on academic probation for poor grades.

Think It Over

Bill, a freshman, slept through his alarm and missed his first math class. He was so ashamed that he "forgot" the next two. It took him four more weeks to overcome his embarrassment and finally make an appointment with the professor, who by this time had no idea of who Bill was, much less how to help him catch up. This is *not* an uncommon story, but it is a trap you can avoid. If you mess up, the faster you deal with it, the easier it will be to clean up.

The most obvious sign you are having trouble in a class is receiving poor grades. But there are other signs of problems as well. Some of these may signal that your ADHD is beginning to interfere with your education. If any of the following are happening, you may need to seek some help:

- Trouble with the professor
- Leaving class feeling you didn't understand the lesson
- Lack of motivation to complete assignments
- Skipping class

- Falling asleep in class

- Change in study habits; spending less and less time on a particular subject

- Procrastination

- Inconsistent work, some weeks you complete assignments and some weeks you lack the motivation

- Asking the professor for extra time to complete assignments or for special consideration

If you begin to notice signs of schoolwork becoming more difficult or you are not able to keep up, ask for assistance as soon as possible. Waiting until you are totally overwhelmed and over your head will only make the problem worse. If you have not applied for accommodations in college, you may want to do so. Accommodations are not retroactive, so whatever you may be allowed, it will only be from this point forward. Past tests and projects will not be able to be redone. (See the section on accommodations later in the chapter for more information on how to request services.)

As soon as you notice signs of struggling, talk with your professor about some options to help you get back on track. Some professors have former students who can tutor you. If you talk with the professor about specific areas causing difficulties, together you may find solutions.

If you don't feel your professor is helping, or is resistant to finding solutions, you can talk with your academic advisor. They are there to help you succeed and know what services are available, including tutoring, coaching, or mentoring, that may help you. The better you get to know your academic advisor, the more options they may be able to offer you.

Do You Need a Tutor?

If you are wondering if you should use a tutor, chances are you should. Usually, you are not going to wonder about using a tutor unless you are already struggling in class. And as soon as you begin struggling, a tutor can help. The sooner you ask for help, the sooner you will be able to get back on track.

Most colleges have drop-in tutoring centers you can visit anytime you are having a problem. You might not be able to understand the assignment or may have been totally lost during class. These programs may charge a small fee, but someone with experience in the subject can help walk you through the information and help you better understand.

The Lowdown

If you are assigned a tutor, spend a little time getting to know each other. Make sure your personalities are a good match and the tutor is at an advanced enough level to be able to answer your questions.

Scheduled tutoring works if you feel you need ongoing help in a certain subject and want to work with a tutor on a regular basis. This is normally scheduled through the tutoring center. There is often a fee for this service.

Some colleges offer group tutoring sessions in certain subjects. This may be free or there may be a small fee. If you feel you may have problems with a certain subject, check with the tutoring center at the beginning of the semester to see if there is a group tutoring program for that class. It may help you to be with other students who are also struggling with the subject.

Some students may be embarrassed to go for tutoring and will avoid it or put it off until it is too late. Remember, it will be more embarrassing to fail the class and need to take it over. Nobody is naturally good at everything. You'll probably have a number of subjects you are good at and can excel at. There is nothing wrong with needing and seeking out help in areas you struggle with.

The Scoop

One study (Zwart & Kalleymeyn, 2001) showed that college students with ADHD had problems with study skills, note taking, summarizing, outlining, and test taking. Another study (Weyandt et al, 2003) indicated difficulties with internal motivation, finding college students with ADHD rely on external factors.

Study Skills

Students with ADHD, whether in elementary school or in college, have a more difficult time in school than students without ADHD. A report compiled by Florida State University identified four specific areas students with ADHD had problems:

♦ **Time management:** Many high school students with ADHD rely heavily on parents to help in creating daily schedules. These students had a difficult time taking on this task themselves. Using appointment books, daily schedulers, and alarms should be incorporated into daily life for students with ADHD.

♦ **Focus and concentration:** As with younger children, college students with ADHD had difficulty concentrating during class and when completing work outside of class. Students with ADHD should continue strategies used in elementary and high school, such as sitting at the front of the classroom, taking notes to make lectures more interactive, and taking short breaks while studying.

♦ **Identifying main ideas:** When studying, it is necessary to be able to differentiate between unimportant information and important facts. Students with ADHD had difficulty summarizing and finding the main idea, therefore spending time studying unnecessary and unimportant information. Learning specific skills such as note taking, outlining, and highlighting or underlining important information can help.

♦ **Test preparation:** Study skills can change depending on whether you are preparing for a multiple-choice test, an essay test, or another type of test. Students with ADHD were found to have a hard time developing different strategies for studying based on the type of tests given. Because of this, students were less prepared for testing. Students may improve test-taking abilities by creating their own test questions and reviewing practice test questions.

Students with ADHD may know and understand the strategies needed to study; however, because of problems with concentration, follow through, and internal motivation skills, they cannot utilize these strategies effectively. Behavior strategies, such as giving yourself rewards for using study skills, can help. For example, a student might study or review notes and underline important facts for one hour, then reward themselves with watching their favorite TV show or getting together with friends.

The Lowdown

When you are assigned a paper, break the paper into chunks with deadlines; for example, research done in one week, outline done in two weeks, rough draft in three weeks, and so on. Put those deadlines on your calendar or organizer and treat them as very real. You'll do better confronting a series of manageable tasks than one overwhelming one.

Self-Advocacy

Part of moving into the adult world is acting as your own advocate. Laws prevent college administrators from sharing information with your parents (unless you sign a release and request information is mailed to your parents). Professors will assume you are an adult and are responsible for your own education. No one will call if you cut school, but they will penalize you at the end. You must be able to talk with administrators in the disability office, your professors, and those in the learning center to request and procure accommodations for yourself when needed.

The following are some tips to help you be your own advocate:

◆ Keep a file. Make copies of your IEP or Section 504 from high school. Make copies of any written requests for accommodations. Keep records of when you spoke with professors and what their response was. Record the date and name of who you spoke with in the disability office and whether or not you were given accommodations.

◆ Set up appointments with your professors. You may want to do this immediately to discuss what you may need to help you succeed in the class. You can discuss your disability, how it impacts your learning, and what accommodations you will be requesting. Some professors will be more than willing to work with you and will offer you additional options and ideas to help stay current with class requirements.

- Set up an appointment with your academic advisor. Discuss your strengths and weaknesses. Besides asking about academic help, such as tutoring services, ask what services the college offers to help further develop areas you feel are weaknesses, for example, social skills classes. Plan to take advantage of everything the college has to offer.

- Make a list of important phone numbers. Program them in your cell phone and keep a copy in your dorm room. You should have phone numbers for your doctor, the infirmary, the pharmacy, extensions of your professors, the disability office, the tutoring or learning center, counselors, your academic advisor, and any other number you may need.

- Find out if there is a support group for students with ADHD on campus. Plan to attend meetings and talk with other students. You will find out which professors are resistant to accommodations, which will work closely with you, and other information to help you succeed. You'll also find support from students who know the difficulties you are going through.

> **Think It Over**
>
> Take the proper steps to manage your disability. If you normally take medication, make sure you continue to do so. Show up for medical appointments. If you are requesting accommodations, it is important to show you are doing whatever is necessary to manage your disability on your own.

When advocating for yourself, remember there is a difference between being assertive and being aggressive. Demanding, demeaning, or getting angry may get you accommodations, but it won't help you build relationships with administrators or professors. Know your rights and follow the proper procedures for requesting accommodations. Always be polite to the people you must deal with. Your college years will be much more enjoyable.

The Least You Need to Know

◆ Before choosing a college, you want to understand your specific needs.

◆ College students with ADHD may be protected from discrimination under the Americans with Disabilities Act.

◆ College students must ask for accommodations in order to be considered eligible for special services.

◆ Colleges may offer services such as tutoring, mentoring, coaching, or resource centers to help students with disabilities.

◆ Asking for assistance as soon as signs of trouble appear can help you alleviate problems later.

Chapter 17

ADHD in Men

In This Chapter

- How symptoms of ADHD may exhibit differently in men
- Driving safety and ADHD
- Difficulties for men with ADHD at work

It is said that ADHD is the most researched childhood disorder. Most of that research done has been based on male children with ADHD. Hyperactivity, impulsiveness, and inattention all have been studied in boys or men. The symptoms listed are based on how they show up in most male children. Because of this, little additional information is written on how ADHD specifically impacts men.

Most men with ADHD face certain problems that appear differently in children, as a whole, and in girls or women with ADHD. Some of these problems may be a result of normal gender differences, and how symptoms of ADHD interact with these differences. This chapter will explore those differences, including increased hyperactivity, driving habits, and why certain comorbid conditions, such as conduct disorders, occur more often in men than in women.

Men vs. Women

In the past few years only a few studies have compared how men and women manifest symptoms of ADHD. For the most part, little difference has been found. Men and women both experience problems at home, and at work, because of symptoms of ADHD. Both are at risk for comorbid conditions.

Men, however, seem to show differences in the following ways:

◆ Men seem to have more symptoms, but women seem to be more impaired, especially emotionally.

◆ Men are more likely to show aggression and antisocial behaviors.

◆ Men tend to have more hyperactivity and motor activity.

◆ Men tend to externalize behaviors while women internalize behaviors.

◆ Men may have a harder time regulating physical and verbal aggression.

◆ Men have more external symptoms.

◆ Men use external situations and things to help control symptoms.

> **Think It Over**
>
> Men are more likely to have conduct disorder or oppositional defiant disorder as comorbid conditions. Women are more likely to suffer from depression or anxiety.

It is not known whether these differences are simply a result of gender differences or if there is actually a difference in ADHD symptoms in males and females.

Difficulty in Accepting Diagnosis

During childhood, three times as many boys are diagnosed with ADHD than girls. In adults, however, the ratio is even. This may be attributed to an increase in women seeking help or a decrease in men seeking help.

During childhood, parents seek help for their children. Since boys are more often hyperactive, the behaviors are more apparent. Girls, more often diagnosed with inattention, may not be brought to the doctor for

ADHD. However, this may reverse in adulthood. Women with ADHD have a harder time coping with the dual demands of work and home and seek help.

Men tend to shy away from medical help, especially help for mental illness or emotional disturbances. ADHD, although medically considered to have a biological basis, is still seen as a mental illness. Men may equate seeking treatment for ADHD symptoms as a weakness. Men are taught to "tough it out," to be strong. Seeking help can be seen as admitting failure.

Men also tend to ignore mental-health signs and focus, instead, on physical signs of illness. ADHD impairments are more emotional or mental and do not manifest in physical symptoms; because of this, men tend to ignore "lack of focus" or "distractibility." These symptoms are seen as personality flaws rather than signs of a disorder.

The Lowdown

Men are more likely to seek out medical treatment when their wife becomes involved in the process. Married men, therefore, seek treatment more often than single men do.

Men may use substance abuse as a way to hide the emotional pain that can accompany years of living with undiagnosed ADHD symptoms. Often doctors, family members, and the men themselves, will focus on the drug or alcohol use rather than looking for, or treating, the underlying ADHD.

Some men, even though diagnosed as a child, will give up on treatment once they reach adulthood. Taking medication or seeing a psychotherapist or a psychiatrist, may be seen as weakness. Men sometimes try to compensate for inattention or distractibility with aggression, or end up with signs of depression or anxiety. Sometimes physical symptoms of stress, such as headaches or heart disease, can develop.

The Peter Pan Syndrome vs. ADHD

The term "Peter Pan Syndrome" was first used by Dr. Dan Kiley in the 1983 book, *Peter Pan Syndrome: Men Who Have Never Grown Up*. Dr. Kiley outlined a disorder that includes the following.

- Immaturity

- *Narcissistic* behavior

def•i•ni•tion

> **Narcissism** is being egotistical, or having a high level of self-love, to the point of excluding everyone else; having a belief that you are more important than all other people.

- Rebellion

- Anger and rage

- Dependency

- Manipulative tendencies

- Unreliability

- Inability to express emotions in a healthy way

- Procrastination or avoidance of responsibilities

- Difficulty with emotional connections

According to the book, men with Peter Pan Syndrome act in an emotionally immature way and, when in relationships, will seek out mothering and nurturing rather than participating as partners and equals in the relationship.

Some men with ADHD are seen as having Peter Pan Syndrome, or simply being immature and refusing to grow up, rather than being diagnosed with ADHD. Spouses of men with undiagnosed ADHD may incorrectly assume their husbands are spoiled and looking for someone to take care of them, rather than suffering from an undiagnosed disorder.

Some ADHD traits, such as procrastination, emotional difficulties, or inability to complete tasks, can appear to be purposeful, or seeking to avoid responsibility. In addition, emotional immaturity is common in individuals with ADHD. Because of that, there may be some confusion as to whether men just don't want to grow up and take responsibility for their lives, or have ADHD. The Peter Pan Syndrome, however, is not a medically recognized syndrome.

Driving and ADHD

Studies have shown men with ADHD have more car accidents than either men without ADHD or women with ADHD. Women with

ADHD tend to have fewer accidents as they age, but the opposite is true for men, the number of accidents increase as they get older.

Drivers with ADHD who weren't taking medication were found to use more aggressive driving strategies and to exhibit riskier behaviors while driving, resulting in more accidents. Medications for ADHD, especially long-acting stimulant medications, decreased the number of accidents in men with ADHD. In addition, men using stimulant medications received fewer tickets for speeding and other moving violations.

The Lowdown

Drivers with ADHD are more likely to run out of gas than those without ADHD. Check your gas tank level every time you turn on your car.

Employment

Although men and women both tend to exhibit symptoms of ADHD that can interfere with their jobs, men tend to view their worth by their job and their earning ability. When their job suffers, so does their self-esteem.

ADHD can negatively impact employment and therefore have a substantial impact on a man's self-esteem. Men with ADHD often hold jobs below their educational and intellectual abilities, leading to lower pay.

Men with ADHD may also have problems at work because:

♦ They may have problems with authority figures.

♦ They may be unclear as to what their position and work responsibilities entail.

♦ They may have poor conflict-resolution skills.

The Scoop

Individuals with ADHD are almost three times more likely to change jobs, and twice as likely to get fired from their job, than people without ADHD.

Employers also tend to view men with ADHD as more impaired than women with ADHD. This could be because societal views still expect more from men in the workplace, and men still hold more and higher management positions than women. These positions usually require a higher level of attention, organization, and focus, so problems in these areas can be more visible.

A man whom one of the authors (DH) treated was a highly successful salesman for his company for a number of years. Due to his success, he was promoted to management. He suddenly found that he could not sit still for more than a few minutes in meetings and could not complete projects in a timely fashion, despite his boss's strong support. His history showed that he had undiagnosed ADHD from childhood. The sales job gave him an outlet for his hyperactivity and fulfilled his need for novelty and shifting focus, but the managerial position required much more concentration and focus.

Adults with ADHD, as a whole, change jobs more often and make less money than their non-ADHD counterparts. Treatment can help improve job function and increase the chance of success at work. Because men are less likely to seek treatment for ADHD, taking this step can be more troublesome for men than for women with ADHD.

The Least You Need to Know

♦ Men tend to be more aggressive and have more external symptoms of ADHD, such as hyperactivity, than women.

♦ Boys are more likely to be referred to the doctor when young, but women are more likely to seek out medical care as adults.

♦ Some adult males with ADHD are seen as having "Peter Pan Syndrome," but may actually have undiagnosed ADHD.

♦ Men with ADHD are at higher risk of having car accidents.

♦ Men with ADHD tend to have more difficulty with self-esteem issues because of problems in their jobs.

Chapter 18

ADHD in Women

In This Chapter

- Estrogen levels impact ADHD symptoms
- ADHD symptoms may worsen during menopause
- Homemaking is boring and difficult for women with ADHD
- Managing a home and working can cause constant overwhelm

Women with ADHD face many unique challenges. Not only are they normally the primary caregivers to their children, they also often work outside the house and must manage symptoms of ADHD on a daily basis. In addition, hormones seem to play a major part in how ADHD medications work and the intensity of inattention and other symptoms.

In this chapter, we'll discuss many of the problems women with ADHD face from puberty through menopause. Mothers with ADHD can be completely overwhelmed by trying to keep up with the demands of managing a house, work, and children. There are plenty of tips in the chapter to help you out. Finally, we talk about the comorbid conditions that are more prevalent in women with ADHD.

Hormones and ADHD

Hormones play a large role in the intensity of ADHD symptoms, as well as in the effectiveness of stimulant medications. Estrogen seems to play a major part, as it does in many mental disorders. As estrogen levels decrease, symptoms of ADHD increase. Girls diagnosed with ADHD prior to puberty may find stimulant medications to be effective in treating symptoms, but once puberty hits, symptoms can vary with the menstrual cycle and medication may seem ineffective at times.

A girl's body metabolizes stimulant medications much quicker after puberty, necessitating a change in dosage or medication. Sometimes, even changing the medication doesn't work during the few years following the start of puberty and rapidly fluctuating hormones.

ADHD and the Menstrual Cycle

A few studies have shown girls and women may need different doses of medication depending on their menstrual cycle. During the early part of the menstrual cycle (pre-ovulation), some women received a euphoric effect from stimulant medications and tended to need less medication to manage symptoms. Higher levels of estrogen at this time in the menstrual cycle may cause this.

The Scoop
The studies conducted on estrogen levels and ADHD medications used amphetamine-based medications (Adderall, Dexedrine, and Vyvanse). It is not certain whether women using methylphenidate (Ritalin and Concerta) would have the same reaction.

During the later phase of the cycle (after ovulation), the same dose of medication might not be as effective. This may be because progesterone levels increase and negate the positive effect estrogen has on cognitive functions.

In the few studies on hormones and ADHD, the level of inattention directly correlated with the menstrual cycle. During times when estrogen levels decrease, inattention increases. Although this may be more noticeable during puberty, it continues to happen throughout a woman's life.

Women with ADHD may have *Premenstrual Dysphoric Disorder (PMDD)*. Moodiness can reach the level of depression. Irritability and low frustration levels intensify and may require medical treatment. Antidepressant medications have been found to be helpful in some women with ADHD for combating PMDD symptoms.

def•i•ni•tion

Premenstrual Dysphoric Disorder (PMDD) is a severe form of premenstrual syndrome (PMS) and affects about 5 percent of all menstruating women. Both PMS and PMDD have symptoms including depression, anxiety, irritability, and tension. PMDD symptoms are more severe and can be disruptive to a woman's life.

It may be helpful to keep a log for several months to track whether hormonal fluctuations are affecting ADHD symptoms. A simple chart where you note the level of symptoms and your mood on a daily basis, together with the beginning and end of your menstrual period can help you and your doctor determine how much hormones are impacting ADHD symptoms. After a few months, you will be able to see if your symptoms increase and decrease during different times of the month. Understanding this will help you to develop strategies to help you cope.

Some ideas for managing symptoms based on your menstrual cycle:

♦ Increase your level of exercise during the last week of your cycle.

♦ If you are using birth control pills, talk with your doctor about those that contain estrogen alone for the first three weeks and only have progesterone during the last week.

♦ Talk with your doctor about whether a low-dose antidepressant medication may help manage symptoms of PMS.

♦ Talk with your doctor about whether increasing the dose of your ADHD medication for the few days before your period begins may help.

Go easy on yourself, eat right, get plenty of rest, especially during the stressful time right before your period begins.

ADHD During Pregnancy

There is very little research about how pregnancy affects symptoms of ADHD. However, many women report that during the first month of pregnancy, symptoms of ADHD worsen, making them feel as if they are in a fog. As the pregnancy advances, symptoms of ADHD decrease. This could be because estrogen levels drop during the first month of pregnancy and then begin to increase.

It is important to remember, however, that stimulant medications may cause heart defects or other problems in fetuses. Some studies have shown a possible correlation between use of stimulant medications and premature birth, low birth weight, growth retardation, and other complications during pregnancy. Some infants also went through withdrawal symptoms. However, these studies looked at high-dose amphetamine use during pregnancy, not ADHD medications, which are taken in much lower doses than the abusive doses studied. There is no specific information on the continued use of ADHD medications during pregnancy, but most doctors recommend stimulant medications be stopped during pregnancy.

> **Think It Over**
>
> It is ideal to use as little medication of any kind as possible during pregnancy, especially during the first three months, when the fetus's nervous system is developing. Only those medications necessary for the health and life of the mother should be used.

Rather than using medication, women who are pregnant may want to use some of the following ideas to control symptoms of ADHD:

- ◆ Use a coach or therapist to help learn strategies for managing symptoms.

- ◆ Cognitive behavioral therapy.

- ◆ Antidepressants, such as Wellbutrin, may be helpful, but aren't necessarily safer than stimulants.

- ◆ Increase structure in daily life.

- ◆ Reduce stress.

- ◆ Use outside help, such as babysitters to help with younger children, or someone to help with cleaning and household chores.

Although breastfeeding is considered optimal, women with ADHD may want to weigh the benefits of breastfeeding with being able to get back on medication. You can discuss options with your doctor and your baby's pediatrician. If you decide to use stimulant medications while breastfeeding, it is best to use short-acting medications and time breast-feeding to occur just before the next dose would be taken, to minimize the baby's exposure as much as possible.

ADHD and Menopause

Perimenopause begins several years before the actual onset of meno-pause. During this time estrogen gradually decreases. Some of the symptoms of perimenopause include:

♦ Irritability

♦ Tiredness

♦ Mood changes

♦ Memory problems, especially in short-term verbal memory and word retrieval

♦ Mental clarity

Women with ADHD may feel these symptoms to a greater degree than women without ADHD. This may be one of the reasons women reach-ing menopausal age visit their doctor, sometimes for the first time, to seek treatment for ADHD symptoms. Once a woman enters perimeno-pause, medications for ADHD may not seem to be as effective as they were previously.

To effectively treat ADHD symptoms during menopause, some women find increasing stimulant medications to be effective. Discuss with your doctor whether this would be a good option for you. Estrogen replacement can sometimes help, especially if ADHD symptoms or mood has worsened. There are some risks with estrogen replace-ment therapy. You should discuss the pros and cons of this treat-ment with your doctor.

The Lowdown

Antidepressants can help women with ADHD who are having a difficult time managing depressive moods during menopause.

Because women with ADHD have special needs during perimenopause and menopause, it is important to find a doctor who has knowledge and understanding of women's issues as well as ADHD in women.

Juggling Work and Home

Today, the majority of women work outside the home. This doesn't mean they don't also work inside the home, being responsible for home-making tasks as well. Most women, therefore, don't hold just one job, but two. They work all day and then come home to work a second job.

The Scoop
Most women with children also work outside the home. Seventy-one percent of women with children under the age of 18 hold outside employment. (National Women's Law Center)

Women are often expected to do it all. They are wives, mothers, daughters, and sisters. They are also employees and business owners. For women without ADHD, raising children and working outside the home can be overwhelming. For women with ADHD, who may have trouble with planning, organization, and follow-through, the task can be daunting and extremely stressful.

Women with ADHD frequently feel as if they work harder but get nothing accomplished. Television and movies show us women who can hold a full-time job and keep an impeccable home, effortlessly. By comparison, the woman with ADHD struggling to get dinner on the table after a full day at work can feel as if they are somehow failing their family when dinner ends up being hot dogs or fast food.

To make matters worse, many women with ADHD suffer in silence, possibly undiagnosed, believing they are somehow inferior because their house is a mess, the electricity was turned off because they forgot to pay the bill, or they were late picking up their child from school—again.

Why Can't I Keep House?

From the time you were young, you were probably taught through words and actions that the job of homemaking fell to the woman. Your mother may have stayed at home, taking care of the cooking and the cleaning. Even if your mother worked outside the home, the majority of the housework probably fell on her shoulders. Although men are contributing to household duties more today than in the past, it does not normally equal the amount of work a woman does.

The job of homemaker is boring and repetitive. You continue to do the same tasks over and over, day after day, week after week. It is a job that requires you to create your own structure and to find your own internal motivation, both difficult areas for women with ADHD.

Managing a home requires you to jump from one activity to another, to work despite continuous distractions and follow through on an endless to-do list. Women with ADHD can feel as if they are in constant overwhelm.

With divorce rates near 50 percent in the United States, many women with ADHD are trying to cope as single parents. Having a child with ADHD increases the chances of your marriage failing. In the majority of divorces, the mother is still the primary caregiver for the children. For women with ADHD, this causes even more stress.

The Lowdown

Hiring a babysitter or hiring someone to help you manage household responsibilities helps many women with ADHD focus on more important things and spend more quality time with their children.

Women as Primary Caregiver

Just as men are pitching in with household duties, they are also pitching in with childcare. But pitching in rarely is the same as sharing responsibilities equally, and the majority of childcare falls to the woman.

From the time children are young, mothers take on the bulk of the work raising their children. Not only do daily tasks, such as feeding and clothing their children, need to get done, but most mothers also:

◆ Coordinate recreational activities, including scheduling and transportation

◆ Provide structure for their children (who may also have ADHD)

- Monitor homework

- Meet with teachers

- Schedule doctor's appointments, make sure everyone gets to appointments, get prescriptions filled

- Handle all paperwork, including school forms, signing tests, and field trip permission slips

Traditionally, women are thought of as the caregivers and are expected to offer support to their spouse, their children, and sometimes siblings and friends. Women are not used to asking for support for themselves. Finding a support group or working with a therapist can help a woman with ADHD deal with the high emotions and frustrations that come with being a mother with ADHD.

Know Your Limitations

For some women with ADHD, working outside the home provides stimulation and adds interest to their daily routine. For them, the boring and monotonous task of caring for the house is easier to handle because their need for stimulation has been met through their job. Holding a job outside the home can provide additional money for the household budget, making it possible to hire outside help for jobs that are just unbearable or never seem to get accomplished.

> **Think It Over**
>
> When parents with ADHD seek treatment for ADHD symptoms, it teaches children ADHD doesn't have to be a liability and isn't a "bad" thing. It teaches children there are positive ways to manage symptoms and succeed in life.

For other women, working outside the home adds an enormous amount of stress. There isn't enough time in the day to accomplish everything, and living in chaos leads to forgotten tasks, incomplete projects, and continuously running to keep up.

Understanding your strengths and limitations can help you manage the household chores better. Focus on the chores that make the best use of your strengths and try to delegate the other chores.

Tips for Women

The tips in this section may help. Some of these tips will work for you while others will not. Choose those that may work for your particular situation.

♦ Make sure you are receiving treatment for your ADHD. Using a combination of different treatments, such as medication and therapy can help you better cope with daily stressors.

♦ Don't "keep up with the Joneses." Decide what is acceptable for your family and be happy with that.

♦ Delegate tasks you are not good at or don't like. Divide up household chores based upon each person's strengths. Take the tasks that are left over and rotate on a weekly basis.

♦ Only take on what you can handle. If having a big sleepover for your child is too overwhelming, invite only one or two children.

♦ Make sure you take care of yourself. Don't give up activities you enjoy in order to care for everyone else. Schedule free time for yourself each day or each week.

♦ Create systems that work with your ADHD instead of trying to use systems that may work for your neighbor or your friend.

♦ Create a priority list and only worry about the items on the top of the list.

♦ Invite company only if you feel prepared. Otherwise, offer to meet friends at a local restaurant instead of your home.

♦ Consider hiring someone to fill in with the jobs you are not able to complete.

♦ Use a tutor for your child instead of spending hours each night trying to complete homework.

♦ Accept that your spouse may be better at some tasks. This doesn't make you inadequate.

> **The Lowdown**
>
> Find a local support group or start one of your own. Surrounding yourself with other women with ADHD can help you feel accepted and give you someone to talk about frustrations with, without feeling judged.

No matter how overwhelming your house may become, the most important part of your household is the people in it. Emphasize everyone's strengths, play with your children, and spend time with your spouse.

Higher Risk for Certain Coexisting Conditions

Women with ADHD may have a higher risk for certain coexisting conditions:

◆ Compulsive overeating

◆ Chronic sleep problems

◆ Substance abuse

◆ Low self-esteem

There are also higher rates of depression, dysphoria, and anxiety than in women without ADHD. These mood disorders seem to impact women with ADHD at about the same rate as men with ADHD. Women, however, seem to suffer from more psychological distress than men. This may be because of the increased demands from caring for home and family as well as working outside the house.

Women who were not diagnosed with ADHD until adulthood may have more signs of depression. They may be more anxious and have lower self-esteem from years of not being able to perform up to expectations and not knowing why. They often have fewer coping strategies than women who were diagnosed as children.

Studies have also shown that wives of husbands with ADHD are more tolerant of symptoms than are husbands of wives with ADHD. Home life, therefore, can be more stressful and this can cause both physical and

> **The Scoop**
>
> Some experts believe there is an increased risk of developing eating disorders in girls and women with ADHD. Low self-esteem may be a contributing factor for a higher incidence rate in anorexia, bulimia, or binge eating.

psychological problems. Although women tend to use more strategies for coping and managing stress than women without ADHD, they are at a higher risk for diseases such as fibromyalgia, which can be related to higher stress levels.

The Least You Need to Know

♦ Estrogen levels impact ADHD symptoms, as estrogen decreases, symptoms worsen.

♦ Some women experience a decrease in ADHD symptoms during pregnancy.

♦ ADHD symptoms can worsen with the onset of menopause.

♦ Women with ADHD often struggle with holding a job, managing a household, and caring for children.

♦ Depression and anxiety are more common in women with ADHD.

Chapter **19**

ADHD Adults as Parents

In This Chapter

- ◆ Treatment helps all family members
- ◆ Parents need to be a team
- ◆ Tips for target problem areas
- ◆ Managing stress and overwhelm

If your child has ADHD, there is a good chance either you or your spouse also has it. Not only can ADHD interfere with your relationship with your spouse, it can cause difficulties in parenting and in your relationship. One study suggests that parents of children with ADHD are almost twice as likely to divorce as parents of children without ADHD.

In this chapter, we'll discuss some of the unique challenges parents with ADHD face when taking care of their family.

Making sure everyone receives treatment is the first step to working together to manage symptoms in all family members. There are also some behavioral strategies parents can implement to help keep the household more organized.

Get Treatment for Yourself

One of the best ways to take care of your children is to take care of yourself. Children with ADHD need routines and structure in their lives and if you are an adult with ADHD, these may be the very areas you have problems with. Medication, if needed, and behavioral strategies can help create a more orderly house and help you help your children succeed. Doctors specializing in treating ADHD often understand the importance of treating the family, rather than the individual. Frequently, children with ADHD are the only ones treated. Without addressing the problems of the family, including adult ADHD, treatment may not work as well.

Support groups can be extremely helpful to parents trying to cope with their own symptoms and disorganization as well as foster good habits in their children. Some support groups may work with adults with ADHD, while others may specialize in parenting children with ADHD. Which type of support group you choose depends on what you are looking to get out of the meetings and where you feel you need the most understanding and support.

def•i•ni•tion

> **Support groups,** often led by a nonprofessional, are groups of individuals dealing with ADHD who come together to provide emotional support, practical ideas, and to exchange information.

Children's success often relies on the support of their parents. Medical, family, and educational strategies all need to be practiced on a daily basis. Medical needs can be even more overwhelming when comorbid conditions are present. Parents are responsible for many different types of responsibilities:

◆ Making doctor's appointments and making sure family members arrive at appointments on time

◆ Getting prescriptions filled

◆ Managing the household, including cleaning, laundry, cooking, getting lunches prepared

◆ Talking with teachers and coordinating extra services at school when needed

◆ Making sure homework is completed

Parents must make sure all of the different components of family life work together, as harmoniously as possible. Adults with ADHD may have trouble managing their own symptoms and juggling home and work. Add in the extra responsibility of children, and every day can be a challenge just to make it to bedtime.

Parents, however, have an opportunity to be a role model for their children. Accepting their diagnosis, seeking out treatment, and making a concerted effort to manage symptoms that interfere with daily life can serve as an example of how ADHD does not need to stop you from succeeding. Parents can show children that treatment for ADHD isn't "bad" or a punishment, but that treatment can help each family member with ADHD function better and contribute to the household.

Make Sure Your Children Get Treatment

Just as much as treatment can help in controlling symptoms of adult ADHD, your children also need treatment. When more than one family member has ADHD, life can be chaotic. Treatment for children may include medication, behavioral strategies, and therapy. A therapist can offer practical advice on dealing with certain situations, as well as providing emotional support for issues such as self-esteem.

For a number of reasons, parents with ADHD sometimes fall short when developing and following through on their child's ADHD treatment. One characteristic of ADHD is the need for instant gratification. Treatment for ADHD may not show immediate results (medication can be effective immediately, but changing behaviors and attitudes can take additional time). Because of this, parents of children with ADHD may become impatient and impulsively end treatment or rely just on medication, without following through on therapy.

Parents may also have a problem being late for or forgetting appointments. This may be construed as not caring about getting help for their child, but could actually be signs of adult ADHD.

Another problem in getting treatment for children is in following through with treatment. Prescriptions for most ADHD medications need to be picked up at a doctor's office each month and brought to the store to have filled. This can result in having prescriptions filled late, losing prescriptions, or forgetting to pick them up or get them filled. Whatever the case, the children go without medication. Even if they get the medication, parents can forget to make sure children take it each morning.

Even though parents face a number of obstacles in both setting up and monitoring a treatment plan, in the end it is well worth the trouble. Using tools such as calendars, online reminders, and cell phone alarms, parents can keep track of doctor's appointments. As children get older, parents may want to start handing more of the responsibility over, teaching their children to manage not only daily symptoms but also overall medical treatment.

> **Think It Over**
>
> Untreated ADHD can lead to poor school performance, low self-esteem, substance abuse, increased auto accidents, and problems in work and relationships.

Work as a Team

Providing consistency includes working with your spouse as a team. Many couples, however, have a hard time doing that. It could be because myths surrounding ADHD still exist. Some parents may feel the child "just needs discipline." Arguments over how to discipline or whether to seek treatment create additional stress in the household and can wreak havoc on any treatment plan.

The parent who has ADHD may be in denial—and deny that anything is wrong with their child. Or the parent who doesn't have ADHD may have no understanding and be unwilling to accept a diagnosis, or adamantly disagree with treatment, to the extent that he or she refuses to allow the child to take medication or visit a therapist regularly.

This seems to happen more often with ADHD than with other conditions. Parents don't argue over whether to get their child eyeglasses or provide them with insulin or make lifestyle changes to help a child with diabetes. For ADHD, a "hidden disability," misunderstandings and long-standing myths can interfere with a child receiving the proper treatment.

Parents need to find a way to work together. ADHD is a chronic disorder that, left untreated, can cause serious problems. Some studies have shown undiagnosed ADHD can lead to substance abuse or additional disorders, such as depression or *oppositional defiant disorder*. Some psychologists offer parent-training sessions, where parents are given tools and strategies to help plan and implement lifestyle changes and behavior-modification programs to help their child succeed. Family counseling can also help in working through many of the issues surrounding raising a child with ADHD. Medical professionals who specialize in treating ADHD often involve the entire family in the treatment process, discussing family dynamics and including problem areas in the treatment plan.

def•i•ni•tion

Oppositional defiant disorder (ODD) is a psychiatric disorder characterized by defiant, hostile, and uncooperative behavior toward authority figures that interferes with daily functioning. Some signs of ODD include frequent arguing, anger, blaming others for their mistakes, and deliberately trying to annoy others.

Inconsistent Discipline and Rules

Effective discipline contains both clear and consistent rules. This is even more important for children with ADHD, but consistency is not always easy when the parents also have ADHD. Parents with ADHD may create rules but lack the follow through. Sometimes the rules are enforced and sometimes they're not; or the rules may be enforced for a while then forgotten, when parents become distracted by a new situation.

Imagine a child who won't clean up his toys. The parents have set

The Lowdown

Proactive discipline at home works with positive-reinforcement methods to prevent certain behaviors rather than using punishment after misbehavior. This type of discipline has been found to be more effective in children with ADHD.

rules that the child must pick up his toys each evening before going to bed. But some nights, his parents are distracted, and toys get left on the floor. Other nights, Mom and Dad are more focused and insist on the toys being put away. The child learns not to pick up toys every night, but to pick up toys only when the parents insist on it; other times, the toys can remain on the floor.

Consistency is what creates rules that are followed on a regular basis. For parents with ADHD, this consistency can be difficult. As children grow, discipline starts to cover more important tasks than cleaning up toys, and there can be problems when children haven't learned the basics of having and following clear and consistent rules.

Many families coping with ADHD indicate that a few specific areas are extremely troublesome. The following provides some suggestions and ideas to help target these areas.

Morning Time

People with ADHD frequently have a difficult time getting up and out in the morning. You can be running late or spend each morning rushing around. Either way, it can mess up the rest of your day. Here are some tips to help your mornings go smoothly:

◆ Set up a routine you can follow every morning. Having the same routine can help keep everyone on track.

◆ Do as much as you can the night before: lay out clothes, prepare lunches, and so on.

◆ Keep a special place for all items needed the next day.

◆ Get ready before getting your kids up.

◆ Set rules: no electronics or television in the morning.

◆ Physical exercise can help.

◆ Go out the door with a hug.

Make sure you start off your day with enough time for your children to eat a healthy breakfast. Inattention and hyperactivity can increase when children don't get the proper nutrition. Although eating a good breakfast is important for everyone, if your children have ADHD, it is absolutely necessary to having a good day in school.

Homework Time

Homework time can last for hours. Your children can miss writing down the assignment, forget important papers or books, and then have a hard time settling down and focusing on the work. Try some of these techniques to make getting started—and getting done—a little easier:

◆ Check with the teacher to see if homework is posted online or if there's a homework hotline to call and see what the assignment is.

◆ Talk with the teacher about what homework problems you are having, can you limit number of math problems, and so on.

◆ Have a homework box with supplies.

◆ Create a distraction-free area for your child to do homework.

◆ Be available to help, but don't hover over the child.

◆ Ask about having a second set of books at home.

◆ Help your child structure homework time.

> **The Scoop**
>
> Between 20 and 30 percent of all children with ADHD also have a learning disability. If your child is experiencing a great deal of difficulty in school, you may want to have him or her evaluated for learning disabilities.

If your child is spending inordinate amounts of time trying to get homework done each night, talk with your doctor. If your child is on medication, you might be able to adjust the dosage to provide more focus time in the afternoon or evening. Homework struggles aren't any fun for you, but they are even less fun for your child.

Transitional Times

Transition time is when one activity switches to another activity, usually involving some waiting or "limbo" time. These are often trouble areas for children (and adults) with ADHD. Throughout the day we have many different transition times to cope with; here are some tips for managing them:

♦ Use visual schedules so everyone knows what to expect next.

♦ Give warnings when one activity is about to end and another one is starting, for example, "in ten minutes we will ...."

♦ Make checklists of the day's activities, check off each one as it's completed, and move to the next one.

Although not always possible, try to schedule more enjoyable activities after less enjoyable ones. It's harder to stop doing something fun and move on to something you don't want to do than to change from something boring to something more interesting.

Bedtime

Children with ADHD have trouble falling asleep. Many say they can't stop their brain from moving at 100 miles per hour and turn off their thoughts long enough to fall asleep. Others can't seem to lie still long enough to close their eyes and relax. This is an ongoing struggle in many households with ADHD.

Here are some tips to help make bedtime more manageable:

♦ Set a bedtime and stick to it. Make sure the bedtime is age-appropriate and insist that your child go to bed at the same time each night.

Think It Over

Not getting a good night's sleep can affect school performance, behavior, and mood in your child. Make sure to discuss any problems with sleep with your child's doctor.

♦ Create a relaxing bedtime; read a story or listen to soothing music together.

♦ Rotate the bedtime routine with your partner. Let your spouse put the children to bed every other night. Bedtimes won't seem so stressful if you share the responsibility.

◆ Have your child take a warm bath before bed. The warm water will help him or her to relax.

◆ Use a white noise machine or a fan in the room to help your child get to sleep.

Children tend to accumulate a great deal of clutter in their rooms, from stuffed animals to posters on the wall. All of this can be stimulating and can stop a child from falling asleep. Declutter your child's room to help her calm down.

Overwhelm in Parent Causes Overwhelm in Household

Being a parent is overwhelming. Being a parent with ADHD is even more so. The enormous task of raising a child (possibly also with ADHD) goes beyond overwhelming and can cause frustration and feelings of inadequacy. Parents with ADHD may feel as if they are spinning their wheels trying to keep up with the never-ending chores. They may have little time left to spend with their children, leaving them full of guilt.

The following are tips for helping parents overcome the constant overwhelm in daily life:

1. Create routines not only for your children, but for yourself as well. Parents with ADHD need structure, and often that structure disappears while rushing around to get all your tasks done. Making a routine and sticking to it can help you accomplish more.

2. Spend quality time with your children every day. Too many times parents feel guilty after having zipped around town, driving to different activities, food shopping, and cooking dinner. Make sure you schedule time each day to focus on your child. Not only will this relieve

> **The Scoop**
>
> At least 50 percent of adults with ADHD also have executive functioning deficits. Parents with both ADHD and executive functioning deficits may have more problems with feeling overwhelmed on a daily basis.

your guilt, it will improve your relationship with your child and help foster self-esteem.

3. Set aside time for yourself each day. Adults with ADHD need time to unwind and destress themselves. This can be especially important during transition times; going from work to home, you may need an extra 15 minutes to adjust to your home responsibilities and mindset. Stop somewhere on your way home to give yourself a few minutes to adjust.

4. Set limits on the activities each person can be involved in at any given time. If you say no more than two activities at a time, your child can sign up for swimming lessons and piano lessons. If he or she wants to add an art class, he or she will need to choose whether to forego swimming or piano lessons. Setting limits will help everyone learn to prioritize their life and interests.

5. Have one day a week for family time. This could be one weeknight where nobody has to go anywhere, or a weekend day that is reserved for the family. This helps everyone slow down and spend time with one another. You can choose quiet activities to do at home, such as game or movie night, or choose to go to the zoo together.

6. Hire a babysitter one night a week. You don't even need to go out! Maybe you want to catch up on household chores or work you need to do. The babysitter could be responsible for helping with homework, cooking dinner, and getting the children ready for bed.

7. Turn off the world. Sometimes we can be overwhelmed because we can always be reached via cell phones, texting, and e-mail. Turn off your phone and computer for a portion of every day. Just knowing you have time without interruption from the outside world can help relieve some stress.

8. Prioritize your life. If you are overwhelmed because you have too much to do and not enough time to do it, decide what tasks are important and work on those. Write down the other tasks if you don't want to forget them, but once you write them down, focus on what you are doing, whether you're helping your child with homework or taking a walk together. Whatever it may be, if you have decided it is important, give all of your attention to it.

9. Start small. When you're overwhelmed, there is too much to do
   and not enough time to do it. You may not even know where to
   start. Choose one thing to complete at a time. Once you've done
   it, move on to the next item.

10. Make household chores part of family time. Set aside 15 minutes
    in the evening for everyone to stop what he or she is doing and
    declutter or clean up a portion of the house. Make the time fun—
    put on some music or have a race. Not only did you get something
    accomplished, but you did so as a family and had fun doing it.

Managing overwhelm is sometimes a matter of simplifying your life.
We continuously add more and more responsibilities, trying to fit as
much as we can into our daily life,
but this stretches our emotional
resources and can leave us drained
and unable to give time and
energy to our family. Eliminating
activities and spending more time
connecting with our family can
reenergize our children, our lives,
and ourselves.

> **The Lowdown**
>
> Your child's success may
> depend on how well you
> manage the daily strug-
> gles with ADHD. Online sup-
> port groups can help parents
> talk with others going through
> the same issues.

The Least You Need to Know

♦ When parents receive treatment for their ADHD, they show their
   children that it's possible—and important—to manage ADHD
   symptoms.

♦ Symptoms of ADHD in parents, such as forgetfulness, may be
   obstacles to treatment for children with ADHD.

♦ Parents' ADHD can interfere with their ability to maintain consistency in discipline for their children.

♦ Overwhelm is a common problem for parents with ADHD.
   Everyday activities can leave parents feeling as if they are spinning
   their wheels but not accomplishing anything.

Chapter 20

ADHD in the Elderly

In This Chapter

- ◆ Why ADHD is underdiagnosed in the elderly
- ◆ The elderly can be hesitant to seek medical treatment
- ◆ Medication concerns in the elderly
- ◆ Anxiety and depression more common in the elderly

Everyone has dreams of what they want to do during retirement. After working for so many years, the luxury of having leisurely days with nowhere to be sounds inviting. But the lack of structure that retirement brings can also mean the inability to make dreams come true for adults living with ADHD. With no organization or semblance of order in their lives, those with ADHD may meander through their days, unable to pay attention long enough to follow through on plans.

Many elderly individuals with ADHD were never diagnosed; ADHD wasn't around when they were in school. For years they may have lived being a social outcast or being considered unreliable. They may withdraw from social activities, avoiding situations for fear of not being accepted or being pushed aside.

Some of the older population may have spent most of their life relying on the organizational skills of their spouse. And now, as they grow old, the spouse either can no longer keep up or may be deceased. They may not even consider seeking medical help for what they view as personality traits.

In this chapter we'll talk about how symptoms of ADHD impact the daily lives of the elderly and why using ADHD medications can be a source of concern. We'll also discuss some of the more common comorbid conditions, how symptoms can change with age, and what types of changes to look for.

Underdiagnosed and Undiagnosed in the Elderly

ADHD is a life-long disorder. It continues to cause difficulties in one's social life, relationships, and occupation throughout adulthood. Today's elderly population is almost certainly underdiagnosed. Since ADHD was previously not diagnosed in adults and ADHD has only been diagnosed with any regularity for a few decades, the majority of elderly people with ADHD were probably not diagnosed as children, and if so, may have been diagnosed with minimal brain dysfunction.

> **The Scoop**
>
> A recent study showed that as many as 32 percent of adults with depression, over 12 percent of adults with anxiety, and almost 10 percent of adults with bipolar disorder also had ADHD, even though medical claims showed only 2.5 percent seeking medical attention for ADHD.

As people retire, much of the structure in their life begins to disappear. Symptoms of ADHD may be more noticeable or become worse. Some research has shown that some symptoms of ADHD may decrease as people age but deficits in executive functioning continue.

When ADHD Goes Undiagnosed

As people age, health care becomes important. Memory, recall, and the ability to follow up may not just be important but may be a matter of remaining healthy. Without diagnosis and treatment, the elderly may:

◆ Forget doctor's appointments.

◆ Forget to schedule appointments.

◆ Forget to take medication as prescribed or on a timed schedule.

◆ Forget important medical follow-up instructions.

Besides medical care, the elderly with undiagnosed ADHD may find it difficult to participate in new activities or enjoy learning new skills. They may avoid social activities and become isolated.

Treatment for ADHD can not only improve daily life but also can improve health by helping elderly patients to better care for themselves and follow through on recommended medical care.

Problems When Diagnosing ADHD in the Elderly

When diagnosing adults with ADHD, one of the problems is in determining symptoms of ADHD from childhood. This can be even more of a problem in the elderly. Normally, adults would be able to corroborate memories with family members or copies of report cards. If this information is not available, doctors can look at other, younger family members. Since ADHD is considered to be genetic, have children and grandchildren been diagnosed with ADHD? This may be an indication of a family history of ADHD.

Symptoms of Age vs. Symptoms of ADHD

Another concern when diagnosing ADHD in the elderly is that symptoms of age can resemble symptoms of ADHD, including mental ones such as mood changes, depression, memory lapses, and problems concentrating. Physical problems can include restlessness and trouble sleeping.

It is important to know when symptoms first began. Are these problems fairly recent or has he or she been struggling with these symptoms for most of their life? For example, a pharmacist sought treatment for anxiety and forgetfulness, indicating these were new symptoms. His wife, however, had accepted his forgetfulness as part of his personality for many years, and, after some discussion, he remembered that in elementary school, he had difficulty sitting still and paying attention.

He had only begun noticing his forgetfulness after his retirement; he had previously been able to manage his symptoms because of the structure of working each day. Once the structure disappeared, his ADHD symptoms became more apparent.

> **Think It Over**
>
> Once women begin menopause they can experience word-retrieval and short-term memory problems. This can sometimes be confused with symptoms of ADHD but may also cause ADHD symptoms to be ignored. A full history is important to discovering whether ADHD is present.

Coping Strategies Developed Through Life

By the time someone reaches retirement age, he or she probably has developed numerous strategies for managing symptoms of ADHD. Some of these strategies may be effective and others may be dependent on external sources.

Symptoms of ADHD may be masked. Forgetfulness may not be readily noticed because a spouse has taken care of scheduling appointments for many years. The spouse may manage finances and help in keeping the household organized. Because a couple has spent years developing a partnership, areas of impairment might be hidden.

Some people have developed other types of coping strategies, such as simplifying their life now that their children are grown, or completing the same tasks on the same day of the week. These strategies may help them cope in certain areas of life but may also cause confusion during the diagnostic process.

Reluctance to Seek Treatment

Some elderly individuals may not seek treatment for ADHD or even believe ADHD is a possibility. After living with symptoms such as disorganization or chronic tardiness throughout their lifetime, these traits may be seen as character flaws rather than symptoms of a disorder. For years, they may have been told to "pull themselves up by their bootstraps" or to "get over it."

Family members may see problems such as inattention, distractibility, or forgetfulness as chronic or ongoing and accept them as "just the way he or she has always been." Family members may accept the extra burden of caring for the elderly family member instead of seeking out treatment.

Finally, especially for the older generation, seeing a psychiatrist or a therapist may be seen as a weakness. There is still a certain negative stigma attached to psychiatric treatment, a belief that you are "crazy."

Medication Concerns in the Elderly

Stimulant medications are the first-line medication treatment for ADHD. These medications increase attention and focus, decrease impulsiveness, and are normally well tolerated when taken as prescribed. In one study, Ritalin, a commonly prescribed stimulant medication, was found to reduce the number of falls and increase cognitive abilities in elderly patients.

The Scoop
Senior citizens, on average, take almost 30 different prescription medications annually and this number is expected to rise significantly. Because of possible interactions, it is important for doctors to know all medications a person is taking before prescribing stimulant medications.

But stimulant medications have side effects that can be dangerous. Some of the concerns include increased heart rate and elevated blood pressure. Stimulants shouldn't be taken by patients with glaucoma.

Although stimulant medications have been used to treat other conditions such as *narcolepsy*, there have not been long-term studies done in the elderly population. Patients need to be aware of side effects and know when to contact their doctor or discontinue use.

def•i•ni•tion

Narcolepsy is a condition that causes excessive daytime sleepiness. A person may feel extreme fatigue or may fall asleep at inappropriate times, such as at work or school.

In addition, when stimulant medications are combined with some other medications, the combination can reduce the effectiveness of one or the other. This includes some over-the-counter medications, supplements, or home remedies. Your doctor and pharmacist should be aware of all medications you are taking, both prescribed and over-the-counter, to be aware of any possible interactions.

Elderly patients may also metabolize medication slower, requiring less medication, and they may be more sensitive to medications.

The Lowdown

Using a seven-day pillbox or case may be helpful. Patients and their families can quickly see what medication they've already taken. This can lower the risk of taking medication twice because of forgetfulness.

Stimulant medications do not need to be taken on a daily basis to be effective, and many people choose to take medication only when needed. However, the risk of forgetting a dose or taking too much remains for elderly patients. Forgetting a dose may cause problems if ADHD symptoms interfere with daily activities, and taking too much medication can cause health problems.

Comorbid Conditions in the Elderly

Elderly patients are three times more likely to suffer from symptoms of depression, stress, or anxiety. Some people report no longer enjoying life, or "losing" days because of depression or not participating in activities.

Depression

As people age, they face the loss of independence. Health issues can interfere with their ability to get around, they may no longer work, and their ability to drive can be impaired. In addition, many are dealing with the loss of their spouse. All of these can take a toll and lead to feelings of sadness and depression. The National Institutes of Health (NIH) indicates that as many as two million older adults have severe depression and another five million suffer from mild symptoms of depression.

For some, years of living with undiagnosed ADHD take an immense toll. Some may have held numerous jobs throughout their lives, never being fully satisfied with how their career turned out. Personal relationships may have failed and, looking back, they see their life as a large failure.

Depression in the elderly can be overlooked. Doctors and family members might focus on the physical health, ignoring signs of depression or assuming symptoms are related to other health issues or grief from losing a spouse. But depression can be serious.

Some signs to watch for:

◆ Increased use of alcohol

◆ Prescription medication abuse

◆ Weight loss not due to physical illness

◆ Loss of interest in eating

◆ Withdrawal from social or family activities

◆ Memory problems

◆ Slower movements

◆ Frequent complaints of aches and pains

◆ Irritability

◆ Wanting to be left alone

◆ Not caring for personal hygiene

◆ Talking or becoming obsessed with death

The Lowdown

Depression in the elderly can be caused by a loss of sense of purpose. Joining a senior center, going out with friends and relatives, and seeking treatment can all help alleviate some of the symptoms of depression.

Some elderly patients may have been misdiagnosed with depression, while signs of ADHD were ignored. Treating depression may help some symptoms of ADHD but additional medical treatment for symptoms such as inattention may still need to be addressed.

Anxiety

Anxiety may be more common in the elderly than depression is. Some researchers believe as many as 7 percent of all older adults suffer from some symptoms of anxiety. Even so, many doctors, family members, and the seniors themselves ignore signs of anxiety, believing them to be normal signs of aging.

It can be difficult to recognize anxiety in older adults for a number of reasons:

◆ Physical symptoms of anxiety may resemble other physical conditions; for example, *heart palpitations* may be seen as the early signs of heart disease.

◆ Memory lapses or problems may be attributed to aging but could be a sign of anxiety.

◆ Agitation could be seen as being temporarily worried about physical illness, or loss of independence, and it may be assumed it will pass.

◆ Many older adults may have signs of anxiety but not exhibit enough symptoms to be diagnosed with an anxiety disorder.

def•i•ni•tion

Heart palpitations are an awareness of the beating of your heart. When the term palpitation is used, many people think of a racing heartbeat, but heart rate can be normal, fast, or slow. Palpitation refers to the intense awareness of your heart beating.

If symptoms of anxiety have lasted for more than six months and don't seem to go away, despite having other situations in your life resolved, you should talk to a medical professional. Treatment of anxiety should begin with your primary doctor. Your doctor may refer you to a therapist for cognitive behavioral therapy. You may also benefit from learning relaxation techniques. Medications such as antidepressants are also helpful in treating anxiety disorders.

The Least You Need to Know

◆ Symptoms of ADHD may become more apparent in retirement, when there is less structure in everyday life.

◆ Symptoms of ADHD may be seen as normal signs of aging, such as forgetfulness, or inattention to detail.

◆ Stimulant medications may interfere with other medications and may need to be closely monitored in older adults.

◆ Depression and anxiety are common comorbid conditions with ADHD, especially in the elderly.

Common Acronyms and Glossary

Acronyms are found in both medical literature and educational documents. Some of these may make no sense until you understand exactly what the letters may be referring to. The following guide should help you better understand written explanations of ADHD and other mental illnesses.

Common Acronyms

AACAP: American Academy of Child and Adolescent Psychiatry

AAP: American Academy of Pediatrics

ACO: ADHD Coaches Organization

AD/HD: The current and medically accepted term for Attention Deficit Hyperactivity Disorder

ADA: Americans with Disabilities Act

ADD: Attention Deficit Hyperactivity Disorder (commonly used but not the official medical term)

ADDA: Attention Deficit Disorder Association

AMA: American Medical Association

APA: American Psychiatric Association or American Psychological Association

ASRS: Adult ADHD Self-Report Scale

CAARS: Conners Adult ADHD Rating Scale

CBT: Cognitive Behavioral Treatment

CDC: Centers for Disease Control

CHADD: Children and Adults with Attention Deficit/Hyperactivity Disorder

DSM: Diagnostic and Statistical Manual

FDA: U.S. Food and Drug Administration

IAAC: Institute of Advancement for AD/HD Coaching

ICF: International Coaching Federation

IDEA: Individuals with Disabilities Education Act

IEP: Individualized Education Program

LD: Learning Disability

NAMI: National Alliance on Mental Illness

NIH: National Institutes of Health

NIMH: National Institute of Mental Health

NLD: Nonverbal Learning Disability

OCD: Obsessive Compulsive Disorder

OCR: Office of Civil Rights

ODD: Oppositional Defiance Disorder

WHO: World Health Organization

Glossary

accommodation   An adjustment, or adaptation, in school or in the workplace, to provide individuals with disabilities a fair working or educational environment.

ADD/ADHD certified coach   Coaches who have received specialized training, have worked with clients for at least 500 hours, and have passed a written and oral test. Currently, the Institute of Advancement for AD/HD Coaching is the only organization specifically providing certification for ADHD coaches.

Adderall (mixed amphetamine salts)   The brand-name stimulant medication commonly prescribed for ADHD. It contains amphetamine and dextroamphetamine.

alternative treatments   This can refer to any treatment that is not considered traditional or conventional. This can also refer to treatments that are based on culture rather than science.

amphetamines   A psychostimulant medication used to treat attention deficit hyperactivity disorder and narcolepsy.

anger management   A process to help individuals reduce the emotional and physical response to situations, or people, which cause rage or infuriation. Anger cannot be erased completely, but the response to it can be controlled through practice.

antidepressant   A psychiatric medication used to stabilize moods. These can be prescribed to treat depression, dysthymia, and some are used to treat anxiety also.

antisocial behavior   Behavior that is outside the norm, that can interfere with relationships, or in an individual's ability to function in society. Examples of antisocial behavior include stealing, hurting other people, and damaging other people's property.

anxiety   An agitated state characterized by extreme worry, apprehension, or a sense of dread.

assessment   A formal evaluation to determine educational or medical needs.

assistive technology   A term used to describe services, or items, which help people with disabilities in educational institutions, or in the workplace.

attention   The ability to concentrate on a single thought, object, or activity for a sustained period of time.

attention deficit hyperactivity disorder   A neurological disorder with the main symptoms of hyperactivity, impulsiveness, and inattention.

attention span   The amount of time an individual can focus and concentrate on a thought, object, or activity.

auditory stimulation   Using music or other sounds to enhance a learning environment.

behavior modification   A program using rewards and consequences in an attempt to increase the frequency of acceptable behaviors and decrease the frequency of unacceptable behaviors.

behavior therapy   A form of psychotherapy that utilizes behavior modification programs in an effort to change undesirable behaviors.

biofeedback   A process of measuring certain bodily functions, such as heart rate, blood pressure, and muscle tension, to help an individual learn methods of controlling these functions and their emotional responses to certain situations.

bipolar disorder   A mental disorder characterized by extreme mood swings. It was previously known as manic depression.

career counselor   Professionals who work with individuals to assess education, experience, skills, abilities, personality, and interests, and then match them with a career.

cerebellar training   An alternative treatment for ADHD that utilizes eye, balance, and sensory exercises. This type of treatment is considered controversial.

chiropractic   A health discipline that works on the belief that disorders and misalignments of the musculoskeletal system affects overall health. This is considered to be an alternative treatment and there is little or no scientific data to indicate chiropractic care can improve symptoms of ADHD.

Clonidine   A medication used to treat high blood pressure that has been found to be useful in conjunction with stimulant medications to reduce side effects and improve sleep. It has also been found to decrease impulsive or oppositional behaviors.

coexisting   An alternate term for comorbid, refers to a condition existing with another condition.

cognitive   A term that refers to mental thought processes using reasoning, memory, perception, and judgment.

cognitive behavioral therapy   A type of therapy that works on discovering the underlying reasons for thought patterns in an effort to change the way individuals react to thoughts, and thereby incorporate more positive behaviors into everyday life.

comorbid   Refers to a disease or condition that exists with another condition. For example, a person can have both ADHD and depression and have symptoms of both disorders.

complementary treatments   Treatments used along with another treatment. These can be traditional treatments, such as two medications being used, or natural treatments, such as adding omega-3 to your diet as well as taking medication.

compulsive hoarding   The continual acquisition of objects without using or discarding any object. This usually results in enormous, and sometimes dangerous, amounts of clutter that can interfere with daily living activities.

Concerta (methylphenidate)   One of the brand-names for methylphenidate, Concerta is a long-acting psychostimulant medication and is one of the most commonly prescribed medications for ADHD.

conduct disorder   A psychiatric diagnosis given when an individual repeatedly shows behaviors that infringe on the rights of others. Individuals with conduct disorder are often verbally or physically abusive toward other people or animals, damage property, or exhibit antisocial behaviors such as stealing, lying, or vandalism.

counseling   A term used when an individual receives assistance from a professional to resolve a problem.

defect of moral control   The name given to a group of characteristics, including impulsivity. The term was created in 1902, by Dr. George Still.

depression   A psychiatric diagnosis characterized by feelings of sadness, hopelessness, and helplessness.

Dexedrine   Brand-name for dextroamphetamine, a psychostimulant medication used to treat attention deficit disorder.

Diagnostic and Statistical Manual of Mental Disorders   A manual containing the diagnostic criteria for all mental-health disorders. This is published by the American Psychiatric Association and is also known as the DSM.

disability A person with a disability is "any individual who has a physical or mental impairment which substantially limits one or more of such person's major life activities."

disability support office The department within colleges that helps to coordinate accommodations or modifications for students with disabilities.

distractibility An inability to sustain attention or having attention diverted to other stimuli on a consistent basis. This can be a symptom of ADHD as well as of anxiety, depression, or schizophrenia.

dyslexia A reading learning disability. Individuals with dyslexia can have difficulties integrating auditory and visual information and spatial relationships.

dysthymia A chronic but less severe type of depression. There are normally less severe and less serious symptoms than in clinical depression but symptoms generally last longer.

emotional disturbance A broad term used to include individuals with a diagnosable mental, behavioral, or emotional disorder. This term is included as a disability in the Individuals with Disabilities Education Act (IDEA).

enabling Doing things for someone who has the physical and mental capacity to do it themselves.

executive functioning A term used to describe brain processes which are responsible for planning, reasoning, organization, managing tasks, and understanding relationships.

Feingold diet An elimination diet first developed by Dr. Benjamin Feingold. The diet eliminates artificial flavors, artificial colors, and preservatives to help decrease hyperactivity. The effectiveness of this diet on ADHD has been debated for several decades.

Food and Drug Administration (FDA) A U.S. government agency that is responsible for regulating and safety of food, drugs, vaccines, and other medical services and products. The FDA must approve all prescription medication.

general practitioner This is your primary care doctor who provides medical care for your overall health. Family doctors can help to coordinate care with various specialists but often do not have specialized training to treat adult ADHD.

genetic   Referring to, or relating to, the genes. ADHD is considered a genetic or hereditary disorder.

gluten   A protein found in rye, wheat, and barley. Gluten is found in most cereals and many types of bread. Gluten-free diets eliminate these foods from your diet. People with celiac disease have a difficult time digesting gluten.

heart palpitations   An awareness of the beating of your heart. When the term palpitation is used, many people think of a racing heartbeat, but the heart rate can be normal, fast, or slow. Palpitation refers to an intense awareness of your heart beating.

herbal supplements   Substances taken from plants and plant extracts to enhance or maintain health. The FDA does not regulate these and their effectiveness in treating symptoms of ADHD has been highly debated.

hereditary   When a characteristic or condition is passed from parent to child through genes, such as blue eyes or blond hair. ADHD is considered to be a hereditary condition.

hoarding   Accumulating, storing, and an inability to discard, a large amount of items for future use.

hyperactivity   Being highly active, usually excessively so. Hyperactivity is one of the main symptoms of ADHD.

hyperfocus   A state of acute mental focus. When someone hyperfocuses, he or she can lose track of time or be oblivious to their surroundings.

hyperkinesis   A term used to describe overactivity or restlessness in children. "Hyperkinetic disorder of childhood" was once used to describe symptoms of ADHD.

hypersensitivity   Also called sensory defensiveness, is an unusual reaction or sensitivity to stimuli taken in through one or more of the five senses (touch, taste, smell, hearing, vision).

impulsivity   Acting without thinking about the possible consequences of the action. Impulsivity is one of the main symptoms of ADHD.

inattention   The inability to pay attention for sustained periods of time. Inattention is one of the main symptoms of ADHD.

independent living skills   Skills needed to perform everyday tasks. This can include time management, planning, scheduling, personal hygiene, laundry, nutrition, and budgeting money.

individualized education program (IEP)   A document that specifies what services and accommodations a student is to receive, as well as the child's current level, how often services will be received, and goals for academic performance.

Individuals with Disabilities Education Act (IDEA)   A U.S. law that governs special education in public schools, and agencies for students with disabilities.

insomnia   Difficulty falling asleep, staying asleep, or waking up too early.

instant gratification   The inability to wait for something you want. People with a need for instant gratification may have trouble with impulse control as well.

intervention   Although generally used to refer to something coming in between or interfering, this term can also be used to describe services and accommodations received at school or work, such as "educational interventions include extra time to take tests."

Intuitiv (guanfacine)   A long-acting medication recently approved for the treatment of ADHD in children. It may also be used in adults with ADHD.

IQ, or intelligence quotient   The ratio of tested mental age to chronological age times 100.

learning disabilities   A learning disability makes learning hard because of problems with processing information, or retrieving information you have previously learned.

major life activity   Includes self-care activities, manual tasks, hearing, speaking, breathing, walking, learning, and work.

manic depression   Previous term used to describe a mood disorder. Now referred to as bipolar disorder.

medically necessary   Services considered medically necessary are those needed for the diagnosis or treatment of your medical condition, are considered to be good medical practice, and are not used for either your or your doctor's convenience.

mental illness   A psychological disorder causing impairment or distress.

methamphetamine   A psychostimulant medication used to treat ADHD. It is stronger than other stimulant medications and used less frequently than other stimulant medications. Brand-names for methamphetamines include Desoxyn and Methedrine.

Methylin   Brand-name medication for methylphenidate, a stimulant medication used to treat ADHD. Can also be used to treat narcolepsy.

Methylphenidate   The most common psychostimulant medication used to treat ADHD. Brand-names for methylphenidate include Ritalin, Concerta, and Methylin.

minimal brain dysfunction   A term used to classify symptoms including hyperactivity and impulsiveness prior to the adoption of the name attention deficit hyperactivity disorder.

modification   A term most often used in educational settings to describe changes or adaptations to curriculum, or procedures. For example, giving an oral test rather than a written test would be a modification.

monopolize   To have possession of, or own exclusively. Therefore, monopolizing a conversation is when you are the only one talking and you do not allow other people to contribute to the conversation.

mood swings   When one feels up one moment and down the next. Periods of elation can be followed by periods of despair.

multimodal treatment   Treatment consisting of various parts, such as medication, therapy, and behavior modification. Multimodal treatment has been found to be the most effective in treating ADHD.

narcissism   Being egotistical, or having a high level of self-love, to the point of excluding everyone else. Having a belief that you are more important than all other people.

narcolepsy   A condition that causes excessive daytime sleepiness. A person may feel extreme fatigue or may fall asleep at inappropriate times, such as while at work or school.

networking   Using personal and business contacts to build additional connections for the purpose of looking for a job or business opportunities.

neurofeedback   Also known as neurotherapy, neurobiofeedback, biofeedback, or EEG biofeedback, this type of therapy uses brainwaves to measure brain activity and provide a better understanding of this to participants. There is some belief that this can lead to a person better controlling brain activity. There is limited scientific data to indicate this is a viable treatment method for ADHD.

noise sensitivity   Being overly sensitive to certain sound frequencies.

nonverbal Usually used in connection with learning disabilities; referring to auditory or visual learning disabilities.

nurse practitioner Nurse practitioners have received additional training
and education in diagnosing illness. Some nurse practitioners specialize in
mental health and can prescribe medications.

obsessive compulsive disorder (OCD) A common mental illness, OCD
is characterized by intrusive thoughts and repetitive actions.

off-label drugs A drug that is prescribed to treat a medical condition
other than the one the Food and Drug Administration (FDA) has approved
it for. The prescribed medications have been approved by the FDA but for
a different medical condition. One study showed that at least one fifth of
all prescriptions written are off-label.

olfactory sensitivity Being overly sensitive to smells. Strong or offensive
smells may be extremely distracting.

omega-3 fatty acids Unsaturated fatty acids that are essential in
humans but cannot be produced by the body. Are considered to im-prove
health, especially in the areas of cardiac and immune system, and rheuma-
toid arthritis. May also have positive benefits on brain function. Omega-3
fatty acids are most commonly found in fish, eggs, flax, and some meats.

oppositional defiant disorder (ODD) A psychiatric disorder characterized by defiant, hostile, and uncooperative behavior toward authority
figures, and interferes with daily functioning. Some signs of ODD include
frequent arguing, anger, blaming others for their mistakes, and deliberately
trying to annoy others.

oral defensiveness Being overly sensitive to textures and tastes of foods.
May only be able to tolerate a few different foods.

organic drivenness A term used in 1933 to describe a brain stem syndrome with symptoms of clumsiness, impulsiveness, and the inability to
engage in quiet activities.

organizational skills The ability to create order, to categorize, and
arrange information or objects to be easily retrievable.

pharmacology The study and practice of using medications to treat
human conditions or diseases.

premenstrual dysphoric disorder (PMDD)   A severe form of premenstrual syndrome (PMS); it affects about 5 percent of all menstruating women. Both PMS and PMDD have symptoms that include depression, anxiety, irritability, and tension. PMDD symptoms are more severe than PMS and can be disruptive to a woman's life.

prevalence   In medicine, prevalence refers to the number of people that have a specific condition, for example, ADHD has a prevalence rate of between 5 and 10 percent in children.

procrastination   Avoiding or delaying doing something.

Provigil (modafanil)   A medication sometimes prescribed off-label to treat ADHD. It is a wakefulness promoting medication approved to treat narcolepsy and excessive daytime sleepiness associated with obstructive sleep apnea. It has not shown to be as effective as stimulant medications in treating ADHD.

psychiatrist   A medical doctor (M.D.) or Doctor of Osteopathy (D.O.) who, in addition to completing medical school, has undergone specialized training and education on the treatment and prevention of mental and emotional disorders. A psychiatrist can diagnose and treat illness as well as prescribe medication. Some neurologists also have experience in treating ADHD, but this is widely variable.

psychologist   A psychologist has received either a Master's degree (M.S.) or a Doctorate degree (Ph.D. or Psy.D.) in psychology. A psychologist can diagnose and treat mental or emotional illness. They cannot prescribe medication in most states, and in the handful of exceptions, require extra training and a license to do so.

psychopharmacologist   These are medical doctors (M.D.) or Doctors of Osteopathy (D.O.) who specialize in treating mental and emotional disorders with medications. Many times psychopharmacologists will work with family doctors or pediatricians to develop a treatment plan for patients with a mental or emotional illness.

psychotherapy   A form of treatment that employs talk therapy and behavior modification to elicit positive change and solve problems. Psychotherapy can be performed by a number of different types of medical professionals, including psychiatrists, psychologists, therapists, licensed clinical social workers, and counselors.

rating scale A collection of questions to determine the number of characteristics and behaviors consistent with ADHD symptoms a person may have. Rating scales have been developed by medical professionals based on symptoms shared by a large number of people.

Rehabilitation Act of 1973 The Rehabilitation Act (RA) of 1973 prohibits discrimination for people with disabilities by the federal government, employers contracted by the federal government, and those institutions receiving federal funds (such as schools and colleges).

Ritalin (methylphenidate) A common pscyhostimulant medication used to treat ADHD. Ritalin is one of the brand-names for methylphenidate.

Section 504 Refers to the U.S. Rehabilitation Act of 1973 to prohibit discrimination on the basis of disability in federal agencies and institutions receiving federal funds, such as schools. This section is used to protect children in elementary and high school.

Section 508 Part of the U.S. Rehabilitation Act of 1973. It requires all people have access to electronic and information technology provided by the federal government.

side effects An adverse or undesired effect resulting from taking a medication.

sleep disorders Disorders that disrupt normal sleep patterns. These can include having trouble falling asleep, waking too early, or waking throughout the night. Sleep disorders can interfere with daily activities and emotional functions.

social anxiety disorder An anxiety disorder characterized by an intense and irrational fear of being scrutinized or judged by other people, causing someone to withdraw from social situations or interaction with other people.

social worker Licensed professionals who can treat and diagnose ADHD and other mental illnesses. They sometimes provide counseling or therapy and work as advocates to help patients locate services and resources within their communities. They cannot prescribe medications.

spectrum disorder A term used in psychiatry to describe conditions associated with a particular disorder, and varying degrees and subtypes of the disorder.

stimulant medications   Commonly used to treat ADHD, they increase dopamine and norepinephrine, neurotransmitters in the brain. It is generally accepted in the medical community that a low level of dopamine in the prefrontal cortex contributes to symptoms of ADHD.

Strattera (atomoxetine)   The first nonstimulant medication approved by the FDA for the treatment of ADHD in children (over 6), adolescents, and adults.

substance abuse   The overuse or dependence on alcohol, illicit drugs, or prescription medication. Substance abuse usually has a negative effect on an individual's mental or physical health.

support group   Groups of individuals dealing with ADHD who come together to provide emotional support, practical ideas, and to exchange information; often led by a nonprofessional.

symptom   A sign of a disease or disorder. The major symptoms of ADHD include inattention, impulsivity, and hyperactivity.

tactile defensiveness   Sensitivity to touch, clothing, such as tags, tight-fitting clothes, and new or stiff fabrics may bother people with tactile defensiveness.

Tenex (guanfacine)   A medication that can be used to control tics. It is also approved for controlling high blood pressure. It is sometimes prescribed off-label to treat symptoms of ADHD but should not be used on children under the age of 12.

therapist   Therapists and counselors generally have at least a Master's degree and most have additional clinical training. There are a number of different certifications and licensing available to therapists and counselors, including: Marriage and Family Therapist, or Clinical Counselors. Therapists and counselors cannot prescribe medication.

therapy   The term therapy can be used as a synonym for treatment, but more often refers to psychotherapy, a form of talk therapy used to help in solving problems or resolving past issues.

tic   Sudden, repetitive, and nonrhythmic motor movements or vocal sounds, such as throat clearing or eye blinking. Tics are different than repetitive movements of seizures or compulsions from obsessive compulsive disorder. Tourette's syndrome includes motor tics and may be a coexisting condition with ADHD.

Tourette's syndrome   Is sometimes a coexisting condition with ADHD and is considered a neuropsychiatric condition. The main symptom of Tourette's syndrome is physical and vocal tics.

undue hardship   When an accommodation requires a significant expense, will lower productivity, or decrease quality.

vision therapy   Also known as visual training, it is a number of different techniques used to strengthen eye muscles and improve visual processing. Some people believe vision therapy can improve symptoms of ADHD, however, there is no scientific data to back up this assumption.

Wellbutrin (bupropion, budeprion)   Brand-name antidepressant some-times used in the treatment of ADHD when stimulant medications are not effective. Is also used as an aid in quitting smoking under the brand-name Zyban.

white noise   Is created by combining all frequencies of sound together. The sound is comparable to gentle sounds of nature such as rainfall or ocean waves. Many adults with ADHD find white noise to be calming.

working memory training   Consists of exercises to improve cognitive performance. Although previously thought to be ineffective, some research has shown promise in using this type of training as a complementary treat-ment for ADHD.

Appendix B

Resources

National Organizations

American Psychiatric Association
1000 Wilson Boulevard
Suite 1825
Arlington, VA 22209
1-888-35-PSYCH or 1-888-357-7924
www.psych.org
apa@psych.org

Attention Deficit Disorder Association (ADDA)
P.O. Box 7557
Wilmington, DE 19803-9997
1-800-939-1019
www.add.org
adda@jmoadmin.com

Children and Adults with Attention Deficit/Hyperactivity Disorder (CHADD)
8181 Professional Place—Suite 150
Landover, MD 20785
301-306-7070
www.chadd.org

Mental Health America (MHA)
2000 N. Beauregard Street
6th Floor
Alexandria, VA 22311
703-684-7722
1-800-969-6642
www.nmha.org

MentalHelp.net
CenterSite, LLC
P.O. Box 20709
Columbus, OH 43220
614-448-4055
www.mentalhelp.net
info@centersite.net

National Alliance on Mental Illness (NAMI)
3803 N. Fairfax Dr.
Suite 100
Arlington, VA 22203
703-524-7600
1-888-999-NAMI or 1-888-999-6264
www.nami.org

National Institute of Mental Health (NIMH)
Science Writing, Press and Dissemination Branch
6001 Executive Boulevard
Room 8184, MSC 9663
Bethesda, MD 20892-9663
www.nimh.nih.gov
nimhinfo@nih.gov

Government Agencies and Information

Americans with Disabilities Act (ADA)
Disabilities Rights Section
U.S. Department of Justice
950 Pennsylvania Ave, N.W.
Civil Rights Division
Disability Rights Section—NYA
Washington, DC 20530
202-307-1198
www.ada.gov

Disability.gov
A government website to connect disabled individuals with information and opportunities.
www.disability.gov

Protecting Students with Disabilities
U.S. Department of Education
400 Maryland Ave, S.W.
Washington, DC 20202
1-800-USA-LEARN
1-800-872-5327
www.ed.gov

Rehabilitation Act of 1973
U.S. Department of Health and Human Services
Office for Civil Rights
Washington, DC 20201
202-619-0403
1-800-368-1019
www.hhs.gov
ocrmail@hhs.gov

Section 508
IT Accessibility & Workforce Division (ITAW)
Office of Governmentwide Policy
U.S. General Services Administration
1800 F Street N.W.
Room 1234
Washington, DC 20405
202-208-7420
www.section508.gov
section.508@gsa.gov

U.S. Equal Employment Opportunity Commission
(Agency responsible for enforcement of ADA)
131 M Street N.E.
Washington, DC 20507
202-663-4900
Automated Frequently Asked Questions:
1-800-669-4000
www.eeoc.gov

Advocacy Resources and Legal Information

The following is a listing of organizations providing services, resources, or information to help protect the rights of individuals with mental illness in the workplace, in education, and as a patient.

ActiveMinds
An organization working to remove the stigma of mental illness on college campuses and create a comfortable environment for college students with mental illnesses.
2647 Connecticut Ave, N.W.
Suite 200
Washington, DC 20008
202-332-9595
www.activeminds.org
info@activeminds.org

American Bar Association on Mental and Physical Disability Law
740 15th Street N.W.
9th Floor
Washington, DC 20005
202-662-1570
www.abanet.org/disability/home.html
cmpdl@abanet.org

American Civil Liberties Union
1400 20th Street N.W.
Washington, DC 20036
202-457-0800
www.aclu.org

The Campaign for Mental Health Reform
A collaborative effort of 18 national mental-health organizations.
1101 15th Street N.W.
Suite 1212
Washington, DC 20005
www.mhreform.org
info@mhreform.org

Consortium for Citizens with Disabilities
A coalition of national disability organizations to ensure independence,
empowerment, integration, and inclusion of children and adults with
disabilities.
1660 L Street N.W.
Suite 700
Washington, DC 20036
202-783-2229
www.c-c-d.org
info@c-c-d.org

Disability Rights Education and Defense Fund
An organization founded to help advance civil and human rights of
individuals with disabilities through advocacy, training, public policy,
and legislative development.
2212 Sixth Street
Berkeley, CA 94710
1-800-348-4232
www.dredf.org
info@dredf.org

Judge Bazelon Center for Mental Health Law
Legal advocate for people with mental illnesses.
1101 15th Street N.W.
Suite 1212
Washington, DC 20005
202-223-0409
www.bazelon.org

Mental Disability Rights International
An international advocacy agency promoting full participation in society
of people with mental disorders.
1156 15th Street N.W.
Suite 1001
Washington, DC 20005
202-296-0800
www.mdri.org
mdri@mdri.org

National Association for Rights Protection and Advocacy
An organization that looks to empower individuals that are mentally disabled.
P.O. Box 40585
Tuscaloosa, AL 35404
205-464-0101
www.narpa.org
narpa@aol.com

National Disability Rights Network
Protection and advocacy for individuals with disabilities.
900 Second Street N.E.
Suite 211
Washington, DC 20002
202-408-9514
www.ndrn.org
info@ndrn.org

National Empowerment Center
Provides information, referrals, and speakers and has conducted research into how people with mental illness recover.
599 Canal St.
Lawrence, MA 01840
978-681-6426
www.power2u.org
info@power2u.org

World Federation for Mental Health
An international organization working to improve the treatment and care of individuals with mental health concerns around the world.
12940 Harbor Drive
Suite 101
Woodbridge, VA 22192
703-494-6515
www.wfmh.com
info@wfmh.com

Job and Employment Assistance

GettingHired.com
1545 U.S. Rt. 206
First Floor
Bedminster, NJ 07921
1-866-352-7481
www.gettinghired.com

Resources for individuals with disabilities looking for employment. It includes a listing of companies reaching out and seeking to hire people with disabilities. The site also offers a resumé tool, a career assessment test, training for interviews, and advice on looking for a new career.

Job Accommodations Network (JAN)
P.O. Box 6080
Morgantown, WV 26506-6080
1-800-526-7234
www.jan.wvu.edu

The Job Accommodations Network works with people with disabilities to find and maintain employment. It provides a free consulting service to help people become more employable, a listing of individualized work site accommodations, a database of searchable accommodation suggestions, and information on self-employment.

Rehabilitation Services Administration (Vocational Rehabilitation)
U.S. Department of Education
400 Maryland Ave., S.W.
Washington, DC 20202
1-800-872-5327
www.ed.gov/about/offices/list/osers/rsa/index.html

Provides job training, financial assistance, and employment placement services to individuals with disabilities who meet eligibility requirements.

Support Groups

The following organizations either have a network of support groups or provide a listing of support groups around the country.

ADDCoach4U
Listing of U.S. Support groups
www.addcoach4u.com/support/usadhdsupportgroups.html
Listing of Canadian support groups
www.addcoach4u.com/canadianadhdsupportgroups.html
Listing of international ADHD support groups
www.addcoach4u.com/internationaladhdsupportgr.html

ADDResources.org
223 Tacoma Avenue South #100
Tacoma, WA 98402
253-759-5085
www.addresources.org
office@addresources.org

Attention Deficit Disorder Association
Provides a directory of support groups.
P.O. Box 7557
Wilmington, DE 19803-9997
1-800-939-1019
www.add.org
adda@jmoadmin.com

The Center
Listing of support groups for women with ADHD.
www.ncgiadd.org/members/support_grp.cfm
support@ncgiadd.org

Children and Adults with Attention Deficit/Hyperactivity Disorder (CHADD)
8181 Professional Place—Suite 150
Landover, MD 20785
301-306-7070
www.chadd.org

Depression and Bipolar Support Alliance
Network of over 1,000 support groups nationwide.
730 N. Franklin Street
Suite 501
Chicago, IL 60654-7225
1-800-826-3632
www.dbsalliance.org

Mentally Ill Chemically Addicted (MICA)
Free support groups nationwide. Contact your local mental-health association for information about a local chapter.

Mental-Health Professional Directories

The following websites provide directories of medical professionals who treat ADHD. Because the authors cannot be responsible for outcomes, the following sites are listed without recommendation but are listed here for your convenience.

ADDConsults.com
www.addconsults.com
info@addconsults.com

ADDitude **magazine**
directory.additudemag.com

ADDResources.org
www.addresources.org/adhd_directory.php

ADHDNews.com
www.adhdnews.com/find-adhd-professionals.asp

Attention Deficit Disorder Association (ADDA)
www.add.org
adda@jmoadmin.com

The Center
www.ncgiadd.org
support@ncgiadd.org

Children and Adults with Attention Deficit/Hyperactivity Disorder (CHADD)
www.chadd.org

Moms with ADHD
www.momswithadhd.com

ADHD Coaching

The following organizations and websites provide information on ADHD coaches, coaching credentials, and directories for locating ADHD coaches. Some of the previous websites may also provide directories for coaches.

ADD Coach Academy
ADD Coach Training Program with a directory of coaches.
1971 Western Avenue #106
Albany, NY 12203-5066
1-800-915-7702
www.addcoachacademy.com
ask@addca.com

ADHD Coaches Organization, Inc.
Association for ADHD coaches and also provides a directory of coaches specializing in ADHD.
701 Hunting Place
Baltimore, MD 21229
1-888-638-3999
www.adhdcoaches.org

International Coaching Federation
An international organization providing independent certification of business and personal coaches.
2365 Harrodsburg Rd.
Suite A325
Lexington, KY 40504
1-888-423-3131
www.coachfederation.org
icfheadquarters@coachfederation.org

Magazines and Publications

***ADDitude* magazine**
39 West 37th St.
15th Floor
New York, NY 10018
646-366-0830
www.additudemag.com
letters@additudemag.com

ADDvance Focus Series
Available online; archives of articles previously published in *ADDvance* magazine.
www.addvance.com/bookstore/focus.html

ADHD Report
A clinical newsletter published by Dr. Charles Barkley.
www.russellbarkley.org/clinical-newsletter.htm
Jody.Falco@guilford.com

Attention **magazine**
Magazine published by Children and Adults with Attention Deficit/
Hyperactivity Disorder (CHADD). Published six times per year, subscription included with membership to CHADD.
www.chadd.org

Books

Knowledge is important in learning how to manage symptoms of ADHD.
The following is a list of books currently available on the subject.

Adamec, Christine. *Moms with ADD: A Self-Help Manual.* Dallas, Taylor
Trade Publishing, 2000.

Hallowell, Edward M., and John J. Ratey. *Answers to Distraction.* New York,
Pantheon Books, 1995.

Hallowell, Edward M., and John J. Ratey. *Delivered from Distraction:
Getting the Most out of Life with Attention Deficit Disorder.* New York,
Ballantine Books, 2005.

Hallowell, Edward M., and John J. Ratey. *Driven to Distraction: Recognizing
and Coping with Attention Deficit Disorder from Childhood Through
Adulthood.* New York, Touchstone, 1994.

Halverstadt, Jonathan Scott. *A.D.D. & Romance.* Latham, Taylor Trade
Publishing, 1998.

Kelly, Kate, and Peggy Ramundo. *You Mean I'm Not Lazy, Stupid or Crazy.*
New York, Scribner, 1993.

Kolberg, Judith, and Kathleen G. Nadeau. *ADD-Friendly Ways to Organize
Your Life.* New York, Brunner-Routledge, 2002.

Koretsky, Jennifer. *Odd One Out: The Maverick's Guide to Adult ADD.*
Plattekill, Vervante, 2002.

Matlen, Terry. *Survival Tips for Women with AD/HD: Beyond Piles, Palms, &
Post-its.* Plantation, Specialty Press/A.D.D. Warehouse, 2005.

Nadeau, Kathleen G. *ADD in the Workplace: Choices, Changes, and Challenges.* Florence, Brunner/Mazel, 1997.

Nadeau, Kathleen G. *Adventures in Fast Forward: Life, Love, and Work for the ADD Adult.* Florence, Brunner/Mazel, 1996.

Nadeau, Kathleen G. *Understanding Women With AD/HD.* Silver Spring, Advantage Books, 2002.

Novotni, Michele, and Randy Petersen. *What Does Everybody Else Know That I Don't?: Social Skills Help for Adults with Attention Deficit/ Hyperactivity Disorder.* Plantation, Specialty Press/A.D.D. Warehouse, 1999.

Pera, Gina. *Is It You, Me, or Adult A.D.D.: Stopping the Roller Coaster When Someone You Love Has Attention Deficit Disorder.* San Francisco, Alarm Press, 2008.

Quinn, Patricia O. *When Moms and Kids Have ADD (ADD-Friendly Living).* Washington, DC, Advantage Books, 2004.

Quinn, Patricia O., Nancy A. Ratey, and Theresa Maitland. *Coaching College Students with AD/HD: Issues and Answers.* Silver Spring, Advantage Books, 2000.

Ratey, John J. *Spark: The Revolutionary New Science of Exercise and the Brain.* New York, Little, Brown and Company, 2008.

Ratey, Nancy. *The Disorganized Mind: Coaching Your ADHD Brain to Take Control of Your Time, Tasks, and Talents.* New York, St.Martin's/ Griffin, 2008.

Sarkis, Stephanie Moulton, Ph.D. *10 Simple Solutions to Adult ADD: How to Overcome Chronic Distraction & Accomplish Your Goals.* Oakland, New Harbinger Publications, 2005.

Solden, Sari. *Journeys Through ADDulthood: Discover a New Sense of Identity and Meaning with Attention Deficit Disorder.* New York, Walker & Company, 2002.

Websites and Online Resources

ADD at About.com
Add.about.com

ADD Classes
www.addclasses.com

ADHD Resources
www.adhdresources.org

ADHDCentral
www.adhdcentral.com

Attention Deficit Disorder Association
www.add.org

Centers for Disease Control
www.cdc.gov/ncbddd/adhd/facts.html

Children and Adults with Attention Deficit/Hyperactivity Disorder
www.chadd.org

HelpGuide on Adult ADHD
www.helpguide.org/mental/adhd_add_adult_symptoms.htm

National Institute of Mental Health-ADHD
www.nimh.nih.gov/health/topics/attention-deficit-hyperactivity-disorder-adhd/index.shtml

National Resource Center on AD/HD
www.help4adhd.org

WebMD
www.webmd.com/add-adhd

ADHD Online Communities

ADHD Forums
www.addforums.com

ADHD Moms on Facebook
www.facebook.com/ADHDMoms

ADHDCentral
www.adhdcentral.com

Friends of Quinn
www.friendsofquinn.com

HealthyPlace
www.healthyplace.com/adhd

MedHelp ADHD Community
www.medhelp.org/forums/ADD---ADHD/show/175

Medpedia
www.medpedia.com/communities/18-Adult-ADDADHD

Revolution Health
www.revolutionhealth.com/forums/mental-behavioral-health/
adhd/?ipc=B00232

Wellsphere ADHD Community
www.wellsphere.com/add-adhd-community/211912

ADHD Blogs

The following are a list of blogs currently available online about ADD/
ADHD. The authors do not endorse any blog or take responsibility for the
content in these blogs. This list is provided for your convenience.

ADD/ADHD Blog
Dr. Kenny Handelman
www.addadhdblog.com

ADD/ADHD Blog
Keath Low
Add.about.com/b/

AdderWorld
Bryan Hutchinson
www.adderworld.com/

ADHD and Marriage Blog
Dr. Ned Hallowell and Melissa Orlov
www.adhdmarriage.com

ADHD Blog
Dr. Donna Krutka
www.everydayhealth.com/blog/a-doctors-personal-take-on-adhd/
category/adult-adhd/

ADHDCentral Blog
Eileen Bailey
www.healthcentral.com/adhd/c/1443

ADDiva Blog
Linda Roggli
www.addiva.net/posts/

Adult ADD and Money Blog
John MacKenzie
www.adultaddandmoney.com

Adult ADHD Blog
ADDitude magazine
www.additudemag.com/adhdblogs/1/

Adult ADD Strengths
Pete Quily
adultaddstrengths.com/

Jeff's A.D.D. Mind
Jeff
jeffsaddmind.com/aboutMy ADD/ADHD Blog

Tara McGillicuddy
www.myaddblog.com

You and Me ... and Adult AD/HD
Gina Pera
adultadhdrelationships.blogspot.com

Appendix C

References

Chapter 1: About ADHD

Goldstein, Sam. Historical Perspectives. *Journal of Attention Disorders*, November, 2006.

Levy, Sol. Post Encephalitic Behavior Disorder—A Forgotten Entity: A Report of 100 Cases. *American Psychiatric Association*, June, 1959.

Images in Psychiatry: Charles Bradley, M.D., 1902-1979. *American Psychiatric Association*, July, 1998, 155:968.

Juhn, Greg, David R. Eltz, Kelli A. Stacy, (reviewers). Causes of ADHD. *ADAM Health Encyclopedia*, March 5, 2007. www.healthcentral.com/adhd/understanding-adhd-000030_3-145.html.

Surman, Craig. Neurobiology and the Genetics of ADHD: An Expert Interview with Stephen V. Farone, Ph.D. *Medscape CME*, June 8, 2007. URL:cme.medscape.com/viewarticle/557612?rss.

DSM-IV, published 1994, revised 2000. *American Psychiatric Association*.

Seidman, L. J. Neuropsychological Functioning in People with ADHD Across the Lifespan. *Pediatric Psychopharmacology Clinical and Research Program: Harvard Medical School*, 2006.

Bowes, Mark. ADHD in Adults: Definition and Diagnosis. *NeuroPsychiatry Review*, Vol. 2, No. 1, February, 2001.

Mannuzza, Salvatore. Adult ADHD: Obstacles to Diagnosis. *NYU Child Study Center.* www.aboutourkids.org/articles/adult_adhd_obstacles_diagnosis.

Szedgedy-Maszak, Marianee. Driven to Distraction. *U.S. News and World Report*, April 18, 2004.

Wender, Paul. Adult ADHD. *MedicineNet.com*, March 10, 2004.

Prediction of ADHD in Boys and Girls Using the D-KEFS. *Archives of Clinical Neuropsychology*, Vol. 23, Issue 3, pp. 283-293, May, 2008.

American Psychiatric Association Practice Guidelines for the Treatment of Psychiatric Disorders. *American Psychiatric Association*, p. 1401, 2006.

Chapter 2: Debunking Myths About ADHD

Booth, Becky, et al. Myths About ADD/ADHD. *Attention Deficit Disorder Association.*

Wilens, Timothy E., Stephen V. Faraone, Joseph Biederman, and Samantha Gunawardene, eds. 2008. Attention Deficit Hyperactivity Disorder. *National Institutes of Health. U.S. Department of Health and Human Services.*

Wilens, Timothy E., et al. Does Stimlulant Therapy of Attention-Deficit/Hyperactivity Disorder Beget Later Substance Abuse? *Pediatrics*, Vol. 111, No. 1, pp. 179-185, January, 2003.

Jensen, Peter (reviewer). Attention-Deficit/Hyperactivity Disorder. *National Alliance on Mental Illness (NAMI)*, May, 2003.

Ellison, Phyllis Anne Teeter. Myths and Misunderstandings. *Attention* magazine, Children and Adults with ADHD, 2003.

Rabiner, David. ADHD/ADD in Girls. *Attention Research Update*, 2006.

Giedd, Jay. ADHD and Substance Abuse. *Medscape*, ADHD Expert Column Series, June 3, 2003.

Effects of Stimulant Medication on Cognitive Performance of Children with ADHD. *Clinical Pediatrics*, Vol. 44, No. 5, pp. 405-411, 2005.

Deciding on a Treatment for ADHD. *Children and Adults with Attention Deficit/Hyperactivity Disorder (CHADD)*, National Resource Center for ADHD, January, 2008.

FAQ-The Feingold Program. *Feingold Association of the United States*, updated Sept 30, 2008.

An ADHD Med without Side Effects. *ADDitude* magazine, February 18, 2008.

Hallowell, Edward. Exciting New Findings on Fish Oil. *The Hallowell Center*, June, 2007.

Hawkins, Ernest N., and Steven D. Ehrlich (reviewers). Omega-3 Fatty Acids. *University of Maryland*, May 1, 2007.

ADHD-Unproven Treatments. *American Academy of Pediatrics*.

Complementary and Alternative Treatments. *National Resource Center on ADHD*, March, 2006.

Bernard-Bonnin, Anne-Claude. The use of alternative therapies in treating children with attention deficit hyperactivity disorder. *Canadian Pediatrics Committee*, 2003.

Chapter 3: Related Conditions

Giedd, Jay. ADHD and Substance Abuse. *Medscape*, ADHD Expert Column Series, June 3, 2003.

CHADD Professional Advisory Board. AD/HD and Coexisting Disorders (WWK 5). *CHADD, in association with U.S. Centers for Disease Control and Prevention (CDC)*.

Adler, L.A. Diagnosing and Treating ADHD and Comorbid Conditions. *Journal of Clinical Psychiatry*, November 6, 2008.

Surman, Craig B. H. ADHD and Comorbid Conditions. *Medscape*, Psychiatry and Mental Health, June 28, 2007.

Watkins, Carol. AD/HD Comorbidity: What's Under the Tip of the Iceberg? *Northern County Psychiatric Associates*, February 5, 2002.

Brown, Thomas E., ed. *ADHD Comorbidities: Handbook for ADHD Complications in Children and Adults*. Washington, DC; London, England: American Psychiatric Publishing, Inc., 2009.

Rostain, Anthony, L. Treatment Resistance in Youths with ADHD and Comorbid Conditions. *Psychiatric Times*, Vol. 24, No. 12, October 1, 2007.

Bipolar Disorder. *PDR Health*, Thomson-Reuters, 2009.

Crites, Russell. Bipolar or ADHD. *Excel Digital Press*, 2006.

Chapter 4: Medical Treatment of ADHD

Wood, Derek. ADHD Management: The Necessity of Psychotherapy. *Mental Health Matters*, Clinical paper, February 2, 2009.

Herkov, Michael. What is Psychotherapy? *PsychCentral*, December 10, 2006.

Jensen, Peter, (reviewer). Attention-Deficit/Hyperactivity Disorder. *National Alliance on Mental Illness (NAMI)*, May, 2003.

Wilens, Timothy E., Stephen V. Faraone, Joseph Biederman, and Samantha Gunawardene, eds. Attention Deficit Hyperactivity Disorder. *National Institutes of Health. U.S. Department of Health and Human Services*, 2008.

The American Psychiatric Publishing Textbook of Psychopharmacology, Fourth Edition. Washington, DC; London, England: American Psychiatric Publishing, Inc., 2009.

Stahl, Stephen, M. *Essential Psycopharmacology: The Prescriber's Guide, Revised and Updated Edition.* Cambridge: Cambridge University Press, 2006.

Chapter 5: Alternative and Complementary Treatments

ADDitude Magazine Scientific Advisory Board. Alternative ADHD Treatment. *ADDitude* magazine, 2008, New Hope Media.

Wilens, Timothy E., Stephen V. Faraone, Joseph Biederman, and Samantha Gunawardene, eds. Attention Deficit Hyperactivity Disorder. *National Institutes of Health. U.S. Department of Health and Human Services*, 2008.

Complementary and Alternative Treatments. *National Resource Center for ADHD in conjunction with U.S. Centers for Disease Control.*

Chapter 6: Coaching

Ratey, Nancy, and Peter Jaksa, eds. *The ADDA Guiding Principles for Coaching Individuals with Attention Deficit Disorder.* Hyde Park: ADDA Subcommittee on ADD Coaching, 2002.

Coaching and ADHD in Adults. *National Resource Center on AD/HD.*

Glossary. Updated March 27, 2008. *Medicare*, the Official U.S. Government Site, HHS.gov.

Chapter 7: ADHD in Marriage

McCarthy, Laura Flynn. Married to ADHD: Relationship Advice for You and Your Spouse. *ADDitude* magazine, January, 2007.

Hoffman, Matthew, (reviewer). ADHD in Marriage and Romantic Relationships. *WebMD*, May 18, 2008.

Tuckman, Ari. Integrative Treatment of Adult ADHD. *New Harbinger Publishers*, 2007.

Ellis, Amy. ADHD and Intimate Relationships. *Attention Deficit Disorder Resources*, 2003.

Marriage and Partnerships. *National Resource Center on AD/HD*, 2002.

Chapter 8: Other Relationships

Bensing, J. Chris. How Does Attention Deficit Disorder Affect Co-Worker Communication and Organizational Assimilation? *The Murray State University Journal of Undergraduate Research*, 2007.

What Helps-Disclosure and Accommodations in the Workplace. *Learning Disabilities Association of Ontario.*

Andrews, Joan, and Denise E. Davis. *A.D.D. Kaleidoscope: The Many Facets of Adult Attention Deficit Disorder*, 97-111. Hope Press, 1997.

Tuckman, Ari. *Integrative Treatment of Adult ADHD*, 191-228. Oakland New Harbinger Publishers, 2007.

A Closer Look at Numbers. *WebMD*, Mental Health Center, March, 2009.

Chapter 9: Communication

Mehrabian, A., and M. Wiener. Decoding of inconsistent communications. *Journal of Personality and Social Psychology* (1967), 6:109-114.

Inference of attitudes from nonverbal communication in two channels. *Journal of Consulting Psychology*, 31:248-252.

Carpenter, Siri. Wait, Don't Tell Me! *Monitor Psychology*, Vol. 31, No. 10, American Psychological Association, November 10, 2000.

Weaver, Jane. How Much Forgetfulness Is Too Much? *MSNBC.com*, November 28, 2004.

Goleman, Daniel. 1991. Non-Verbal Cues Are Easy to Misinterpret. *The New York Times*, September 17.

Chapter 10: Managing Symptoms in the Workplace

Quinn, Patricia. Stretch Your Attention Span: ADHD at Work. *ADDitude* magazine, January, 2007.

How ADHD Affects the Workplace. *Mental Health America of Illinois (MHAI)*.

Buckley, John E. Relative Pay Rates Among Census and Occupational Groups. *Bureau of Labor Statistics*, 2003.

"Hyperactivity." *The American Heritage Science Dictionary*. Retrieved July 28, 2009. Dictionary.com.

Kessler, R. C. et al. The Prevalence and Workplace Costs of Adult ADHD in a Large Manufacturing Firm. *Psychology Medicine*, 137-147, January, 2009.

AD/HD Predominately Inattentive Type. *Children and Adults with Attention Deficit Hyperactivity Disorder (CHADD)*, 2004.

Chapter 11: Protecting Yourself at Work

Employment Opportunity Complaint Processing Regulations (29 CFR Part 1614). *Equal Employment Opportunity Commission*, 21 April 2003.

Legal Issues for Adults with ADHD in the Workplace and Higher Education. *National Resource Center on AD/HD.*

The Rehabilitation Act of 1973. *Equal Employment Opportunity Commission,* February 20, 2009.

Disability Discrimination. *Equal Employment Opportunity Commission,* June 1, 2009.

Kitchen, Suzanne Gosden. Accommodation and Compliance Series: Employees with Attention Deficit-Hyperactivity Disorder. *Job Accommodation Network,* updated September 4, 2008.

Guidelines for Succeeding in the Workplace with AD/HD. *National Resource Center on AD/HD.*

Chapter 12: Finding the Right Job

Giwerc, David. The ADHD Entrepreneur. Attention Deficit Disorder Association.

Silvestri, George T. Considering Self-Employment: What to Think About Before Starting a Business. Occupation Outlook Quarterly, 1999.

Self-Employment Statistics. The Center for Ethics and Entrepreneurship, November 5, 2008.

Hallowell, Edward. Career Advice for Finding the Right Work for ADHD. *ADDitude* magazine, October/November, 2006.

Fellman, Wilma R. Making ADD-Friendly Career Choices. Attention Deficit Disorder Association.

Tuckman, Ari. Find a Job and Love It. *ADDitude* magazine, Adult ADHD Career Advice, Winter, 2008.

Chapter 13: Time Management and Procrastination

Ratey, Nancy. The Disorganized Mind: Coaching Your ADHD Brain to Take Control of Your Time, Tasks, and Talents, 89-129. New York, St. Martin's Press, 2008.

Sarkis, Stephanie. 10 Simple Solutions to Adult ADD: How to Overcome Chronic Distraction & Accomplish Your Goals, pp. 50-60. Oakland New Harbinger Publications, 2006.

Time Management: Learning to Use a Day Planner. Approved by CHADD Professional Advisory Board, Children and Adults with Attention Deficit/Hyperactivity Disorder (CHADD), 2003.

Novotni, Michele. Stop Pracratinating! ADHD Time Management Strategies. *ADDitude* magazine, February, 2006.

Saisan, Joanna, Jeanne Segal, Jaelline Jaffe, Tina DeBenedictis, Melinda Smith, Robert Segal. Adult ADD/ADHD: Signs, Symptoms, Effects and Getting Help. Helpguide.org, March, 2009.

Chapter 14: Tackling Hypersensitivities, Budgets, and Clutter

Stein, Martin T. Tactile Defensiveness: More Common in Girls Than in Boys with ADHD. *Journal Watch Pediatrics and Adolescent Medicine*, April 16, 2008.

Simon, Harvey (reviewer). Attention Deficit Hyperactivity Disorder. *A.D.A.M. Health Encyclopedia*, December 27, 2007.

Johnson, Mary Jane. Having ADD and Being Hypersensitive: Is There a Connection? *Attention Deficit Disorder Association*, 1998.

Greenberg, Rosalie. What is Sensory Hypersensitivity. In *Bipolar Kids: Helping Your Child Find Calm in the Mood Storm*. Cambridge, Da Capo Press, 2007.

Money Management for Adults with ADHD. *National Resource Center for ADHD*, 2003.

Dunn, W. The impact of sensory processing abilities on the daily lives of young children and their families: a conceptual model. Infants and Young Children, 9(4), 23-35, 1997. International Society on Early Intervention (Journal)

Maidment, Karron. Compulsive Hoarding Syndrome. *Obsessive Compulsive Foundation*, 2009.

Chapter 15: Managing Emotions

Baker, Don. ADHD, Anger Awareness and Management. *Attention Deficit Disorder Resources*, 2004.

Kubose, Shauna. Symposium Report: Current Opinion on Management of Neurologic Disorders. *Neurology Reviews*, Vol. 8, No. 2, February, 2000.

Brown, Thomas E. ADD/ADHD and Impaired Executive Function in Clinical Practice. *Current Attention Disorder Reports*, 1:37-41, 2009.

Muncu, Bonnie. Break the Chains of Shame. *Thrive with ADD*, 2009.

Trail, R. R. *Molecular Explanations for Intelligence*, pp. 141-152. West London, Ondwelle Publications, 2006.

Searight, H. Russell, et al. Adult ADHD: Evaluation and Treatment in Family Medicine. *American Academy of Family Physicians*, November 1, 2000.

What Do Mood Swings Feel Like? *National Center for Health and Wellness*, 2006.

Flanagan, John C. Overwhelm. *TraumaTherapist.com*, 2006.

Chapter 16: ADHD in College

Taymans, Juliana M. Selecting a College for Students with Learning Disabilities or Attention Deficit Hyperactivity Disorder. *LDOnline*, 2001.

Sandler, Michael. The College Quest. *ADDitude* magazine, 2007.

Larosse, Mayda. Accommodations for Postsecondary Students with ADHD. *Job Accommodation Network*, West Virginia University, 1999.

Top 5 Things to Learn Before You Go Away to College. *ECampus Tours*, July 2, 2005.

Prevatt, Frances, Abigail Reaser, Briley Proctor, and Yaacov Petscher. The Learning/Study Strategies of College Students with ADHD. *Department of Educational Psychology and Learning Systems*, Florida State University, 2007.

IDEA, ADA, IEP'S, and Section 504 Plans: What Happens in College? *Rutgers University*, 2008.

Strock, Margaret. Attention Deficit Hyperactivity Disorder. *National Institute of Mental Health*, 2006.

Being Your Own Advocate. *National Center for Learning Disabilities*, 2007.

Being Your Own Advocate. *Canadian Mental Health Association*, 2004.

Chapter 17: ADHD in Men

Busko, Marlene. Sex Differences in Brain Activity Seen During Memory Task in Adult ADHD. *Medscape*, Medical News, October 23, 2007.

Weiss, Margaret, Lily Trokenberg Hechtman and Gabrielle Weis. *ADHD in Adulthood: A Guide to Current Theory, Diagnosis, and Treatment*, pp. 25-27. Baltimore, Taylor & Francis US, 2001.

Ellison, Anne Teeter, and Sam Goldsten. *Clinician's Guide to Adult ADHD*, p. 197. San Diego, Academic Press, 2002.

Barkley, Russell, Kevin R. Murphy and Mariellen Fischer. *ADHD in Adults: What the Science Says*, pp. 208, 336. New York, The Guilford Press, 2007.

Gershon, Jonathan. A Meta-Analytic Review of Gender Differences in ADHD. *Journal of Attention Disorders*, 2002, Vol. 5, No. 3, 143-154.

Rucklidge, Julia J. Gender differences in ADHD: implications for psychosocial treatments, pp. 643-655. *Expert Review of Neurotherapeutics* (April, 2008), Volume 8, Number 4.

Cassels, Caroline. Male Drivers With ADHD Have More Collisions as They Age. *American Psychiatric Association*, May 19, 2009.

Ludvigsen, Mykle. Marketing Mental Health Literacy ... to Men. *BC Partners for Mental Health and Addictions Information*, March 10, 2003.

Canadian Men Reluctant to Consult Mental Health Services. *ScienceDaily*, May 22, 2009.

Men's Mental Illness: A Silent Crisis. *Canadian Mental Health Association*.

Definition of Peter Pan Syndrome. *MedicineNet.com*, March 4, 1999.

Kiley, Dan. *The Peter Pan Syndrome: Men Who Have Never Grown Up*. New York Avon Books, 1995.

Quily, Pete. Men with Adult ADHD. The Effect on Their Families. *Adult ADD Strengths*, April 25, 2006.

U.VA. Study Finds Ritalin Improves Driving for Young Men with ADHD. *University of Virginia*, March 1, 2000.

Zoler, Mitchel L. ADHD often persists as boys become men: the boys with ADHD had greater prevalence of a variety of psychiatric disorders as young adults. *Pediatric News Magazine*, December 1, 2004.

Chapter 18: ADHD in Women

Nadeau, Kathleen. Women with ADHD in the Workplace: Juggling the Dual Responsibilities of Home and Work. *Attention Deficit Disorder Resources*, 2000.

Johnson, Caitlin A. Women Suffer in Silence with ADHD. *CBS News*, May, 2007.

Nadeau, Kathleen. Women and AD/HD. *National Center for Gender Issues and AD/HD*, 2004.

Solden, Sari. *Women with Attention Deficit Disorder: Embrace Your Differences and Transform Your Life*. Nevada City, Underwood Books, 2005.

Women and AD/HD. *Children and Adults with Attention Deficit/ Hyperactivity Disorder (CHADD)*, 2004.

Surman, Craig B. H. Treating ADHD During Pregnancy. *Medscape*, Psychiatry and Mental Health, December 27, 2005.

Quinn, Patricia. Medications to Treat AD/HD and Their Use During Pregnancy. *National Center for Gender Issues and AD/HD*, 2002.

Sogn. ADHD and Menopause. *WebMD*, July 26, 2006.

Sorgen, Carol, (reviewer). ADHD-Not Just for Boys. *WebMD*, July 5, 2005.

Chapter 19: ADHD Adults as Parents

Rabiner, David. The Impact that Having a Child with ADHD has on Parents' Satisfaction with Family Life. *Attention Deficit Disorder Resources*, 1998-2009.

Elias, Marilyn. Children who have ADHD Can Strain Marriages. *USA Today*, October 20, 2008.

Barclay, Laurie. Parents of Children with ADHD May Have ADHD Themselves. *Medscape Today*, January 4, 2009.

Wender, Paul. Adult ADHD. *WebMD*, Live Events, March 10, 2004.

Matlen, Terry. Parents with ADHD. *AddConsults.com*, August 15, 2005.

Executive Functions in Parents with ADHD. *Psychiatric Times*, Vol. 18, No. 11, 1 November 2001.

Chapter 20: ADHD in the Elderly

About Psychiatric Medications. *Real Mental Health, Inc.*, March 2006.

Parker-Pope, Tara. Ritalin for Senior Citizens. *The New York Times*, June 28, 2008.

Successful methylphenidate treatment for ADHD in an elderly woman (Case Report). *The Brown University Geriatric Psychopharmacology Update*, 2008. www.AccessMyLibrary.com.

Wetzel, Martin W. and William J. Burke. Addressing Attention-Deficit/ Hyperactivity Disorder in Later Adulthood. *Clinical Geriatrics*, Volume 16, Issue 11, October 1, 2007.

Survey of adults reveals life-long consequences of ADHD. Health & Medicine Week, *NewsRX*, 2004. www.AccessMyLibrary.com.

Matlin, Terry. ADHD in the Elderly. ADHDCentral.com, http://www. healthcentral.com/adhd/c/57718/24812/adhd-elderly.

Anxiety in the Elderly. *HealthyPlace.com*, February 17, 2007.

Chakraburtty, Amal. Anxiety Often Missed in Elderly. *WebMD*, May 22, 2006.

Segal, Jeanne. Depression in Older Adults and the Elderly. *Helpguide.org*, 2008.

Nauert, Rick. Undiagnosed ADHD in Adults. *PsychCentral.com*, October 30, 2006.

Prescription Drug use by Senior Citizens. *Minnesota Board on Aging*, 2005.

Index

CHECK OUT THESE
BEST-SELLERS

More than 450 titles available at booksellers and online retailers everywhere!

U.S. HISTORY GRAPHIC ILLUSTRATED
978-1-59257-115-4

Word Search Puzzles
978-1-59257-900-6

Glycemic Index Weight Loss
978-1-59257-855-9

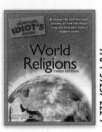
World Religions
978-1-59257-222-9

U.S. History Graphic Illustrated
978-1-59257-785-9

Calculus
978-1-59257-471-1

Positive Dog Training
978-1-59257-483-4

Personal Finance in Your 20s & 30s
978-1-59257-883-2

Learning Spanish
978-1-59257-908-2

Wine Basics
978-1-59257-786-6

Windows 7
978-1-59257-954-9

Music Theory
978-1-59257-437-7

The Perfect Resume
978-1-59257-957-0

Organizing Your Life
978-1-59257-966

Walt Disney World
978-1-59257-888

idiotsguides.com
ALPHA